Function	CUA Key Sequence	M
Help (Context Sensitive)	Shift+F1	
Hide Bars	Alt+Shift+F5	View ➤ Hide Bars
Horizontal Line	Ctrl+F11	Graphics ➤ Horizontal Line
Indent	F7	Layout ➤ Paragraph ➤ Indent
Insert/Typeover	Ins	
Justify Full	Ctrl+J	Layout ➤ Justification ➤ Full
Justify Left	Ctrl+L	Layout ➤ Justification ➤ Left
Justify Center	Ctrl+E	Layout ➤ Justification ➤ Center
Justify Right	Ctrl+R	Layout ➤ Justification ➤ Right
Macro Record	Ctrl+F10	Tools ➤ Macro ➤ Record
Macro Play	Alt+F10	Tools ➤ Macro ➤ Play
Margins	Ctrl+F8	Layout ➤ Margins
Merge	Shift+F9	Tools ➤ Merge
Merge End of Field	Alt+Enter	
Merge End of Record	Alt+Shift+Enter	
New Document	Ctrl+N	File ➤ New
Open Document	Ctrl+O	File ➤ Open
Page View	Alt+F5	View ➤ Page
Page Full Zoom	Shift+F5	
Paste	Ctrl+V	Edit ➤ Paste

The ABCs of WordPerfect® 6.0 for Windows™

Alan R. Neibauer

SYBEX®

San Francisco Paris Düsseldorf Soest

Coordinating Editor: Joanne Cuthbertson
Developmental Editor: Steve Lipson
Editor: Armin Brott
Project Editor: Valerie Potter
Technical Editor: Richard Nollet
Book Designer and Artist: Ingrid Owen
Screen Graphics: Cuong Le
Typesetter: Thomas Goudie
Production Assistant: Lisa Haden
Indexer: Nancy Guenther
Cover Designer: Archer Design
Cover Illustrator: Richard Miller

Screen reproductions produced with Collage Plus.

Library of Congress Card Number:9386064
ISBN: 0-7821-1384-2

Manufactured in the United States of America
10 9 8 7 6 5 4 3 2

Dedicated to Barbara Neibauer

acknowledgments

Being faced with writing a book on a major upgrade such as WordPerfect 6.0 for Windows can be daunting. Producing the book in a timely fashion while creating a fresh, enhanced format can be overwhelming. Fortunately, I was not alone. The professionals at Sybex were there all along, providing the assistance and support needed to meet this challenge head-on.

Joanne Cuthbertson, coordinating editor, and Steve Lipson, developmental editor, successfully cultivated this book and the new ABC's format. Armin Brott edited the book, maintaining a rigid schedule while carefully fine-tuning the text to perfection. Val Potter coordinated the flow of disks and papers without missing a beat.

My thanks also to technical editor Richard Nollet, typesetter Thomas Goudie, screen graphic artist Cuong Le, production assistant Lisa Haden, and indexer Nancy Guenther. The efforts of designer Ingrid Owen translated the concept of this new format to reality. Thanks also to Dianne King and Dr. Rudolph Langer, as well as the other people at Sybex whose efforts contributed to this book.

My deepest thanks and respect go to Barbara Neibauer. She spent quite a few nights perched over the printer, monitor, and copy machine, organizing papers, handling last minute details, and providing the humor and support that keep a writer going.

contents at a glance

table of contents

part two

EDITING YOUR WORK 33

part three

FORMATTING YOUR DOCUMENTS 111

lesson 8

Changing the Appearance of Characters 113

lesson 9

Formatting Lines 135

part four

▶ introduction

Just when you thought Windows word processing couldn't get any better, along comes WordPerfect 6.0 for Windows.

Packed with extra features and versatility, WordPerfect 6.0 combines the most powerful features of state-of-the-art word processing with the graphics and design features of desktop publishing. Here's one program that can do it all—memos and letters; professional reports, booklets, and brochures; even spreadsheets, charts, and graphs.

Yet with all of its capabilities, WordPerfect is easy to use. Equipped with this book, you'll soon be using WordPerfect to prepare all sorts of documents. Whether you already use the Windows or DOS version of WordPerfect, or are a new WordPerfect user, you'll be creating professional-looking documents that you may never have imagined possible.

HOW TO USE THIS BOOK

This book combines all of the elements you need to become productive as quickly as possible. In fact, like WordPerfect 6.0 for Windows, this book is an exciting update of a best-seller. We've fine-tuned the renowned SYBEX ABCs series for today's busy reader, mixing our own no-nonsense, direct style with a blend of tips, tricks, and hints. Here's a book you can keep by your computer, at the office or at home, without embarrassment.

In *The ABCs of WordPerfect 6 for Windows,* you'll get a concise step-by-step guide that you can immediately apply to your own work—you don't have to type some silly document that we've made up for you. (But if you need some more structured practice, you'll find it in this book as well!)

You can learn each key WordPerfect function in minutes. Each is covered in a short two-page lesson, and contains everything you need, including a graphic showing what you should look for on the WordPerfect screen.

You'll also find useful hints, tips, and tricks about the procedure. Here, you'll learn how the function works, some shortcuts, or items to watch out for. Each item is clearly marked to help you decide which are important for you to read.

Before diving into WordPerfect, take a look at the "WordPerfect Basics" section that follows this introduction. This short section shows you how to work with WordPerfect, its menus, and its dialog boxes. If you are a new Windows user, you'll also find this section invaluable.

Once you're familiar with the WordPerfect screen and Windows, you can use this book in several ways:

- Read from start to finish to learn WordPerfect 6.0 for Windows in a linear fashion. Don't worry about slogging through a lot of dense material or complicated instructions you don't need—you'll be typing and printing documents in a few minutes!

- Need a quick reference or refresher? At the beginning of each lesson is a handy reference showing where you'll read about key features. Go directly to the step-by-step guide describing the feature, and follow the steps.

- Something not go exactly as planned? Interested in more details? Check out the tips, tricks, or hints at the end of each section.
- Need a little hands-on practice to reinforce your skills? Check out the optional exercises (Let's Do It!) after each major part of the book.

tip — **When you see this icon, you'll find a handy tip or shortcut for performing the task.**

for more... — **When you want some more information, look for this icon. Here, you'll find additional details about the task or a cross-reference to related lessons.**

power bar — **This icon means that you can perform the task quickly using a mouse and the Power Bar.**

button bar — **This icon means you can perform the task using a mouse and the Button Bar.**

oops! — **Refer to these notes to troubleshoot problems or to help you when something appears not to work properly.**

new feature — **Features new to WordPerfect 6.0 for Windows are explained where you see this icon.**

warning! — **Pay close attention when you see this icon—it'll save you a lot of trouble later.**

WHAT THIS BOOK CONTAINS

We've divided this book into four parts to complement the way you work and learn. In Part One, Quick Start, you'll learn how to start WordPerfect, type, save, and print documents. You'll learn how to use the Power Bar and Button Bar, how to change your view of your documents, and how to zoom the screen to reduce or enlarge the display. All this, and more, in two short lessons!

With the basics under your belt, you'll learn how to edit documents in Part Two. There are lessons on opening documents, deleting and inserting text, correcting mistakes, and moving and copying text. You'll also learn how to insert a date, repeat keystrokes, and create templates to speed up repetitive functions. There's also a special section on using Windows to work with up to nine documents at a time.

Part Three concentrates on formatting. You'll learn how to change the appearance of text and how to insert symbols, icons, and foreign-language characters. There are lessons on centering text, aligning it at the right margin, indenting and numbering paragraphs, changing line spacing, and setting tabs. You'll learn how to change margins and page sizes, and even create envelopes and booklets automatically. Part Three also explains how to add headers, footers, watermarks, and page numbers.

In Part Four you'll learn about some of WordPerfect's special features. After reading these lessons, you'll be able to create tables and multicolumn newsletters, add graphic lines and borders, create form letters, and record macros. You'll learn how to check your spelling, and how to use the thesaurus and grammar checker to improve your vocabulary and grammar. Finally, you'll learn the basics of desktop publishing—how to add graphics, rotated text, custom drawings, and charts to enhance your documents.

At the end of each part, you'll find some short exercises (Let's Do It!). These take you step-by-step through a sample document, performing the key tasks described in that part. Follow the exercises if you're not sure how something should work, or if you want to strengthen your skills before using them in your own documents.

▶ WordPerfect basics

Working with WordPerfect for Windows is really very easy. Because it is a Windows application, you interact with it the same way you would with any other Windows program.

If you are an experienced Windows user, you'll immediately feel comfortable using WordPerfect. But to learn about the WordPerfect screen, and about some of the program's unique features, such as multipurpose dialog boxes, take a few minutes to read this section.

If you are new to the Windows environment, you will find it an easy and convenient way to work with your computer. This section will show you how to communicate with WordPerfect. You'll learn about the WordPerfect screen, how to give commands, and how to select options using the mouse, keyboard, menus, and dialog boxes.

If you have never used a graphic interface before, or do not have a mouse, there's no need to be intimidated by the following discussion of menus, mice, and dialog boxes. Just take your time working through this section until you feel comfortable. A little practice will go a long way toward making you a confident WordPerfect user.

USING A MOUSE WITH WORDPERFECT

Although a mouse is not absolutely necessary to use WordPerfect for Windows, it certainly makes things a lot easier. With a mouse, for example, you just point to the function you want to perform and click the left mouse button. A mouse is particularly useful if you use graphics, since it allows you to change the size and position of graphic boxes and lines without using a single keystroke!

A mouse will be a worthwhile investment that will quickly pay off in time and trouble.

There are several types of actions you can take with the mouse:

- You will see a symbol on the screen, called the *pointer*, indicating the position of the mouse. The shape of the pointer will depend on its location on the screen. When an instruction says to point to something on the screen, move the mouse on your desk until the pointer is on top of the object on the screen.

- *Click* means to place the mouse pointer on an object, then quickly press and release the left mouse button. In some instances, you will see an instruction to click the right mouse button, but unless that button is specified, use the left one.

- *Double-click* means to click twice—quickly. If you double-click and nothing occurs, then you didn't click fast enough—don't wait before each click.

- To *drag* means to place the mouse pointer on an object, press *and hold down* the left mouse button, then move the mouse. Do not release the mouse button until you reach a specified location.

USING THE KEYBOARD

Though it is certainly easier to use WordPerfect if you have a mouse, you can get by with the keyboard alone. Most mouse commands or actions can also be performed by using a few keystrokes. You'll either have to press a particular key by itself, or together with another key. In this book, keystrokes that should be pressed together are separated with a plus sign. The combination Alt+F5, for example, means that you should press and hold down the Alt key, press and release the F5 key, then release the Alt key.

CONVENTIONS USED IN THIS BOOK

Throughout this book you will get concise instructions on how to perform WordPerfect functions. In most cases, you can follow the instructions whether or not you have a mouse.

Most instructions tell you to select an option. *Selecting* an item means to chose it in a way that performs some action. To select an item with the mouse, point to the item with the mouse pointer then click the left mouse button (unless the right button is specifically given in the instruction). We'll discuss selecting menu and dialog box items with the keyboard a little later.

To *highlight* something means to place the cursor at the option so its name appears in reverse. Highlighting does not perform any action immediately but prepares the option for some action. Highlighting is usually performed with the keyboard to prepare an item for selection. For example, you can highlight a Menu Bar option without displaying its pull-down menu.

Often, you have to select more than one item to perform a WordPerfect function. Rather than tell you to select File, then select Print, then select Page, each of the items you must select are separated by the ➤ symbol. For example,

Select File ➤ Print ➤ Page

means to select these three items in turn as they appear on the screen.

Many WordPerfect options also have shortcut keys—key combinations that you can press instead of selecting items from the screen. You'll see shortcut keys listed (in parentheses) after the select instruction, like this:

Select Layout ➤ Paragraph ➤ Indent (F7)

This means you can either select Layout, then Paragraph, then Indent, or simply press F7. The shortcut keys are particularly useful if you don't have a mouse.

As a Windows application, WordPerfect uses shortcut keys that conform to the Windows environment and that are compatible with earlier versions of WordPerfect for Windows. These are the keystrokes explained and illustrated in this book.

UNDERSTANDING THE WORDPERFECT SCREEN

The WordPerfect screen contains the Title Bar, Menu Bar, Button Bar, and Power Bar at the top of the screen, and the Status Bar at the bottom of the screen.

The screen is composed of two types of windows—the WordPerfect application window and document windows. Document windows allow you to display and work with as many as nine different documents at the same time.

The Title Bar

The Title Bar on the top of the screen displays the name of the document on which you are working. Document1 will be replaced by the name you give to a document. The Title Bar also has three control boxes which govern the WordPerfect application window:

- The Control Menu box (the rectangle) at the left end of the Title Bar lets you exit WordPerfect, reduces the program to an icon (so you can work with another program while WordPerfect is still running), or switches you to another application.
- The Restore button at the right end (the two triangles) changes the size of the WordPerfect window. When you use the restore button to reduce the size of the window, the button becomes a single up-pointing triangle, called the maximize box, which returns the window to full-screen size.
- The Minimize button (with a single triangle pointing down) just to the left of the Restore button, also reduces WordPerfect to an icon.

The Menu Bar

The Menu Bar displays the menus from which you select commands to work with your documents. On the left of the Menu Bar is a Control Menu box that you can use to close the document window. The Restore button on the right of the Menu Bar lets you change the size of the document window, or reduce it to an icon.

The Button Bar

The Button Bar contains buttons you click with the mouse to access a WordPerfect function. The icon (picture) and caption on each button explain the function it performs. For example, you'd use the button with the word Envelope and the picture of envelopes to quickly format and print an envelope.

You'll learn how to use the Button Bar, and how to display other bars that perform additional functions.

The Power Bar

The Power Bar contains buttons you click with the mouse to perform common word processing functions. The icon on each button represents the function it performs.

You'll learn how to use the Power Bar to streamline your word processing. In many cases, you can complete a word processing session using just the Button- and Power Bars to communicate with WordPerfect.

The Status Bar

The Status Bar gives you information about your document and the current state of WordPerfect. The name of the font you're using and the size of your text appears on the left side of the Status Bar. The center section of the bar displays additional information as you perform certain WordPerfect functions. For example, the word Insert means that you are in the Insert mode—existing characters will move over and down to make room for new characters that you type.

The information on the right of the Status Bar lets you know where the cursor is located in the document:

Pg The number of the page you are currently viewing on the screen

Ln The distance of the cursor from the top of the page

Pos The distance of the cursor from the left edge of the page

The area between the Power- and Status Bars is the *text region*. The text region is where your document appears as you type. While you're in the text region, the cursor is a thin vertical line called the *insertion point*, which indicates where the next character you type will appear. Its position is indicated in the Status Bar. You can use either the mouse or the directional arrow keys to move the cursor to the place you want to type, insert, or delete characters. You can place the insertion point before or after a character on the screen, but *not* on or under it as with the cursor in a DOS application.

WORKING WITH MENUS

Selecting a Menu Bar option with the mouse or keyboard displays a pull-down menu. A pull-down menu lists specific operations that you can perform. Figure B.1, for instance, shows the pull-down menu for the File option. Notice that the first option on the menu is highlighted, or appears in reverse. This means that it is ready to select or activate. In some pull-down menus, certain options may appear gray, or dimmed. These options are not currently available to be selected but must first be activated by performing some other function.

Menu Bar shown with pull-down menu for the File option

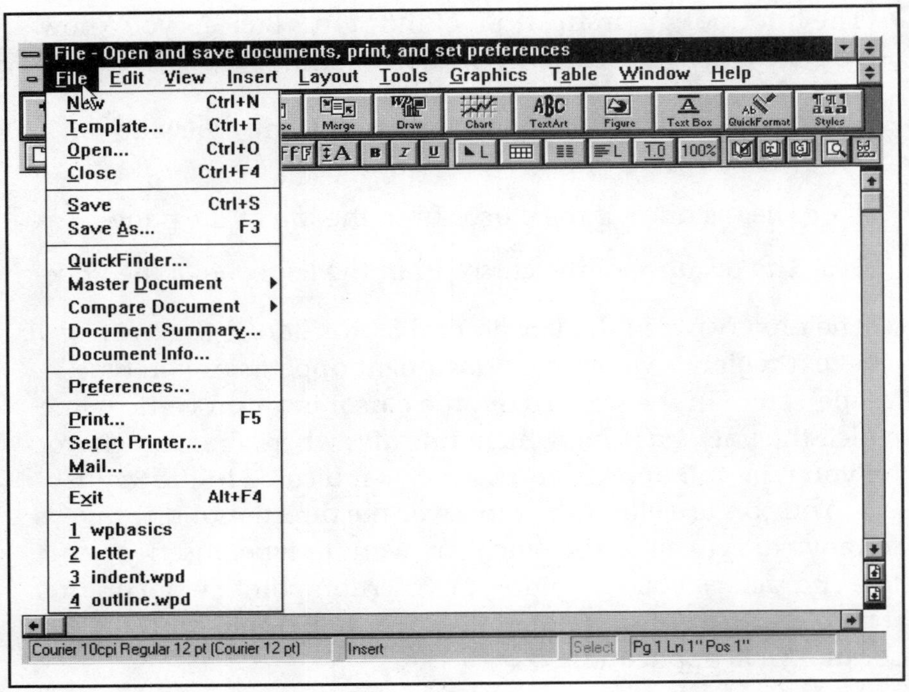

If the function has an alternate shortcut key, it will be listed next to the command, such as F3 next to the menu option Save As.

Other options in pull-down menus contain special symbols. An ellipses (...) means that selecting the option will display a dialog box containing additional choices from which you must select. Selecting an option with the ➤ symbol will display another pull-down menu. A ✓ next to a menu option shows that it has been turned on, or selected.

Here's how to use menus:

- To display a pull-down menu, click on the option with the left mouse button, or hold down the Alt key and press the underlined letter of the function.

- To display another pull-down menu, click on another menu bar option, or press the → or ← keys.
- To select a pull-down menu option, click on the option with the mouse button, press the underlined letter, or press the ↓ or ↑ key to highlight the option and press Enter.
- To cancel a menu, click elsewhere on the window or press the Esc key.

WORKING WITH DIALOG BOXES

Selecting a menu item or performing a function may display a dialog box. A dialog box contains additional options and requires some type of input by either clicking the mouse or typing on the keyboard. While some dialog boxes only present a few options, others can be quite complex. The dialog boxes shown in Figure B.2, for example, contain a number of different types of options.

Moving within a Dialog Box

You move from item to item in a dialog box by clicking the mouse in the item you want to change.

With the keyboard, press Tab to move forward, Shift+Tab to move backward through the options. You can also press Alt and the underlined letter of the option.

Text Boxes

A text box is an area where you can type information using the keyboard. Move into a text box by clicking it with the mouse, by pressing Alt and the underlined letter of the option, or by using

Dialog boxes contain options from which you can select

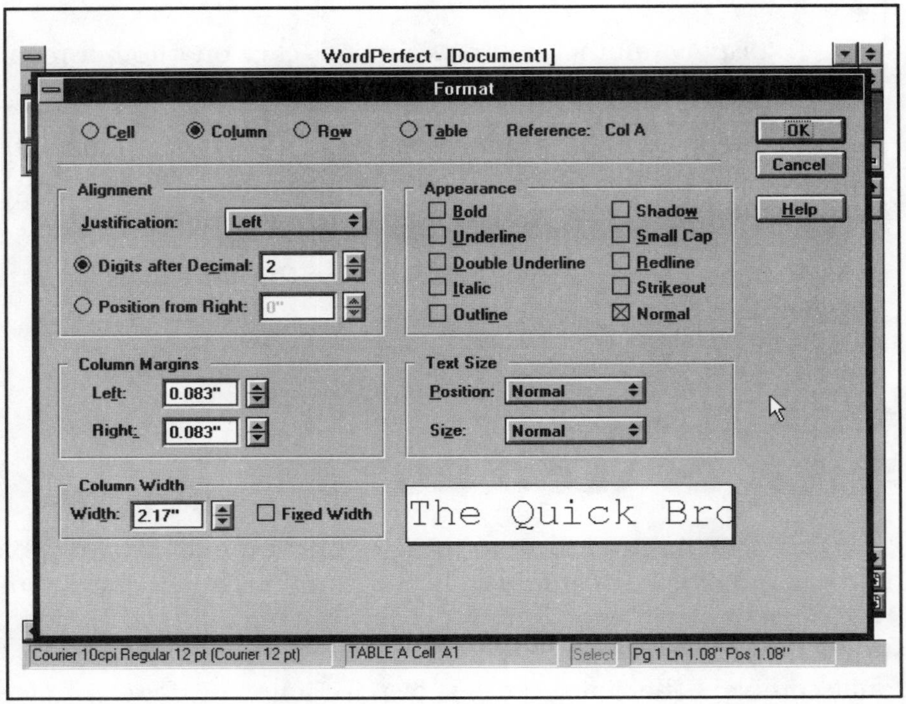

the Tab, Shift+Tab, or one of the arrow keys. Then, type the value or setting you want for that option. *Do not* press Enter after typing the settings unless you are done selecting options in the dialog box. Pressing Enter accepts the settings and removes the dialog box from the screen.

Most text boxes already contain an entry or setting. If the box is highlighted, the current contents will be erased when you start typing a new entry. If the text is not highlighted, you must first delete the current contents before entering new information.

To the right of some text boxes is a smaller box with up and down pointing arrows separated by a line. You can increase or decrease the value in the text box by clicking on these arrows.

With the keyboard, select the text box and press ↑ or ↓ to change the value in the text box.

Drop Down List Box

You'll see other boxes with up and down pointing arrows, but without a line between them. This indicates that there are additional choices for that option in a drop-down list box. A drop-down list box shows a list of available options.

To see the list, point to the arrow, then click and hold down the mouse button. Once the list is displayed, drag the mouse down to select, or highlight, your choice. With the keyboard, select the item, press Alt+↓ to display the list box, then press the ↑ or ↓ key to select your choice. You can also press the ↓ or ↑ to cycle through the items without displaying the list. Each time ↑ or ↓ is pressed another item in the list appears.

You cannot type information directly in one of these boxes—you can only select an option from the drop-down list.

List Box

Other list boxes are already displayed on the screen. To select an option from the list box, click on it with the mouse. Using the keyboard, select the list box, then press the ↑ or ↓ to select the option.

Check Boxes

A check box is a small square next to an option that you may select. When you select a check box, WordPerfect places an X in the box indicating that the option is turned on. Selecting a check box that already contains an X will remove the X and turn off the option. In many cases, check boxes are grouped together. Within the group, they are usually non-exclusive, so you can check more than one box at a time. For example, Figure B.2 shows a group of check boxes in the Appearance section. You can click on both the bold and underline check boxes in the group to print characters that are both boldfaced and underlined.

Radio Buttons

A radio button is a circle next to an item. When you select a radio button, a black dot appears in the center, indicating it is turned on.

Radio buttons come in exclusive groups. Choosing one radio button in the group automatically turns off any other button in the same group that was already turned on. For example, in Figure B.2 there are four radio buttons on the top row of the dialog box. Only one of these buttons can be selected at a time.

Command Buttons

Command buttons carry out an action and act on the entire dialog box. Many dialog boxes have command buttons labeled OK and Cancel. Clicking on OK or pressing Enter removes the dialog box from the screen and puts its settings into effect. Clicking on Cancel or pressing Esc removes the dialog box without accepting your changes.

Other dialog boxes contain a button labeled Select. After choosing an option from the dialog box, choose Select to accept the settings.

When you click on a command button that has an ellipses (...), another dialog box containing additional choices will appear.

Graphic Sample

Many WordPerfect dialog boxes contain a graphic illustration showing how your choices affect the document. Figure B.2, for instance, shows how text will appear. As you select options in the box that affect text, the characters in the illustration will change to reflect your settings.

Refer to the illustration as you make your choices. When the sample appears as you desire, choose OK or Select to accept the settings and return to the document.

If the dialog box does not contain an illustration, you have to exit the dialog box to see how your settings affect the document.

Multipurpose Dialog Boxes

Radio buttons are sometimes used to control multipurpose dialog boxes. The options displayed in a multipurpose dialog box depend on which radio button is selected. The dialog box in Figure B.2, for example, is controlled by the row of radio buttons on the top of the box. The Column button is selected, so the dialog box contains options that relate to columns. If you click on another radio button in the group, different options will appear in the other parts of the dialog box.

CHANGING TO WORDPERFECT FOR WINDOWS

If you are a WordPerfect for DOS user, you may prefer to use the keystroke combinations you are already familiar with. To change to the DOS-compatible keyboard:

1. Select File ➤ Preferences
2. Double-click on the Keyboard icon.

3 Click on WPDOS Compatible in the list that appears

4 Choose Select, then Close.

WordPerfect for Windows will now respond to the DOS version shortcut keys, and these keystrokes will appear next to the function names in pull down menus.

Keep in mind that the instructions and figures in this book illustrate the *Windows* shortcut keys. No matter which keyboard you select, you can follow all of the menu selection and mouse instructions in this book. However, if you change to the DOS keyboard, substitute the DOS keystroke when you use a shortcut key rather than the mouse or menu to perform a function.

1 part one

QUICK START

Even with all of its power and versatility, WordPerfect for Windows is remarkably easy to use. You can produce professional-looking newsletters and other publications almost as quickly and easily as you can create a short memo or letter.

It you still need convincing, just work through the two short lessons in this part. You will learn how to start WordPerfect for Windows, and how to write, save, and print documents. If you can learn all of this in just two lessons, imagine what you'll be able to accomplish after you're done with this book!

It's So Easy

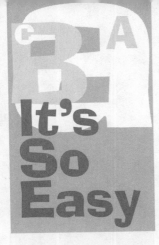

Starting WordPerfect

The tasks in this lesson will get you started with WordPerfect for Windows by teaching you the most basic features. You'll learn how to start WordPerfect, how to enter text, how to get on-screen help, how to change the display mode and magnification, and more.

If you have not yet installed WordPerfect on your computer, carefully follow the installation instructions supplied with the program, then come back to this lesson. If WordPerfect for Windows is already on your computer, you're ready to go!

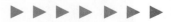

STARTING WORDPERFECT

Starting WordPerfect for Windows is easy. Just make sure that you or someone else has installed WordPerfect and Windows on your computer's hard disk drive, and that your computer, monitor, and printer are all set up as they should be.

1 Turn on your computer and monitor. If your system automatically starts in Windows, skip to step 3.

The Word-Perfect for Windows screen

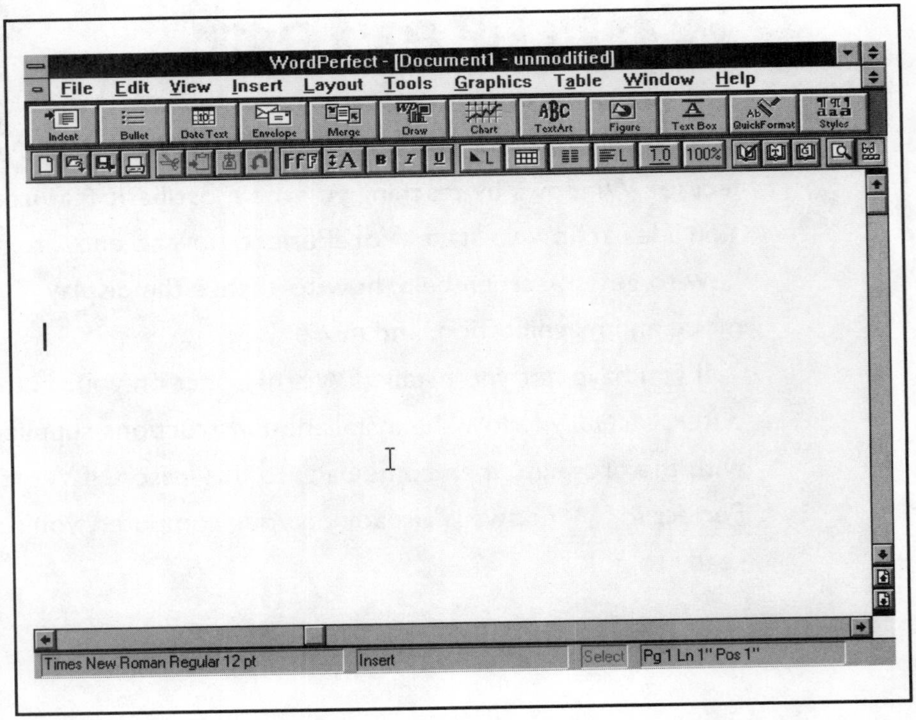

2 Type **WIN** and press Enter to run Windows.

3 Double-click on the WPWin6.0 icon in the WPWin6.0 group window. Your screen will look like the figure.

oops!

Something's wrong

If the WPWin 6.0 group window is not displayed when Windows starts, select Window from the Menu Bar, then click on WPWin 6.0 in the pull-down list.

tip

If you're ready to quit

If you are not ready to continue with this lesson, select File ➤ Exit (or press Alt+F4). If you entered any text on the screen, a dialog box will appear asking if you want to save the document. Select No.

tip

Trouble with the menus?

See WordPerfect Basics to learn how to work with the Menu Bar and pull-down menus, and to learn about the WordPerfect screen.

TYPING IN WORDPERFECT

If you've ever used a typewriter, you'll feel at home in WordPerfect—all of the letter, number, and punctuation keys on the four middle rows of the keyboard work just the same. Here's how it works:

1 Press Tab to insert a tab at the start of a paragraph.

2 Type until you reach the end of the paragraph. *Do not* press Enter when you reach the end of a line. WordPerfect senses when the word you are typing will not fit in the line and

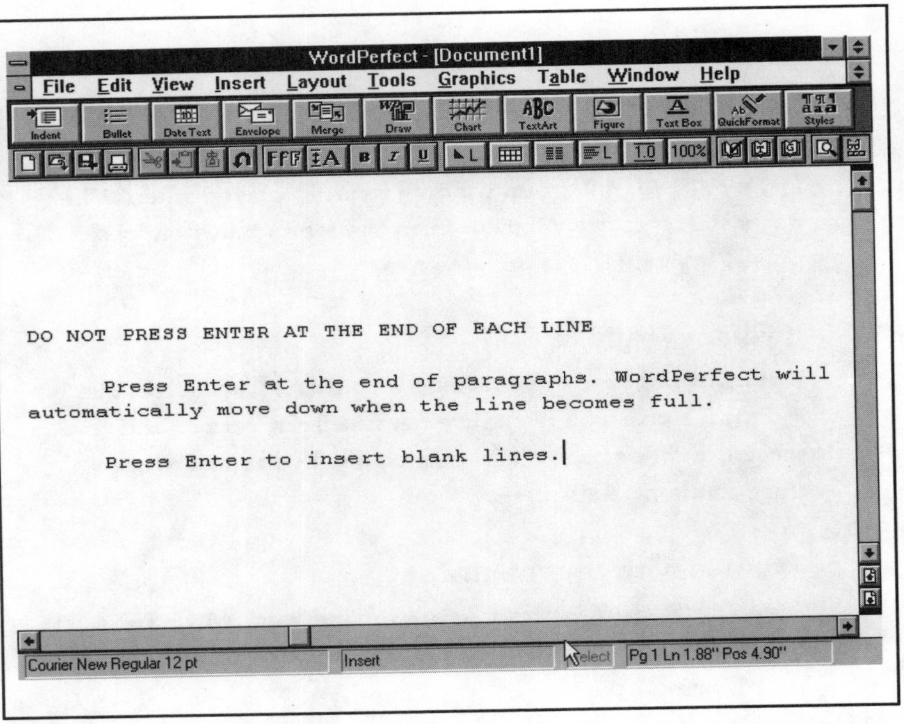

WordPerfect moved the word "automatically" to the next line as it was typed.

moves the word to the next line automatically, as shown in the figure (this process is called *wrapping*).

3 Press Enter to end a paragraph or to insert a blank line.

4 Press Backspace to erase mistakes.

As you type, the insertion point (cursor) moves down the page and the Ln (for Line) indicator in the status line changes. As you pass the last line on the screen the lines at the top scroll up out of view. You can use the Scroll Bars to bring text back into view, as explained in Lesson 3.

tip

Is there still room on the page?

When you reach the end of a page, just continue typing—WordPerfect automatically starts a new page. A line appears across the screen, and the Pg (for Page) indicator in the Status Bar increases by one.

Extra! Extra!

for more...

Taking control of pages

If you want to end one page and begin another before WordPerfect does it automatically, press Ctrl+Enter. See "Inserting Page Breaks" in Lesson 6 for more information.

tip

It's been modified

When you start typing, the word *Unmodified* is removed from the Title Bar. This indicates that you should save the document before exiting WordPerfect—if you're happy with your changes.

GETTING HELP

With a program as feature-laden as WordPerfect, it is easy to forget how some features work. To help jog your memory, WordPerfect has an on-line Help system. WordPerfect Help includes information on menu commands, dialog boxes, and other tools. There are even *coaches* that take you step-by-step through complete word processing tasks. If you need help:

1 Select Help from the Menu Bar to display the Help pull-down menu.

Help Contents window

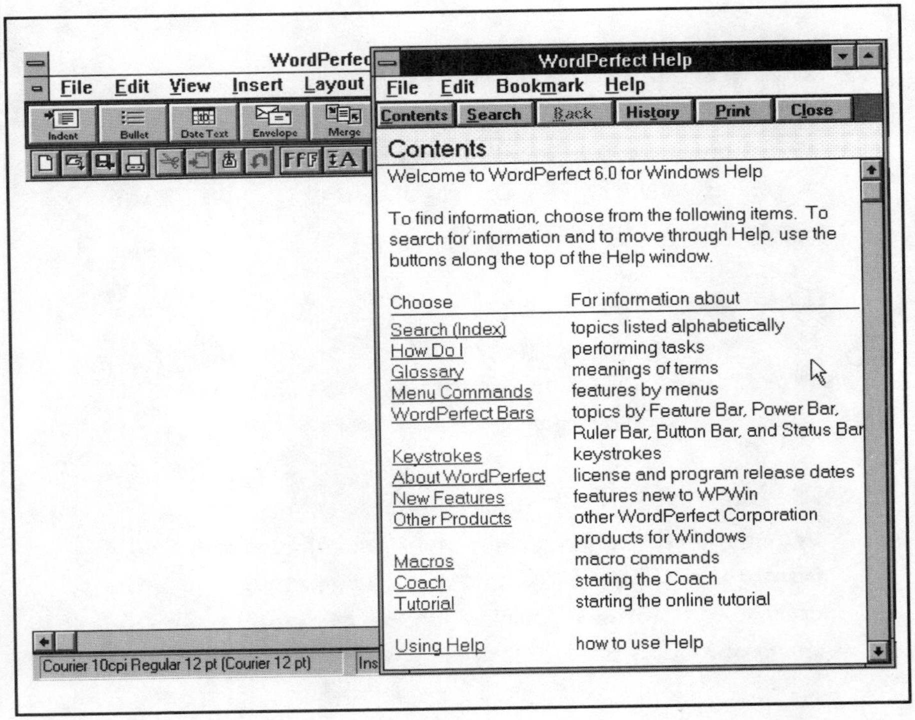

2 To see detailed information, do one of the following:

- Select Contents to display a list of general topics for which help is available, then double-click on the subject you want help with—scroll the list if necessary.
- Select Search for Help On to select from a list of help topics, or to enter the subject for which you need help.
- Select Coaches to display a list of topics for which WordPerfect provides step-by-step instructions.

3 Double-click on the Help window control box (or press Alt+F4) to quit the Help system.

tip

Skip the menu, full speed ahead

WordPerfect also has context-sensitive help that you can use at any time. Just display the menu or dialog box you want help on, highlight the item, and press F1.

new feature

New feature

Step-by-step coaches are new in version 6.0.

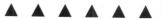

DISPLAYING THE POWER BAR AND BUTTON BAR

Some functions are performed so often when creating documents that WordPerfect has added them to special on-screen elements. The *Power Bar* displays options for performing common functions, such as opening and printing documents and formatting text. The *Button Bar* provides buttons for additional formats and specialized functions, such as creating envelopes, graphics, or charts. When you place the mouse pointer on a Power Bar or Button Bar button, a description of the button's function will appear in the Title Bar.

Use the View menu to turn off and on the Power Bar and Button Bar

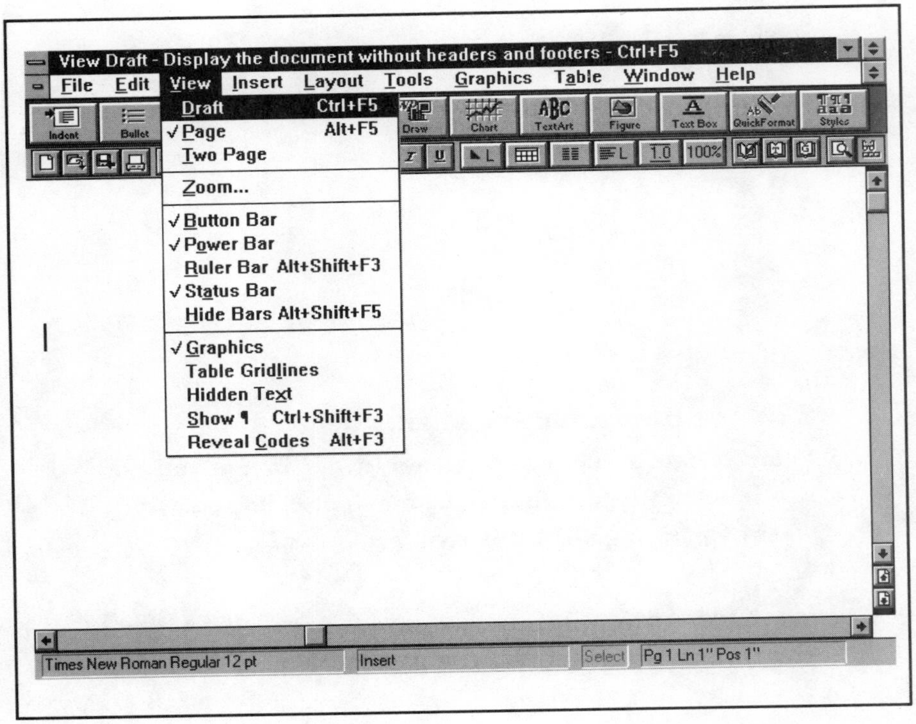

To work with the Power Bar:

1 Select View ➤ Power Bar to display the Power Bar (if it is not already on your screen).

2 Click on the button for the function you want to select.

3 To turn off the Power Bar, select View ➤ Power Bar.

To work with the Button Bar:

1 Select View ➤ Button Bar to display the Button Bar (if it is not already on your screen).

2 Click on the button of the function you want to select.

3 To turn off the Button Bar, select View ➤ Button Bar.

power bar

Quick buttons

Click on the View Button Bar button to alternately turn on and off the Button Bar.

tip

It remembers!

The Button Bar and Power Bar will appear automatically if they were on screen when you exited WordPerfect.

tip

Hiding everything

To remove all the on-screen aids at one time, select View ➤ Hide Bars, then select OK from the dialog box that appears. The Title, Menu, Button, Power, Status, and vertical Scroll Bars will be removed. To display them again, press Esc.

SELECTING BUTTON BARS

WordPerfect has so many useful features that they cannot all fit on one Button Bar. Since buttons are so easy to use, twelve Button Bars are available for performing other frequently used functions. Just select the one you want to display and use.

To select another Button Bar:

1. Point to the Button Bar and click the *right* mouse button to display a list of available Button Bars, as shown in the figure.

Quick menu of Button Bars with a rectangular Button Bar in the background

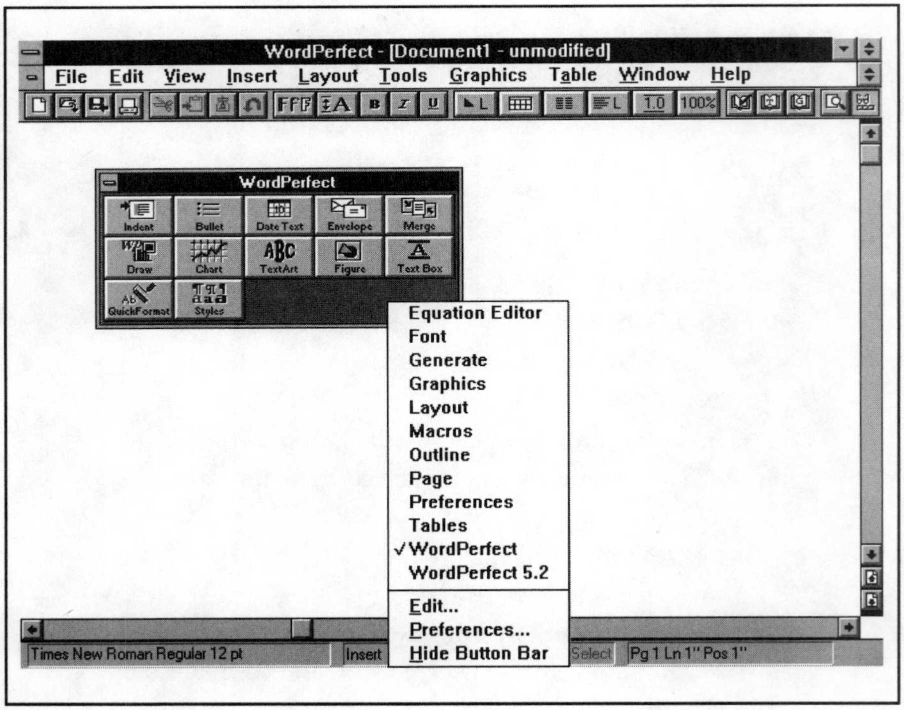

2 Click on the Button Bar you want to display. If all the buttons do not fit on the screen, a Scroll Bar will appear on the Button Bar's right. You use the Scroll Bar to scroll additional buttons into view.

tip

Setting preferences

You can also choose a Button Bar by selecting File ➤ Preferences ➤ Button Bar, double-clicking on the bar you want, then selecting Close. Use the Preferences dialog box to create and customize Button Bars.

tip

WordPerfect remembers

If you turn off the Button Bar—by selecting View ➤ Button Bar—WordPerfect remembers which bar was active. That same bar will appear when you next select View ➤ Button Bar. To choose the default Button Bar again, select WordPerfect from the Button Bar quick list, or from the File ➤ Preferences ➤ Button Bar dialog box.

for more...

Keep reading

See later lessons to learn about the functions performed by these Button Bars.

CHANGING VIEWS

WordPerfect has three view modes: Draft, Page, and Two Page. When you first start WordPerfect, it will be in Page mode and you'll see your document on the screen exactly how it will appear when printed. This includes headers, footers, page numbers, graphics, and blank areas representing the top and bottom margins of the page. In Draft mode, you will also see fonts and graphics, but not headers, footers, page numbers, and margins. In Two Page mode, you will see two complete pages on screen at one time.

You can type, edit, and format documents in all three modes.

Two Page mode showing a document with fonts and graphics

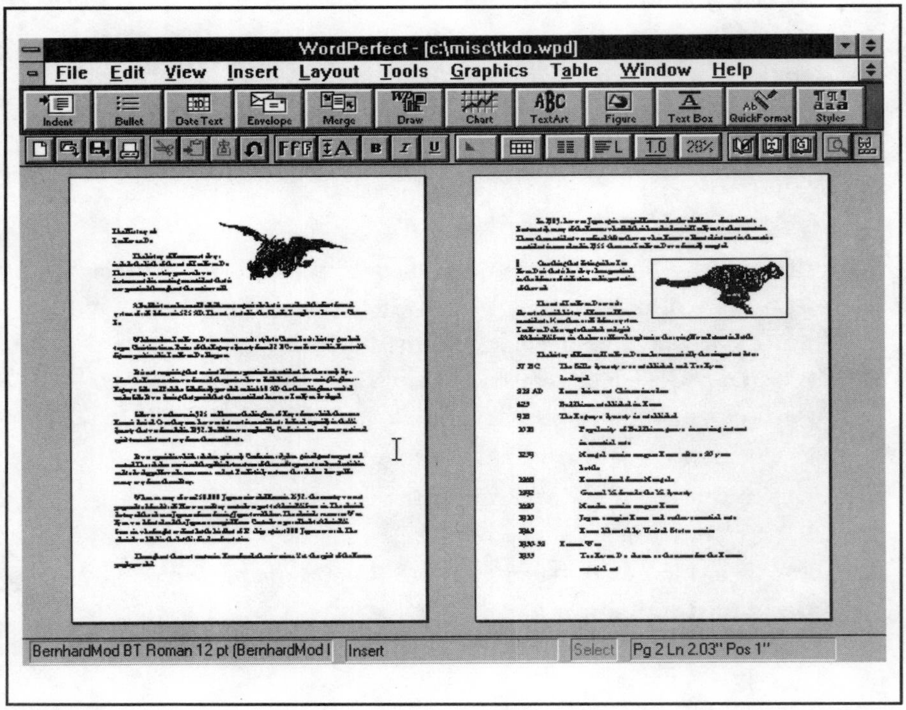

To Change to Draft Mode

- Select View ➤ Draft.

To Change to Page Mode

- Select View ➤ Page.

To Change to Two Page Mode

- Select View ➤ Two Page.

new feature

New feature

Being able to edit facing pages and in magnified modes is new in version 6.0.

tip

Previewing the page

Two Page mode serves as a Print Preview. You can type and edit in Two Page mode, but your text may appear too small to read. Use Two Page mode to see an overview of how your document will appear when printed, and to move graphic images around the page.

CHANGING THE DISPLAY MAGNIFICATION

The default display magnification is set at 100%. This means that the text and graphics appear about the same size on screen as they do on the printed page. You can reduce the magnification to display a full page or more on screen at one time, or enlarge the text to make it easier to read. For example, when set at 200%, the on-screen text and graphics are twice as large as they are on paper.

Document in 150% magnification

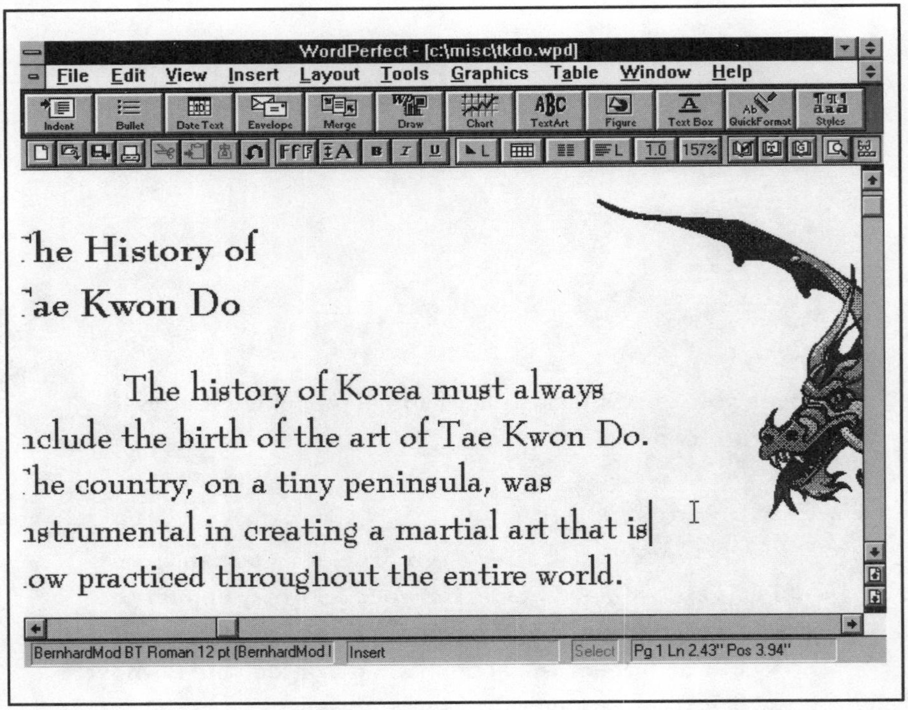

You can edit and format your document no matter what magnification you select.

1. Select View ➤ Zoom.
2. Select a percentage. The options are 50%, 75%, 100%, 150%, 200%, 300%, Margin Width, Page Width, Full Page, and Other (to set a custom magnification).

power bar

Instant zoom

Click on the Zoom button (the one marked 100%) and hold down the mouse button to display zoom options. Drag the mouse to select the desired magnification.

power bar

Full Page preview

Click on the Page Zoom Full button to display one full page in Page View. Click on the button again to return to your previous view mode.

tip

Zoom options

Full Page displays one full page on the screen. Margin Width sets the magnification so text lines fill the width of the window. Page width sets the magnification so the page width fills the screen. With each setting, WordPerfect calculates the percentage of magnification and displays it in the Power Bar zoom button.

It's So Easy

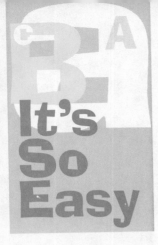

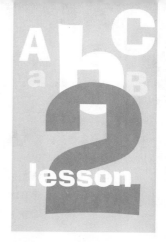

lesson 2

Saving and Printing Documents

When you are done typing a document, you'll need to print it or save it to a disk so you can use it later. Usually, you'll do both. Printed copies are handy for reviewing documents and for distributing your documents to others—even in this age of electronic mail. You will still need to save a document if you want to edit or print it later.

SAVING A DOCUMENT

When you save a document for the first time, you must give it a name. Document names can be from one to eight characters long, plus a three-character extension of your choice.

To save your document for the first time:

1. Select File ➤ Save As (F3) or File ➤ Save (Ctrl+S) to display the Save As dialog box.

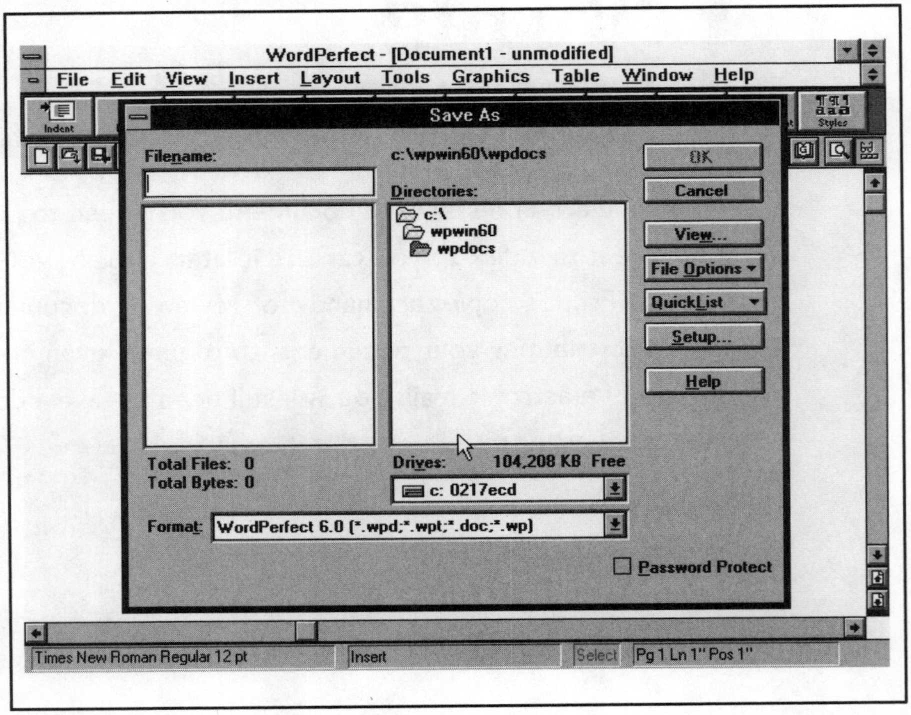

Save As dialog box

2 Type a document name. When WordPerfect saves a document, it automatically adds the extension WPD and saves it in the WPWIN60\WPDOCS directory. If you want another extension, or want to save the file on another disk or directory, type a full path and filename, as in

c:\BUDGET\REPORT.DOC

3 Select OK. The document's name will appear in the Title Bar.

Once you have saved your document, you can save it again (after making changes to it) by selecting File ➤ Save (Ctrl+S).

power bar

Saving documents

Click on the Save button to save a document.

tip

If you use another version

WordPerfect 6.0 saves documents in a format incompatible with earlier versions of WordPerfect. If you want to use the document with WordPerfect 5.1 for DOS as well, select File ➤ Save As, pull down the Save File as Type list box, and select WordPerfect 5.1/5.2 from the list of formats.

oops!

Don't be lazy

WordPerfect saves a temporary copy of your document every 20 minutes. But this is only a safeguard in the event of a power or computer failure. ***You must still save your document yourself before exiting WordPerfect.***

CLEARING A DOCUMENT FROM YOUR SCREEN

Saving a document does not remove it from the screen. This way you can continue working on it.

If you have already saved one document and want to work on another, or if you have changed your mind about what you've already typed and want to start again, you can erase the document from memory by using the File ➤ Close command.

Dialog box seen when trying to close an edited document

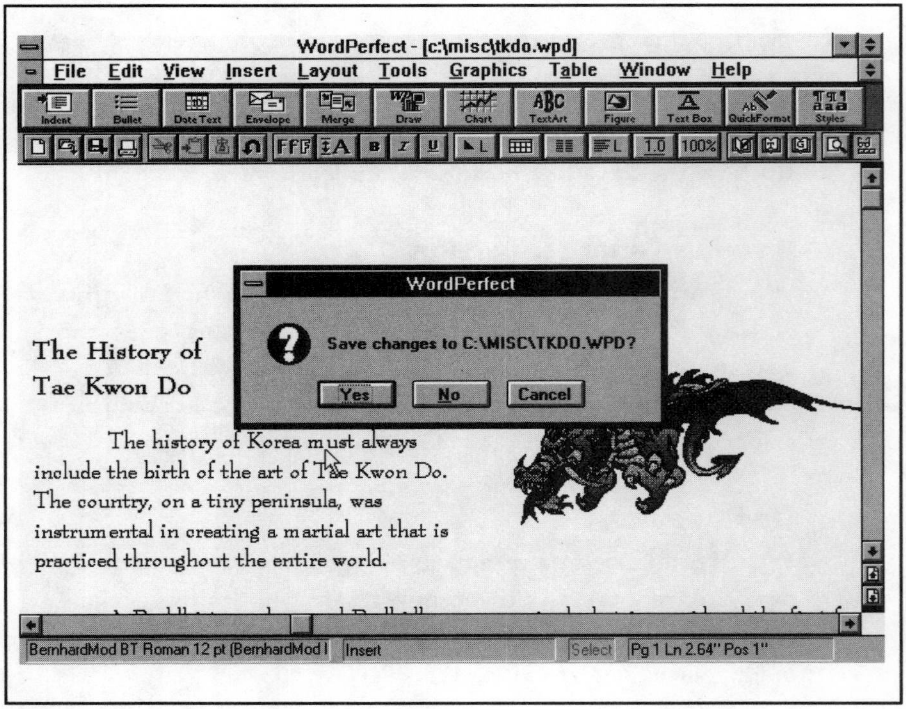

1 Select File ➤ Close (Ctrl+F4).

2 If you made any changes to the document since you last saved it, a dialog box will appear asking if you want to save the document before exiting. Select Yes to save the document, No not to save it, or Cancel to leave the document on screen.

tip ▶ **Using the control box**

You can also close a document by double-clicking on the document's control box. The document control box is on the left side of the Menu Bar, beneath the WordPerfect control box in the Title Bar. Double-clicking on the WordPerfect control box will close WordPerfect.

PRINTING DOCUMENTS

WordPerfect has many powerful printing features. By default, it prints every page in the document on the screen. You can also print just the page you are working on, a bit of selected text, or a series of selected pages. You can print multiple copies by setting the Number of Copies option, and you can speed up the process of printing multiple copies if you set the Generated By option to Printer. You can also select to print odd or even pages, print pages in reverse order, print your document like a booklet, and print a document that's on the disk, without even displaying it.

Print dialog box

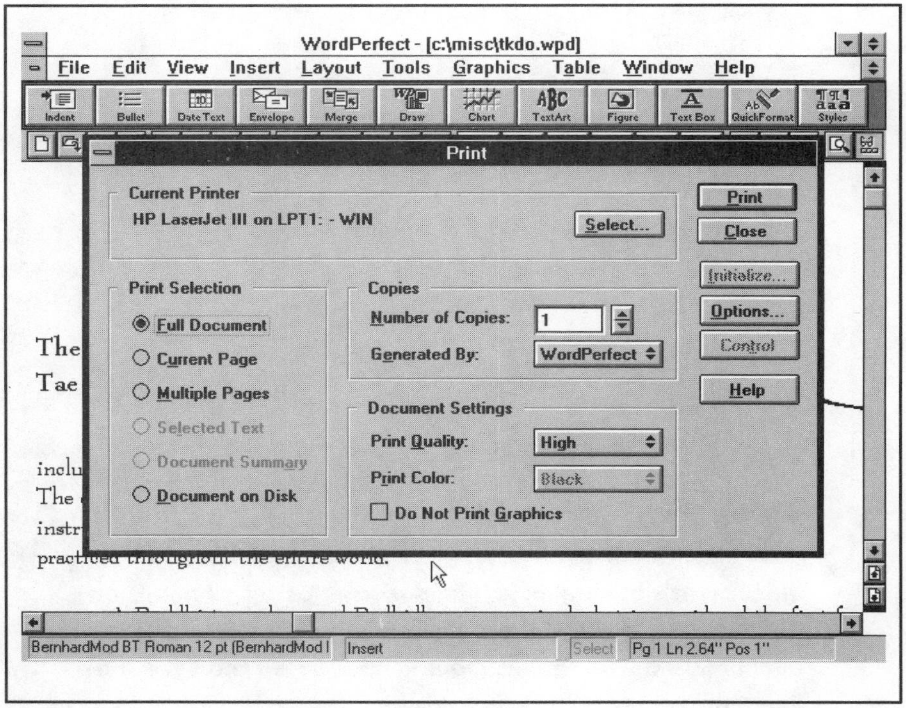

But if you just want a quick copy of your document, the process is easy.

1. Make sure your printer is turned on and ready, and that you have paper.
2. Select File ➤ Print (F5) to display the Print dialog box.
3. Select Print.

power bar

One click printing

Click the Print button to print a document.

tip

Just to be safe, save!

You do not have to save a document before you print it. However, get into the habit of saving documents whether you print them or not. You may print a document, then need it again at some later date.

tip

Speed printing

To print a document using all of the default settings, press Ctrl+P. This sends the document to the printer without first displaying the Print dialog box.

SELECTING YOUR PRINTER

If your document does not print accurately, you may have selected the wrong printer. WordPerfect for Windows can use two different types of printer drivers: the Windows printer drivers that are already installed on your Windows system, or its own printer drivers. WordPerfect can print with almost any printer on the market, so if you currently have the wrong one selected, changing it is a simple matter.

1 Select File ➤ Select Printer. A dialog box appears listing your installed Windows and WordPerfect drivers. The printers are identified by either a Windows or WordPerfect logo.

Select Printer dialog box

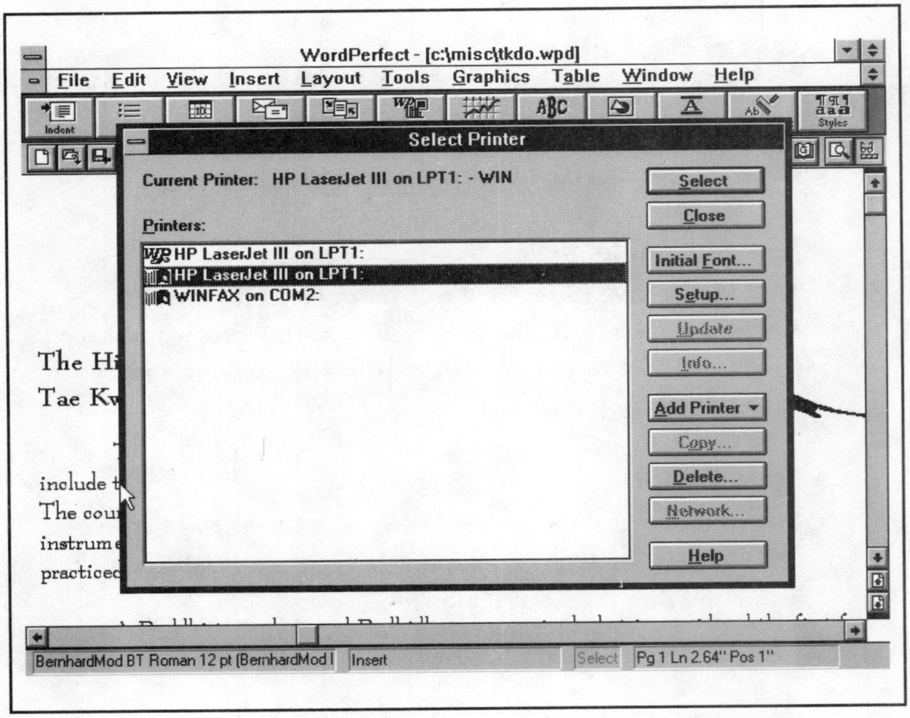

2 Select the printer that is connected to your system.

3 Choose Select.

oops!

Your printer isn't listed

If your printer is not listed in the Select Printer dialog box, select Add Printer. You can then choose to add a WordPerfect or Windows printer driver. If you cannot add your printer using this option, exit WordPerfect and run the WordPerfect Install program.

tip

What printer?

If you cannot find your model printer, try selecting a compatible brand. For dot matrix printers, try an EPSON or IBM Graphics printer. For a laser printer, try one of the HP LaserJet models. If you cannot find a substitute, contact WordPerfect Corporation for updated drivers and printer information.

SAVING DOCUMENTS AND QUITTING WORDPERFECT

When you are finished using WordPerfect, exit the program and return to the Windows Program Manager. You can save a document and exit WordPerfect using one dialog box.

1. Select File ➤ Exit (Alt+F4).
2. If you made any changes to the document since you last saved it, a dialog box will appear asking if you want to save the document before closing. Select Yes to save the document, No not to save it, or Cancel to remain in WordPerfect.

File menu

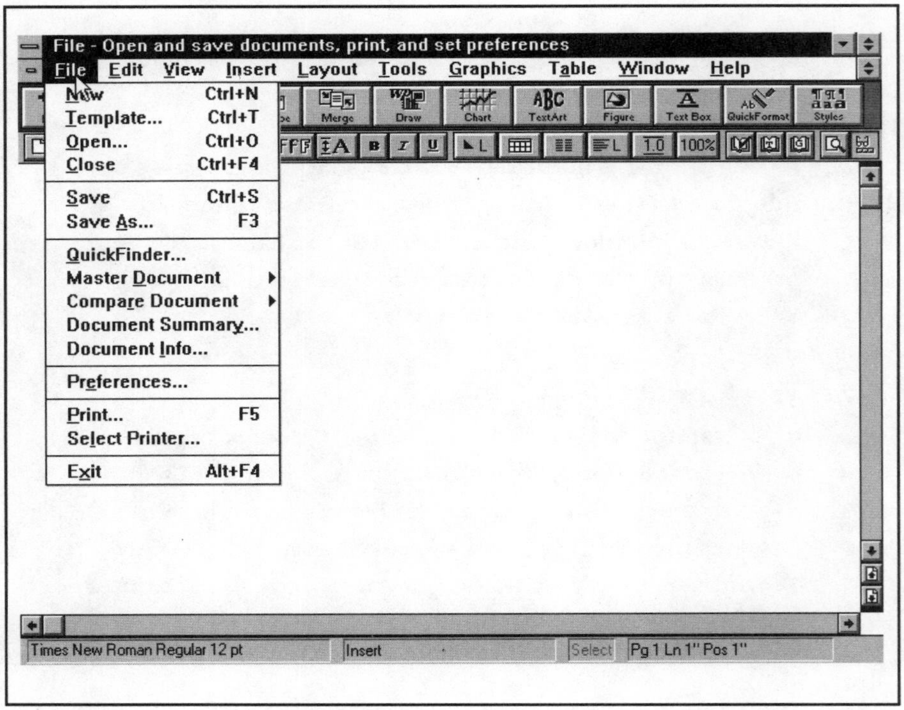

tip **Play it safe**

Always exit WordPerfect and Windows before turning off your computer. If you don't, you could damage files that you'll need later.

tip **Using the control box**

You can also exit WordPerfect by double-clicking on the WordPerfect window control box—the small rectangle on the left of the Title Bar.

Let's Do It!

PART ONE ▶ **Exercises**

Here is a brief exercise that lets you create, save, and print a document:

1. Turn on your computer and monitor.
2. Type **WIN** and press Enter to start Windows.
3. Double-click on the WPWin 6.0 icon to start WordPerfect.
4. Press Tab to indent the first line of the paragraph.
5. Type the following text. Remember, do not press Enter when you reach the end of the line.

   We the People of the United States, in Order to form a more perfect Union, establish Justice, insure domestic Tranquility, provide for the common defense, promote the general Welfare, and secure the Blessings of Liberty to ourselves and our Posterity, do ordain and establish this Constitution for the United States of America.
6. Press Enter twice—once to end the paragraph, a second time to insert a blank line between paragraphs.

▶▶▶▶▶▶▶

7 Press Tab, then type the following:

> **All legislative powers herein granted shall be vested in a Congress of the United States, which shall consist of a Senate and House of Representatives.**

Now let's save the document under the name HISTORY.

8 Click on the Save button on the Power Bar or select File ➤ Save As (F3).

9 Type **HISTORY**.

10 Select OK. The completed text is shown in Figure 1.1.

Now, print the document.

11 Click on the Print button on the Power Bar or select File ➤ Print.

12 Select Print or press Enter.

Finally, let's exit WordPerfect.

13 Select File ➤ Exit.

That's all there is to it!

Figure 1.1: Completed sample text

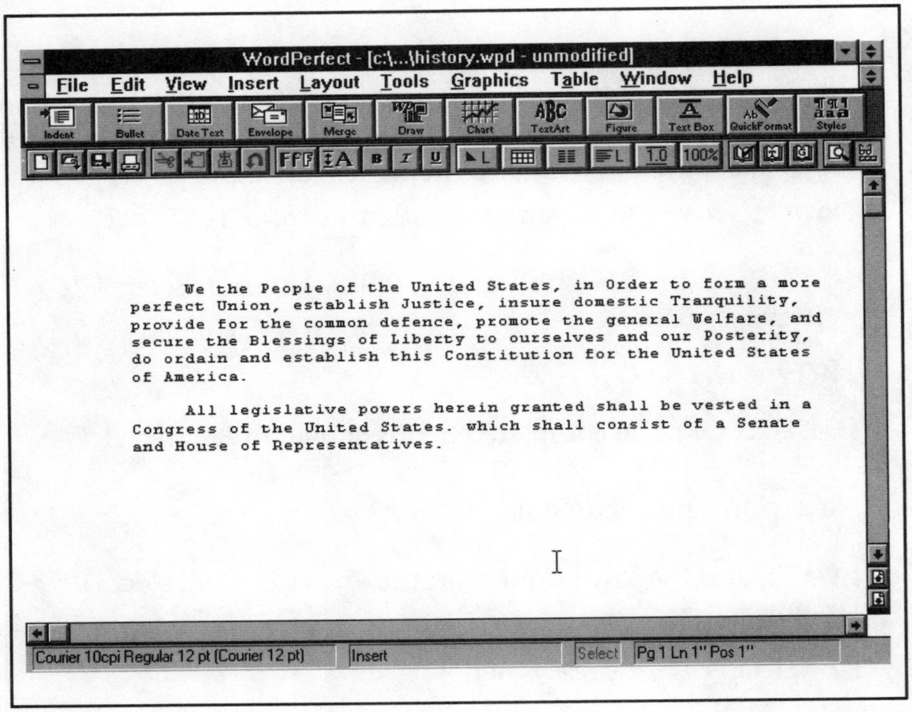
WordPerfect - [c:\...\history.wpd - unmodified]
File Edit View Insert Layout Tools Graphics Table Window Help
Indent
Bullet
Date Text
Envelope
Merge
Draw
Chart
TextArt
Figure
Text Box
QuickFormat
Styles
We the People of the United States, in Order to form a more perfect Union, establish Justice, insure domestic Tranquility, provide for the common defence, promote the general Welfare, and secure the Blessings of Liberty to ourselves and our Posterity, do ordain and establish this Constitution for the United States of America.
All legislative powers herein granted shall be vested in a Congress of the United States. which shall consist of a Senate and House of Representatives.
Courier 10cpi Regular 12 pt (Courier 12 pt)
Insert
Select
Pg 1 Ln 1" Pos 1"

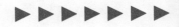

2 part two

EDITING YOUR WORK

Wouldn't it be nice if we never made mistakes? We wouldn't need erasers, correction fluid, or divorce lawyers.

WordPerfect can't make happy marriages, but it can help you avoid embarrassing mistakes in your documents. In the lessons in this part, you will learn how to edit your documents—correcting mistakes before you print.

It's So Easy

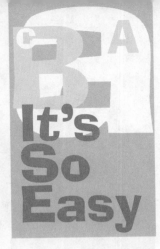

lesson 3

Recalling and Editing Documents

One of the best things about word processing is that you can edit a document as much as you want before printing it. You can print up a draft copy and fine-tune the document—then print the final copy. In this lesson, you'll learn how to open documents you've saved and use some of WordPerfect's basic editing techniques.

OPENING A RECENTLY USED DOCUMENT

You can edit new documents as you type them or existing documents already saved on disk. To edit an existing document, you must first *open* it, or recall it from the disk. WordPerfect makes it easy to open the last four documents you opened or created and saved.

File menu listing recently used documents

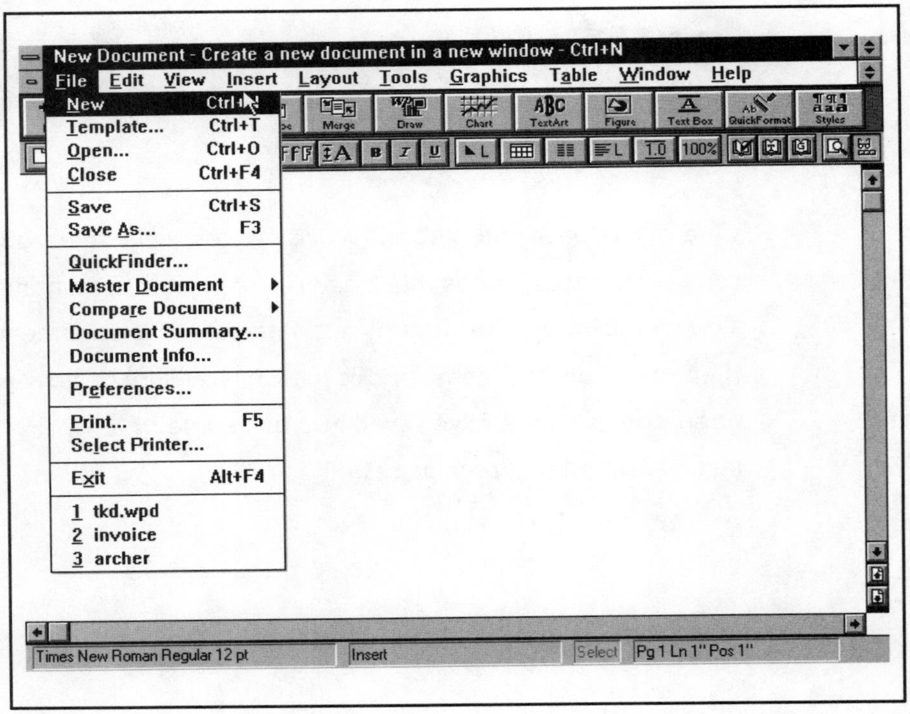

To open a recently used document:

1 Select File. At the bottom of the File menu, WordPerfect lists the last four documents you worked on, as shown in the figure.
WordPerfect does *not* list the path of the file with its name in the File menu. If you recently worked on two files with the same name (but in different locations), both of them will be listed identically.

2 Click on the name of the file you want to open, or press the number next to the filename.

oops!

WPWin error!

If you have already deleted a file from your disk, WordPerfect will display an error message if you try to open it. Click on OK, or press Enter, to remove the error message from the screen.

for more...

What happened?

If you already have a document in the window and open another, WordPerfect will open a second window for the new document. The first document window will be moved to the background. See "Opening Multiple Documents" in Lesson 7.

OPENING A DOCUMENT

To open a document not listed in the File menu, use the File Open command. With File Open, you can open a document no matter where it is located on your disk or when you last worked on it.

To open a document:

1 Select File ➤ Open (Ctrl+O or F4). WordPerfect displays the Open File dialog box as shown in the figure.

2 Double-click on the file you want to open, or highlight the name of the file, then click on OK. Scroll the list if necessary.

File Open dialog box

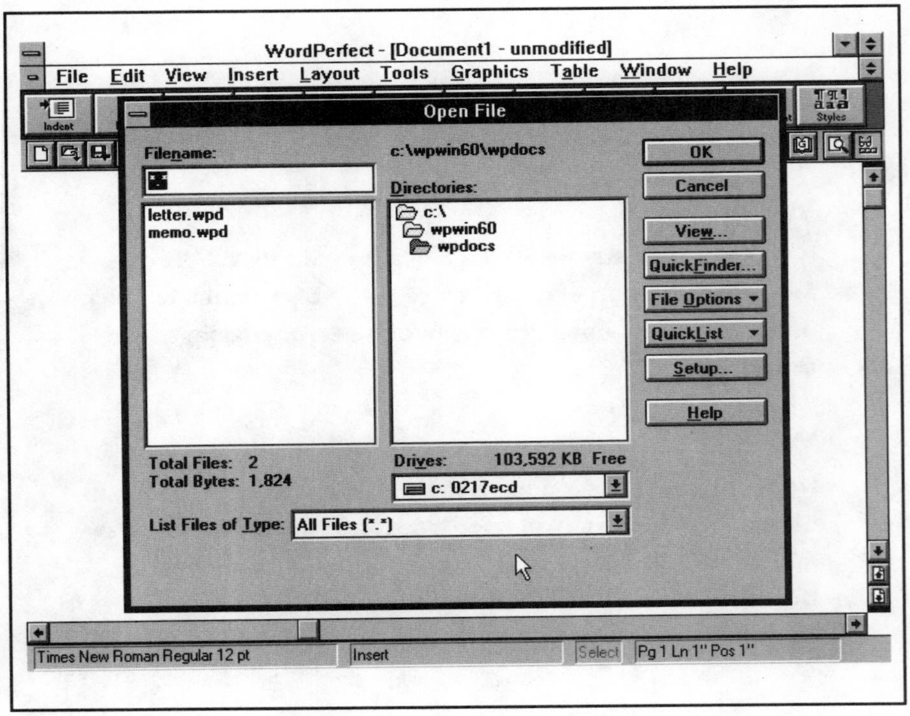

3 If the file you want to open is not listed, do *one* of the following:

- Type the complete path and name of the file in the Filename text box, then select OK.
- Select another directory in the Directories list box—double-click on the root directory (C:\) to list the directories on the drive.
- Select All Files (*.*) in the List Files of Type list.

power bar

One-click opening

Click on the Open button to display the Open File dialog box.

tip

Preview before you open

If you are uncertain which file to open, you can preview it before you open it. Click once on the file name in the list, or Tab into the list and highlight the file name using the arrow keys. Then select View.

tip

Open options

Select File Options in the Open File dialog box to copy, move, rename, delete, or print the highlighted file; to make a file *read-only* (so it can't be changed); to print a list of the file names displayed in the list box; or to create or delete a subdirectory.

TO INSERT TEXT

To insert characters in text you've already typed, you must move the insertion point to the spot where you want to make the changes. Then, when you enter characters within existing text, words to the right will move to make room for your new text.

To move the insertion point:

- Place the mouse pointer where you want to enter, delete, or revise text, and click the left button.

Once you insert or edit text in an opened document, the word *unmodified* is removed from the Title Bar. This indicates that you must save the document before exiting WordPerfect (if you want to keep your changes).

The table on the next page shows ways to move the insertion point using the keyboard.

Insertion Point Movement Keys

KEYSTROKES	MOVES THE INSERTION POINT
→, ←, ↓, ↑	In the direction of the arrow
End	To the end of the line
Home	To the start of the line
Ctrl+→	To the beginning of the next word
Ctrl+←	To the beginning of the current or previous word
PgUp	To the top of the screen
PgDn	To the bottom of the screen

tip

I thought you said it would insert

By default, WordPerfect is in the *Insert* mode. If you press the Ins key (the *0* key on the numeric keypad), the word *Typeover* will appear in the center of the Status Bar. New characters typed will now replace existing ones.

oops!

All I get is numbers

If you press an arrow key and a number appears on the screen, press the key marked Num Lock. This turns off the numeric function.

tip

I can't move the insertion point

You cannot use the mouse or arrow keys to move the insertion point past the last text in the document. Move to the end of the document, then press Enter.

USING THE SCROLL BARS

To move the insertion point to a part of the document that is not in the visible text region, you must use the Scroll Bars.

To use the Scroll Bars:

- To scroll line by line, click the up or down arrow on the ends of the Scroll Bar.
- To scroll screen by screen, click above or below the *scroll box* (the box within the bar), between the up and down arrows.
- To scroll to a relative position in the document, drag the scroll box. For example, drag the box to the middle of the Scroll Bar to display text from the middle of the document.
- To scroll page by page, click on the previous or next page buttons at the bottom of the Scroll Bar.

The table on the next page shows how to scroll the screen using the keyboard.

Scrolling Keys

PRESS...	TO MOVE...
Ctrl+Home	To the beginning of the document
Ctrl+End	To the end of the document
Alt+PgUp	To the top of the previous page
Alt+PgDn	To the top of the next page
PgUp	To the top of the screen, then to the top of the previous screen
PgDn	To the bottom of the screen, then to the bottom of the next screen

tip

Where's the cursor?

Scrolling the screen with the Scroll Bar does not move the insertion point—the Pg and Ln indicators in the Status Bar will show the original insertion point location. After scrolling the screen, click where you want to insert or edit text. If you do not click the mouse, the screen will scroll back to its previous location when you begin typing.

tip

Using Goto

To quickly move to a specific position, select Edit ➤ Goto. A dialog box appears in which you can select to go to a specific page, to the top or bottom of the current page, or to the last insertion point position.

It's So Easy

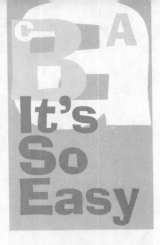

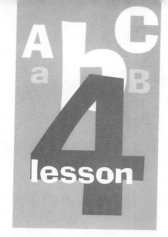

lesson 4

Editing Techniques

The ability to edit a document gives word processing its power and versatility. You can type a document, letting your thoughts flow onto the screen, and not have to worry about making mistakes or how your ideas are arranged on the page. Then, when you've gotten your ideas out, you can go back over the document and edit it into the final form.

SELECTING TEXT

For many editing functions, you must *select* (highlight) text, which makes the characters appear light against a dark background. Once you select text, you can easily delete it, copy it, move it to another location, or change its appearance. You'll learn how to perform all these tasks in the lessons that follow.

To select text by dragging the mouse:

1 Place the mouse pointer at one end of the text.

2 Hold down the left mouse button.

Quick menu displayed by clicking in the left margin

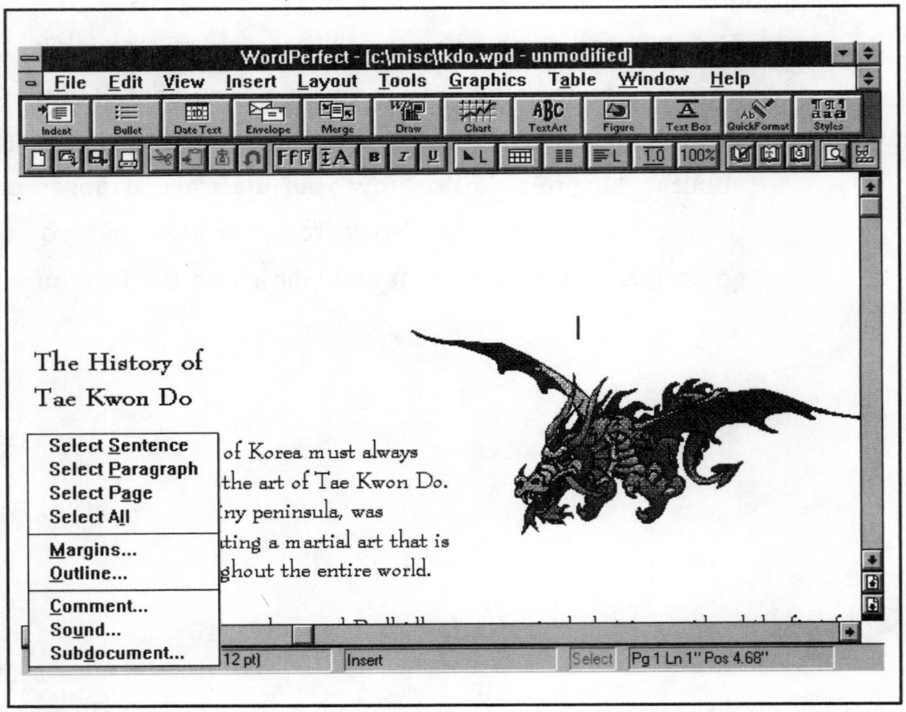

3 Move the mouse pointer while you hold down the left button.

4 Release the mouse button.

To select text with the Quick menu:

1 Point to the sentence or paragraph you want to select and place the insertion point there by clicking the left mouse button.

2 Point to the left margin and click the right mouse button to display the Quick menu shown in the figure.

3 Choose Select Sentence, Select Paragraph, Select Page, or Select All.

To deselect all highlighted text quickly, click the mouse or press F8.

tip ▶ **Quick select**

Click twice to select a word, three times to select a sentence, and four times to select a paragraph. Or, place the insertion point in the sentence or paragraph you want to select, select Edit ➤ Select, then choose Sentence, Paragraph, Page, or All.

oops! ▶ **Where did it go?**

If you press any character key when text is selected, the character will replace all the selected text. If that is not what you intended to do, select Edit ➤ Undo, as explained later in this lesson.

DELETING TEXT

WordPerfect provides many ways to delete characters or erase mistakes.

- To erase characters to the left of the insertion point, press the Backspace key.
- To erase a character to the right of the insertion point, press the Del key.

Quick menu displayed when right clicking in the document with text selected

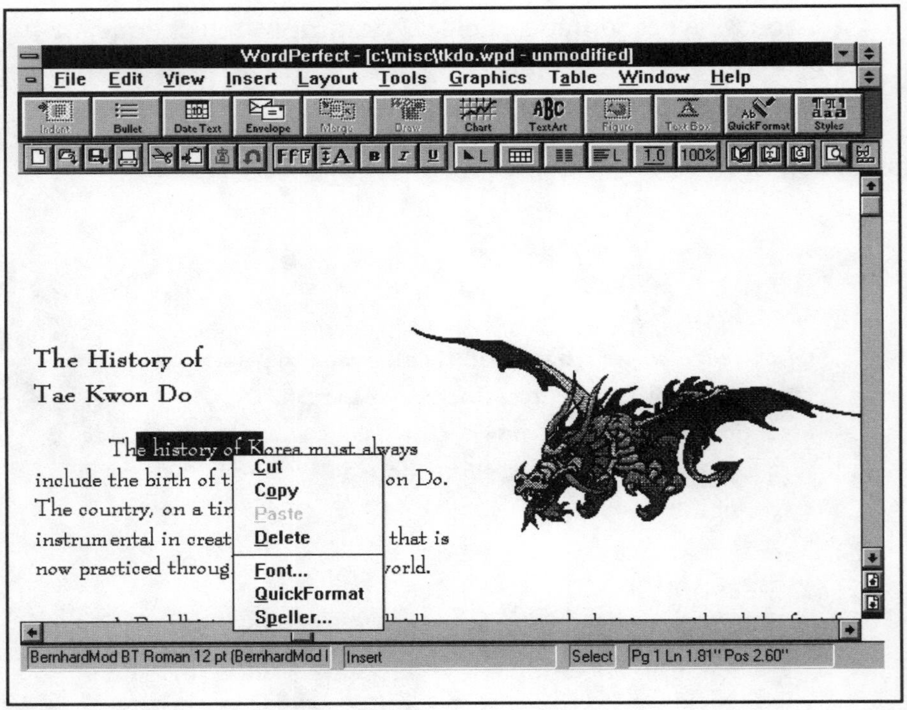

To delete sections of text:

1 Select the text you wish to delete.

2 Press Del or click the *right* mouse button in the text (*not* in the left margin) to display the Quick menu shown in the figure, then select Cut or Delete.

power bar

Quick delete

Click on the Cut button to delete selected text.

tip

So many choices

Press Ctrl+Backspace to delete the current word; press Ctrl+Del to delete from the insertion point to the end of the word, or press Ctrl+Shift+Del to delete from the insertion point to the end of the page. After selecting text, you can also delete it by selecting Edit ➤ Cut or pressing Ctrl+X.

tip

Deleting blank lines

To delete a blank line, place the insertion point before the line and press Del, or place it after the line and press Backspace. You can use this technique to join two paragraphs into one.

USING UNDELETE

If you erase text by mistake, you may be able to restore it without having to retype it. WordPerfect remembers the last three deletions you made using the Del or Backspace keys.

To restore deleted text:

- Select Edit ➤ Undelete (Ctrl+Shift+Z) to display the Undelete dialog box shown in the figure. The last deletion you made will reappear highlighted at the position of the insertion point.

Undelete box

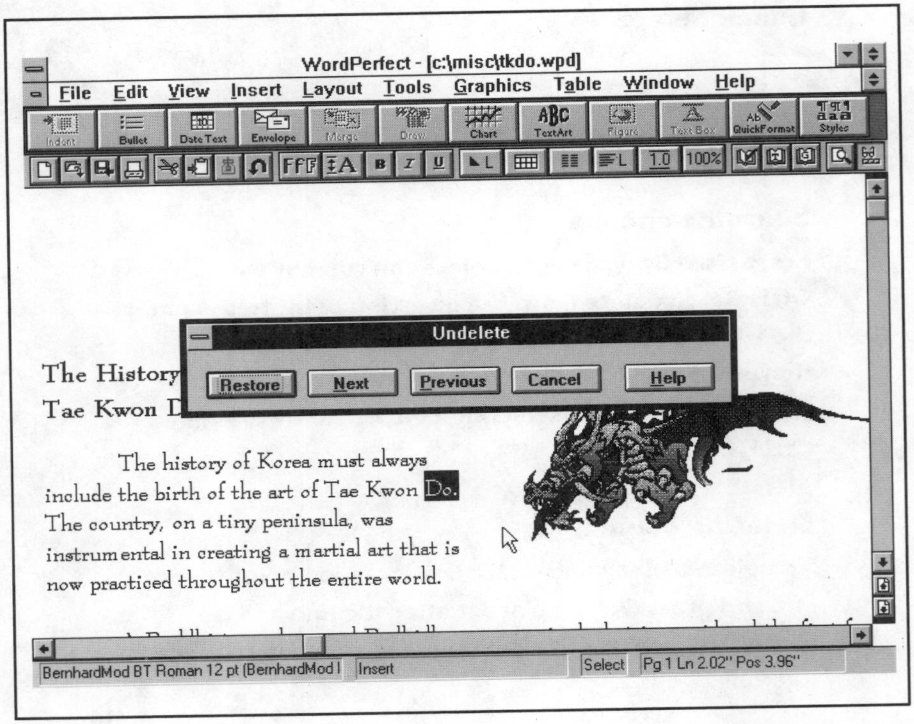

2 Choose one of the following:

- Select Restore to restore the text at that location on the screen.
- Select Previous or Next to cycle between the last three deletions.

oops! **I can't get it back!**

Undelete will not restore text erased by selecting Edit ➤ Cut. **To restore such text, see "Using Undo" on the next page.**

tip **Restoring text in its original location**

To restore the text at its original position, first move the insertion point to where you deleted the text. Then, undo your deletion.

tip **Making duplicate copies**

Restoring text does not remove it from WordPerfect's memory. You can restore it again—to make a copy of it—as long as it is one of the last three deletions made. For other ways to copy text, see "Copying Text" in Lesson 5.

USING UNDO

The Undo command cancels the last editing or formatting you performed on your document. You can use Undo to delete the last bit of text you typed, delete text you just restored by mistake, return recently formatted text to its original condition, or reverse just about any WordPerfect operation.

The Edit menu

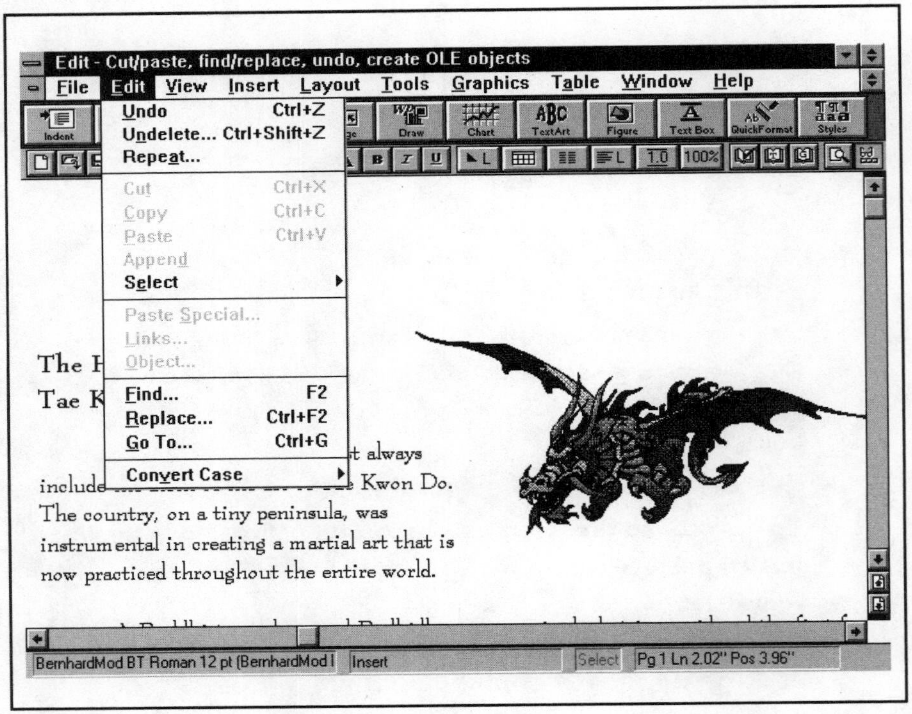

To undo your last action:

- Select Edit ➤ Undo (Ctrl+Z), as shown in the figure.

You can select Undo again to cancel the last undo operation. Undo restores deleted text in its original location, even if you moved the insertion point.

power bar ▶ **Click to undo**

Click on the Undo button to undo your last action.

tip ▶ **Always try Undo first**

If you deleted text by selecting Edit ➤ Cut, you cannot restore it using the Undelete command. If you *do* try to use the Undelete command, you will no longer be able to restore it using Undo. So, try using Undo first to restore text. If the correct text is not restored, just select Undo again to cancel the operation.

tip ▶ **Undelete versus Undo**

When you use Del or backspace, the text is stored in an "undelete" area that can hold the last three deletions. You can restore this text by selecting Edit ➤ Undelete (or pressing Ctrl+Shift+Z). Text deleted using Edit ➤ Cut is stored in a separate retrieval area, which can only hold one deletion. Restore the text using Edit ➤ Undo or Edit ➤ Paste.

SEARCHING FOR TEXT

If you spend a lot of time scrolling through documents looking for a particular word or phrase, you can save time by using WordPerfect's Find feature. WordPerfect can search an entire document for a specific set of characters in seconds.

To locate specific text:

1 Move the insertion point to the location where you want the search to begin. To search the entire document, press Ctrl+Home before searching.

Find Text dialog box

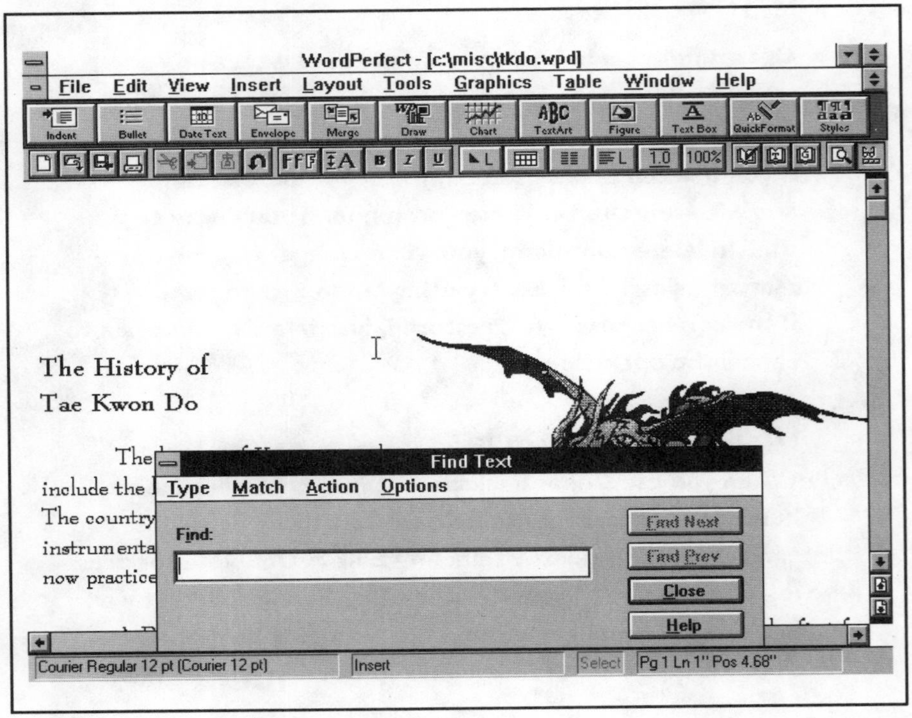

2 Select Edit ➤ Find (F2) to display the Find Text dialog box shown in the figure.

3 Type the characters you want to locate.

4 Press Enter or select Find Next to begin the search. Select *Find Prev* if the text is before the insertion point position.

WordPerfect will highlight the next occurrence of the text. The Find dialog box remains on the screen after WordPerfect locates the text. To find the next occurrence of the same text, select Find Next.

If the text is not found, a dialog box appears with the message *Not Found*. Select OK or press Enter to remove the message—the insertion point will be in its original position.

tip ▶ **Search options**

Pull down the Match menu in the Find dialog box to select Find options. Select *Whole Word* to locate only entire words that match the search text, not just the characters themselves. Select *Case* to match the case of the characters as you enter them in the Find dialog box. Select *Font* to search for text in a specific font, or to locate any text in a specific font.

tip ▶ **Search for codes**

To locate a formatting code, select Match ➤ Codes, then double-click on the code you want to locate. To find a specific code (where multiple options are available), select Type ➤ Specific Codes, then double-click on the specific format.

REPLACING TEXT AUTOMATICALLY

Have you ever misspelled the same word several times in one document or realized that you've made the same mistake over and over? In situations like this, you can use the Replace command to automatically locate any text and replace it with something else.

To replace text automatically:

1 Move the insertion point to where you want the replacements to begin.

Find and Replace text dialog box

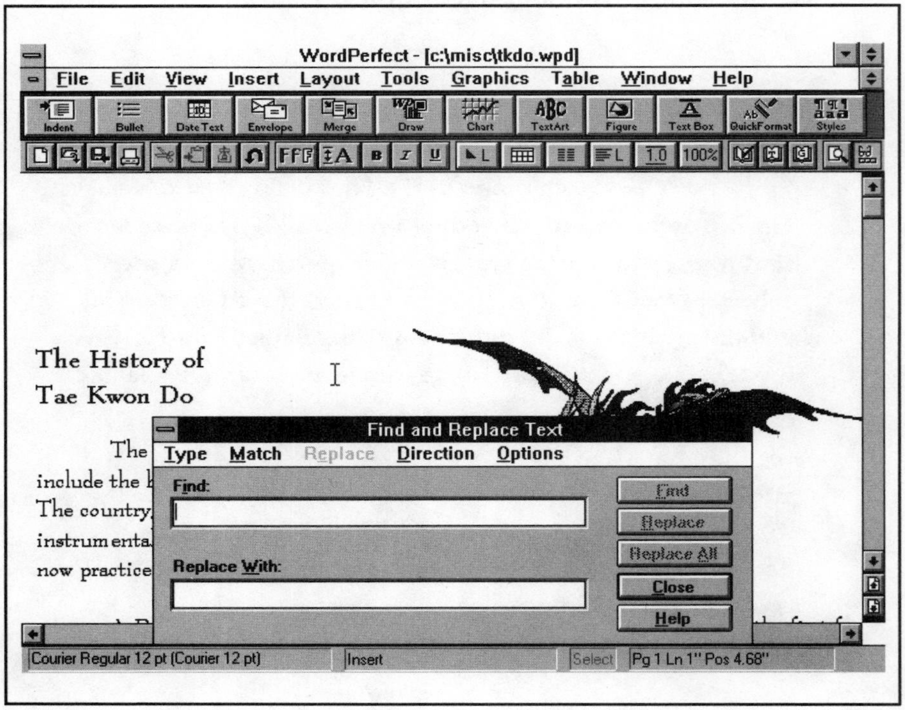

2 Select Edit ➤ Replace (Ctrl+F2) to display the Find and Replace Text dialog box.

3 Type the text you wish to replace, then press Tab.

4 Type the text you want to insert.

5 Select Replace All.

6 WordPerfect will change all the occurrences of the text. Select Close to remove the Find and Replace dialog box.

oops!

Where did it all go?

Don't forget a Replace With entry. If you leave the entry blank, WordPerfect will *delete* the text it locates.

tip

Save your document first

As a safeguard, save your document first before making an automatic replacement. If the wrong text is replaced or deleted, you can restore the original text by selecting Edit ➤ Undo.

tip

Additional replacement options

Select Find to locate the next occurrence of the text without changing it. Select Replace to replace the text and locate the next occurrence. Select Direction, then choose either Forward or Backward to change text after or before the insertion point. To replace a specific number of matching occurrences, select Options ➤ Limit Number of Changes and enter the number desired.

SAVING EDITED TEXT AND BACKUP COPIES

When you save a document for the first time, you have to enter its name in the Save As dialog box. To save it again after making changes, select File ➤ Save—this time, the Save As dialog box will not appear, and the changed file will be saved immediately, overwriting the original.

If you want to use the Save command but keep the original version on the disk unchanged, set WordPerfect to make backup copies. Then, when you save a document, WordPerfect gives the original copy the extension .BK! and saves the new version with the original name. This type of backup is called an Original Document Backup.

As a safeguard, WordPerfect automatically makes another type of backup for you—called a Timed Backup. Every ten minutes, WordPerfect saves all open documents to temporary files so you won't lose too much work if your machine goes haywire before you've had a chance to save the document. When you next start WordPerfect, you can open these timed backup files, then edit or save them as desired.

To change backup options:

1. Select File ➤ Preferences, then double-click on File to display the dialog box shown in the figure.
2. At the Minutes text box, enter the interval for making timed, or automatic backups.
3. Select Original Document Backup to make backup copies when you save or exit a document.
4. Select OK then Close to return to the document.

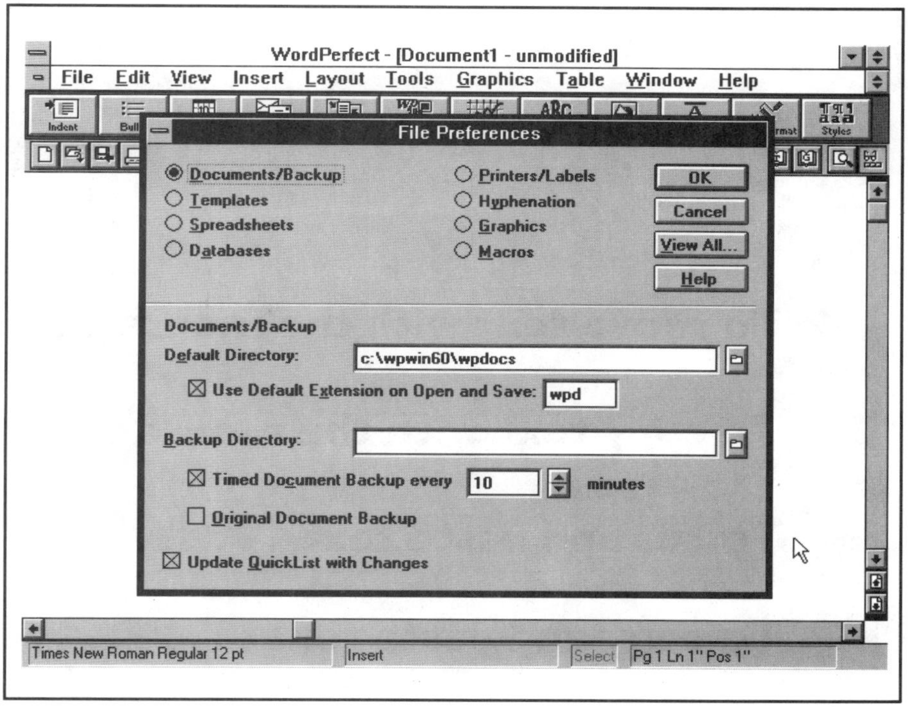

File Preferences dialog box

tip

Do not rely on timed backups!

Although WordPerfect automatically makes a temporary backup file, these files are deleted when you exit the program without saving your document. To avoid losing your data, save regularly with File ➤ Save.

tip

Other file options

You can use the settings in the File Preferences dialog to change the default directory and file extension for your documents.

It's So Easy

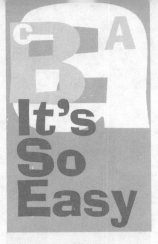

lesson 5

Moving and Copying Text

Selecting text gives you the ability to make changes to entire sections of your document at the same time. You already know how to delete and print selected portions of a document. In this lesson, you'll learn how to move, copy, and save selected portions of text.

MOVING TEXT WITH THE MOUSE

When you *move* text, you delete it from one location in a document and place it at another. The quickest way to move text is by using the mouse to *drag and drop*. This means you drag the text to where you want it to appear, and drop it there.

You can use drag and drop to move text anywhere in the document, even to a location that has already scrolled off the screen.

Text ready to be moved with drag and drop

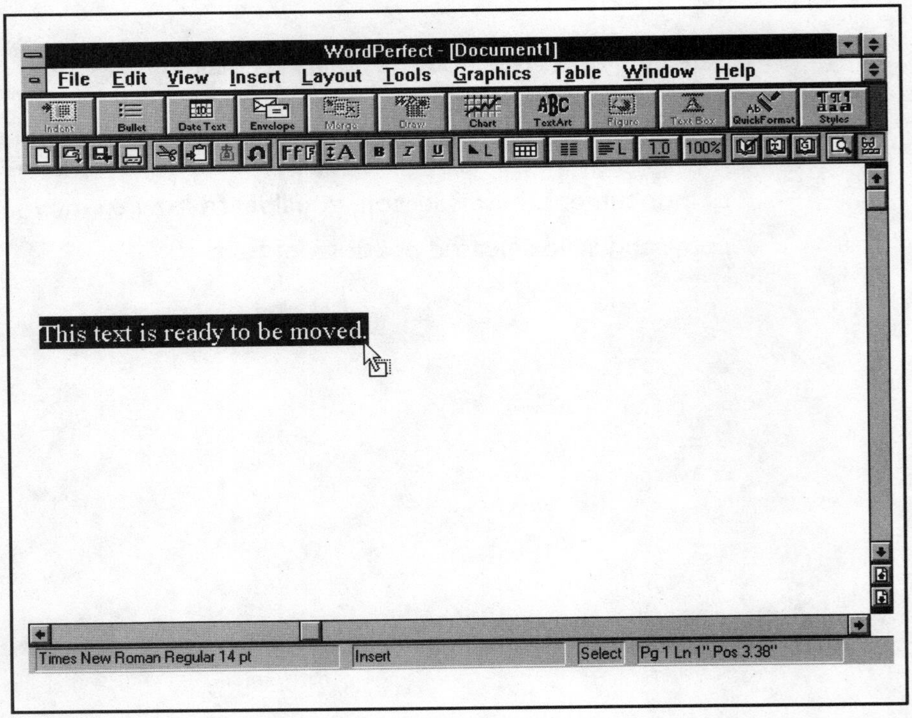

To move text by drag and drop:

1. Select the text you want to move.
2. Place the mouse pointer on the selected text, then press and hold down the left mouse button.
3. Drag the mouse pointer to the location where you want to insert the text. The screen will scroll if you move the pointer to the top or bottom of the screen.
4. Release the mouse button.

tip

Too slow?

If your screen scrolls too slowly when you move text to a location not visible on the screen, use the Cut and Paste options, as described later in this lesson.

oops!

Change your mind?

The text isn't actually moved until you release the mouse button. If you decide not to move the text after you begin dragging the mouse, move the pointer back onto the selected text, then release the mouse. If you change your mind after releasing the mouse, select Edit ➤ Undo (Ctrl+Z).

for more...

Keep reading

To move text to another document, see "Moving Text Between Documents" in Lesson 7.

COPYING TEXT WITH THE MOUSE

When you *copy* text, you insert a duplicate of it at another location. The original text is not deleted from the document. You can copy text using drag and drop, in a procedure almost identical to moving text. The only difference is that you use the Ctrl key.

Text ready to be copied with drag and drop

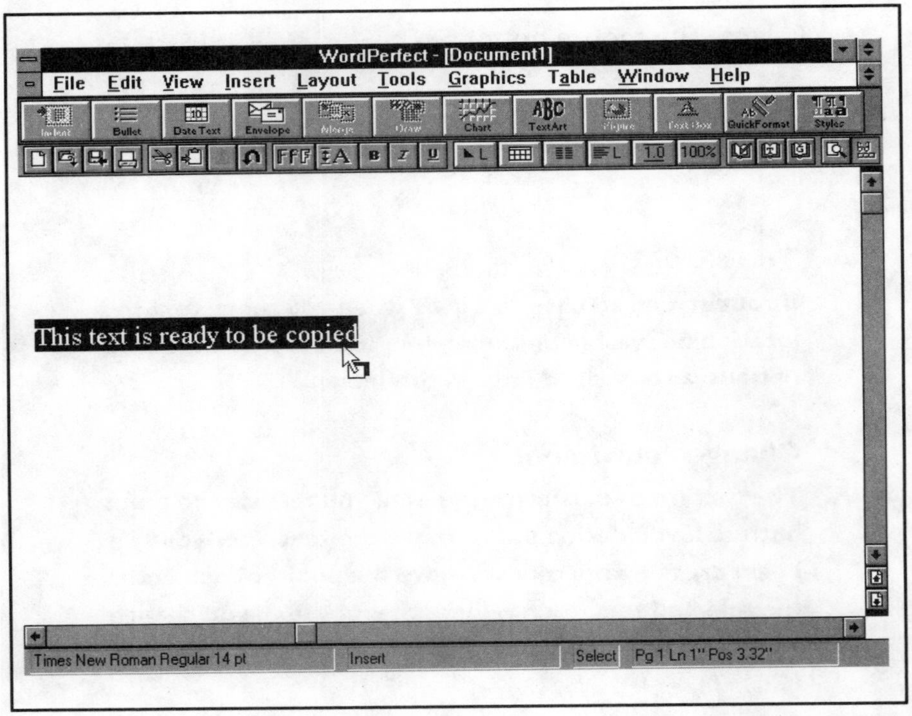

To copy text by drag and drop:

1 Select the text you want to copy.
2 Place the mouse pointer on the selected text, then press and hold down the left mouse button.
3 Drag the mouse point to the location where you want to insert the text.
4 Press and hold down the Ctrl key.
5 Release the mouse button.

tip

Copy or move?

As long as you do not release the mouse button, you can either move or copy the selected text. Press the Ctrl key to copy the text, release it to move the text. If you decide to move, rather than copy, the text, release the Ctrl key before releasing the mouse button.

If you decide not to copy the text after all, release the mouse button then select Edit ➤ Undo (Ctrl+Z).

for more...

Keep reading

To copy text to another document, see "Moving Text Between Documents" in Lesson 7.

MOVING TEXT WITH CUT AND PASTE

Drag and drop is convenient, but you may want to move text using the Cut and Paste commands instead. You'll need to use Cut and Paste to move text between documents.

To Cut and Paste text:

1. Select the text you want to move.
2. Click the *right* mouse button to display the Quick menu, then select Cut. The text disappears from the screen. You can also select Edit ➤ Cut (or press Ctrl+X).

Quick menu displayed when the mouse pointer is beyond the left margin and text is not selected

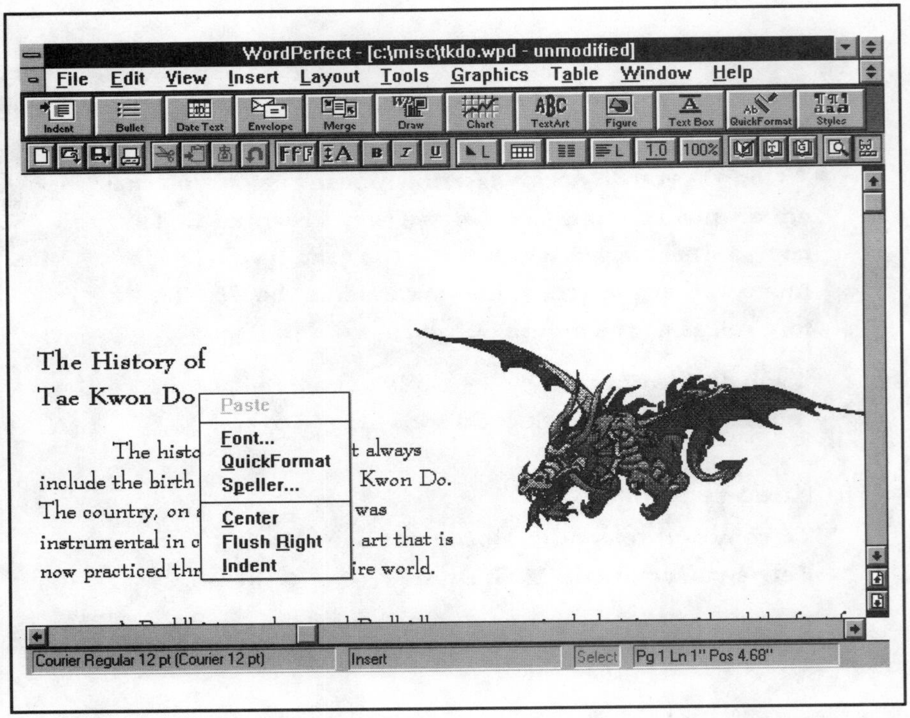

3 Position the insertion point where you want to place the text. If you decide not to move the text, place the insertion point at its original location.

4 Click the *right* mouse button to display the Quick menu shown in the figure and select Paste. You can also insert the text by selecting Edit ➤ Paste, or pressing Ctrl+V.

power bar

Click to Cut and Paste

Click on the Cut button to delete the text, then click on the Paste button to insert it.

tip

Pasting multiple copies

Cut text will remain in the clipboard until you cut other text. To insert another copy of the text at some other location, move the insertion point, then select Edit ➤ Paste again.

tip

Appending text to the clipboard

To add other selected text to clipboard without deleting the original contents, select Edit ➤ Append.

COPYING TEXT WITH COPY AND PASTE

You can also copy text from the Quick menu or the Edit menu. The original text is not deleted from the document. You can copy as much text as you want, and as many times as you want.

To Copy and Paste text:

1 Select the text you want to copy.

2 Click the *right* mouse button to display the Quick menu, then select Copy, or select Edit ➤ Copy (Ctrl+C).

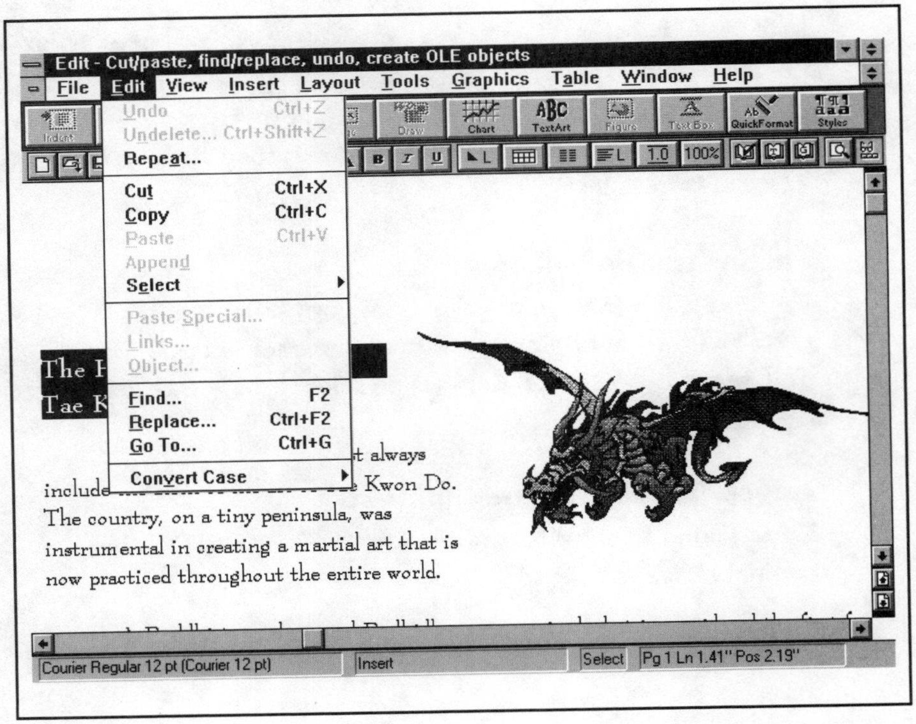

Edit menu with Copy option available

3 Position the insertion point where you want to place a duplicate of the text.

4 Click the *right* mouse button to display the Quick menu and select Paste.

power bar

Click to Copy and Paste

Click on the Copy button to place a copy of the text into the clipboard, then click on the Paste button to insert it. Select Edit ➤ Paste or press Ctrl+V.

tip

Making multiple copies

To insert another copy of the text at some other location, move the insertion point, then select Edit ➤ Paste again.

SAVING SELECTED TEXT

Sometimes as you write, you create a phrase or paragraph that you know you can use somewhere else. Rather than leave it in the current document, you can save the text as a separate file on the disk. Just be sure to store the saved text with a new name. If you give it the name of the existing document, the original will be replaced.

To save a portion of text:

1 Select the text you want to save.

Save Block dialog box

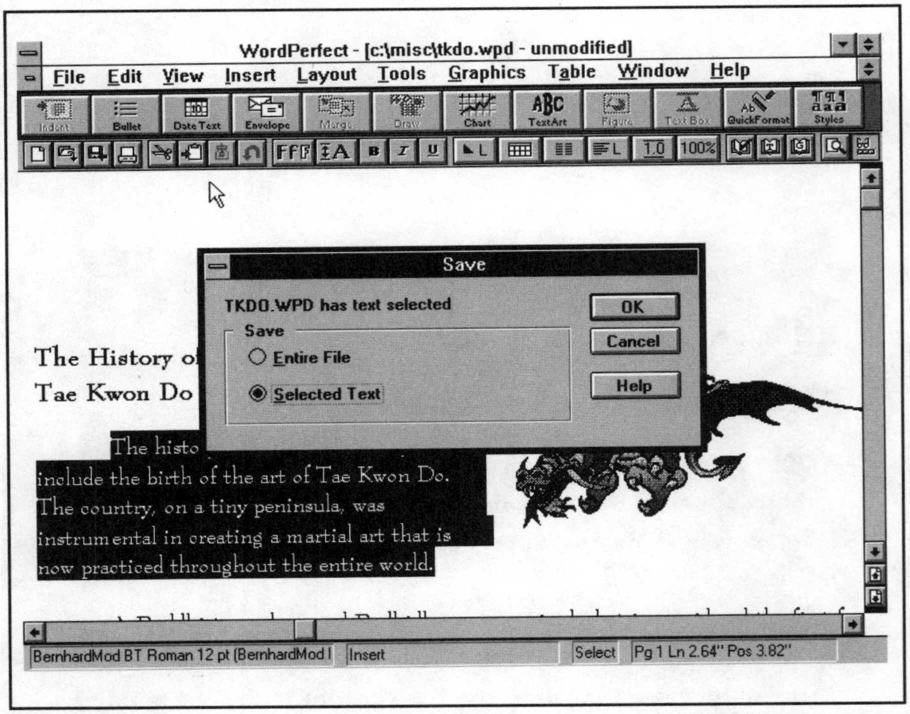

2 Select File ➤ Save (Ctrl+S) to display the Save dialog box, as shown in the figure.

3 Select OK to display the Save As dialog box.

4 Type the name you wish to save the highlighted text under.

5 Select OK.

tip ▶ **Save the entire document**

If you change your mind and want to save the entire document, click on Entire File, then on OK.

tip ▶ **Duplicate file names**

If there already is a document with the same filename that you give the selected text, you will be asked if you want to replace it. Select No, then enter another filename.

tip ▶ **Where did the formatting go?**

Only the text and codes within the highlighted block are saved. The formatting codes outside of the block—even those that would affect it when printed—are not included in the saved document. To learn more about codes, see Lesson 6.

It's So Easy

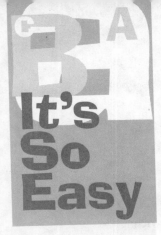

lesson 6

Fine Tuning Your Documents

The editing techniques you've learned so far are sufficient for most simple editing, but you'll also want to take advantage of WordPerfect's comprehensive array of special editing capabilities. You may not use the techniques you'll learn in this lesson for every short note you write, but they are invaluable for fine-tuning your documents.

WORKING WITH CODES

Keys such as Tab and Enter do not display any characters on the screen. They do, however, affect the format of the text by inserting invisible codes that can be deleted just like any other character. To see which codes are in your document, and to delete individual codes, you reveal them in a separate window at the bottom of the screen.

To reveal codes:

- Select View ➤ Reveal Codes (press Alt+F3). Your screen will look much like the figure.

WordPerfect screen with codes revealed

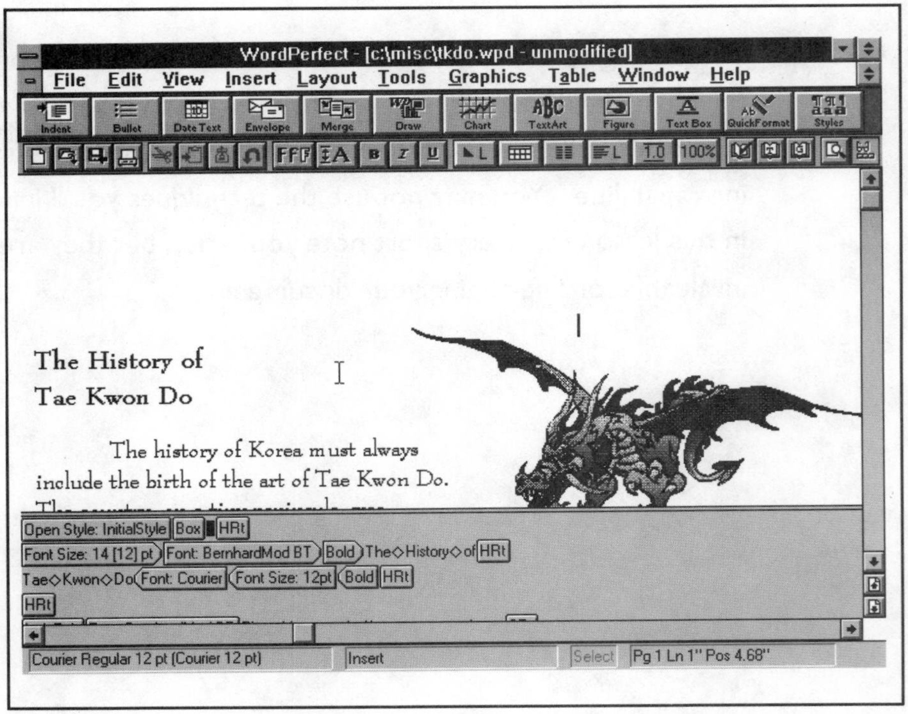

If you want, you can leave the codes revealed as you continue writing.

To remove the display of codes:

- Select View ➤ Reveal Codes again (or press Alt-F3).

Don't worry if some of the codes look complicated or mysterious.

tip

When things go wrong

Reveal codes whenever the text on the screen just doesn't appear correct. You may have entered a code by accidentally pressing the wrong function key.

tip

Common codes

As you use WordPerfect you'll become familiar with the important codes. The position of the cursor is shown highlighted. Hard carriage returns (created by pressing the Enter key) are represented by HRt, soft carriage returns (added by word-wrap) are shown as SRt, tabs are Tab, and spaces are small diamonds.

new feature

Code placement

WordPerfect automatically places codes in a logical order. Codes that affect the entire document will be placed first, followed by codes that affect pages, paragraphs, lines, and finally characters. WordPerfect deletes duplicate or redundant codes.

INSERTING THE DATE

We use dates in letters and many other documents. You can have WordPerfect insert the correct date automatically as either text or as a code. When you insert the date as *text*, today's date is inserted into the document just as if you typed it yourself. If you ever use that document again, you'll need to remember to update the date.

When you insert the date as a *code*, however, today's date will be inserted and appear just as if you had entered it as text, but it will change automatically if you open or print the document some other day. So, if you start a letter on one day and include the date as a code, then complete and print the letter on an-

Insert Date menu

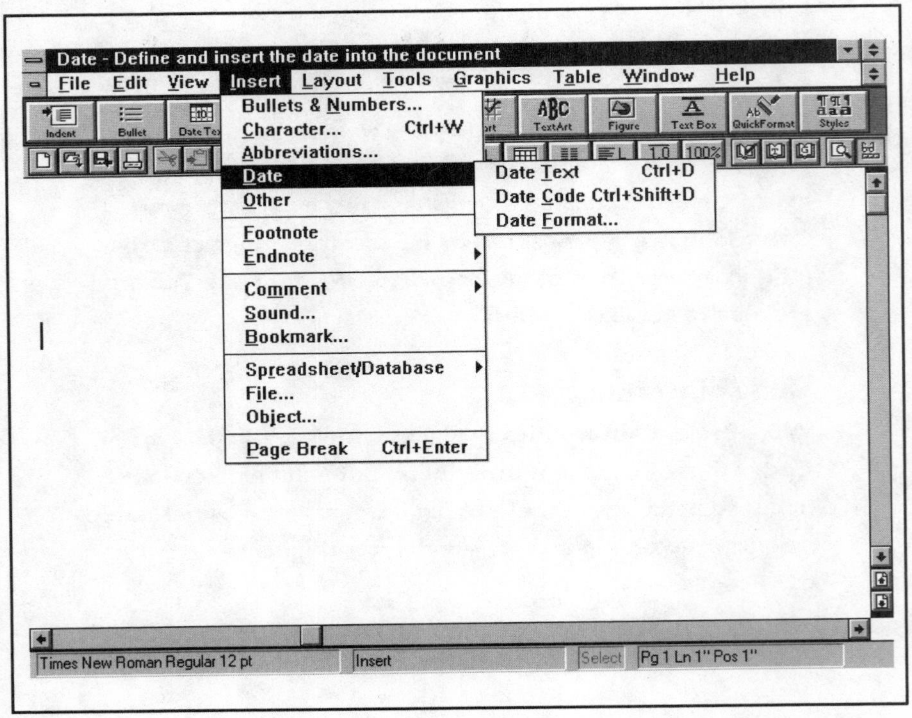

other day, the printed copy will show the date that you printed the letter.

To insert the date:

1. Select Insert ➤ Date to see the options shown in the figure.
2. Select Date Text to insert the current date as text, or select Date Code to insert the date as a code.

tip ▶ **Date shortcut**

Press Ctrl+D to quickly insert the date as text, or press Ctrl+Shift+D to insert the date as a code.

tip ▶ **Using the date code**

Do not use the date code function if you want a reminder when the letter was originally written or mailed. When you later open the document, the current date will appear.

tip ▶ **Erasing the date code**

When you enter the date as a code, the date appears on screen but it is stored as a single code in the document. To erase the date, you only need to press Del or Backspace once, as if you were deleting a single character.

button bar ▶ **Click the date**

Click on the Date Text button to insert the date as text.

CHANGING DATE FORMATS

WordPerfect's default date format is the one you'll probably use most often. However, WordPerfect provides twelve common date formats to choose from. You can also create your own custom date formats. For more information, see "Creating Custom Date Formats" later in this lesson.

To select a date format:

1. Select Insert ➤ Date ➤ Date Format to display a dialog box listing common date formats, as shown in the figure.
2. Select one of the formats.

Document Date/Time Format dialog box

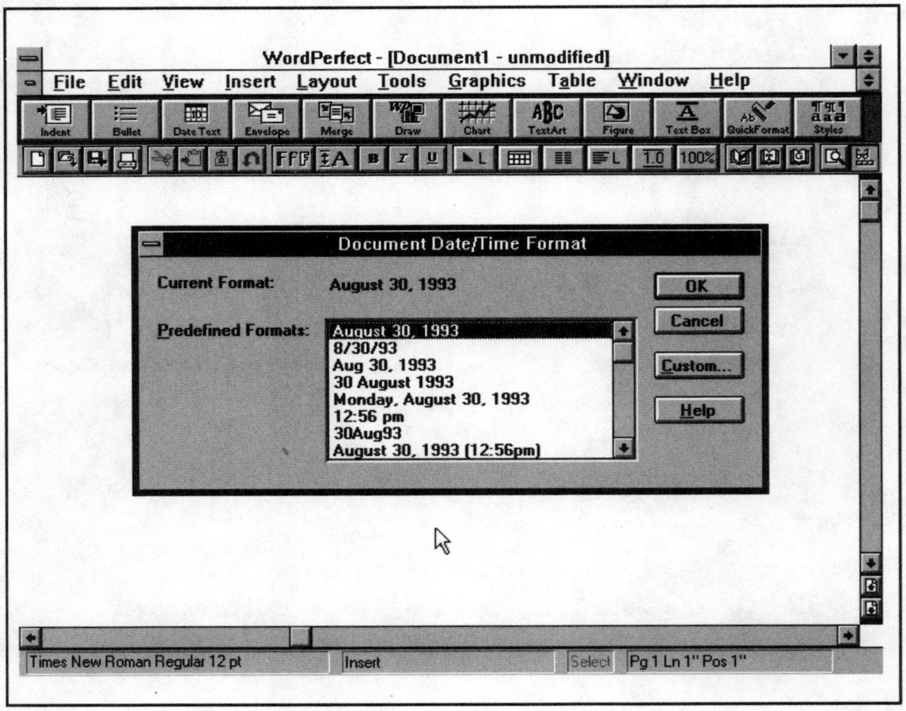

3 Select OK.

4 Insert the date as text or code.

for more...

Formatting existing dates

Dates entered as a code following the insertion point will change automatically to conform to the new date format. To change dates already inserted, place the insertion point at the start of the document before selecting a new format. Dates already entered as text will *not* be affected.

tip

A personal log

Select a date format that contains both the date and time, then use it to record your activities, log phone calls, or maintain accounts for billing purposes.

CREATING CUSTOM DATE FORMATS

If you do not like any of the date formats provided by WordPerfect, you can create your own. You can include Roman numerals in dates and even add the seconds to times.

To create your own date format:

- Select Insert ➤ Date ➤ Date Format ➤ Custom to display the dialog box shown in the figure. The box shows the current format in an Edit Date Format text box, a list of date codes, and a list of time codes.

Custom Document Date/Time Format dialog box

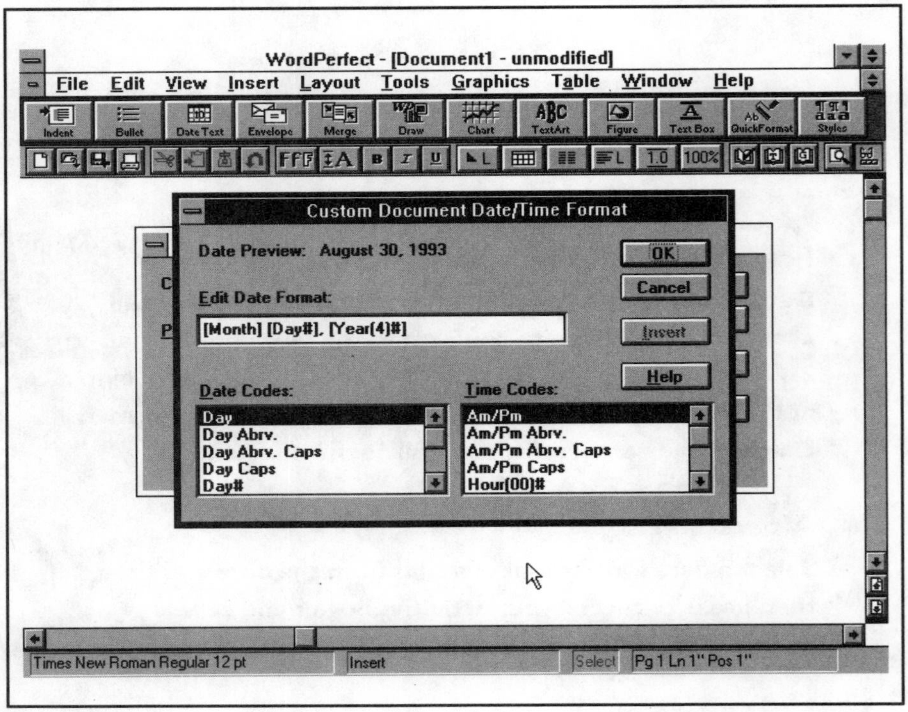

2 Select the desired codes from the date and time code lists. Double-click on the code or highlight the code and select Insert. The code will appear in brackets in the Edit Date Format box.

3 Add any desired spacing, punctuation, or text, in the Edit Date Format box and then select OK.

4 Select Insert ➤ Date, then Date Text or Date Code, to insert the date into your document.

for more...

Use these examples to help create custom formats:

Codes...	**Result...**
[Day], [Month] [Day#], [Year(4)#]	Sunday, June 12, 1993
[Hour(24)#]:[Minute#]: [Seconds#]	13:12:34
[Year(4), Roman#]	MCMXCIII
Day [Day#] of [Month] in [Year(4)#]	Day 12 of June in 1993

Extra! Extra!

REPEATING KEYSTROKES

Sometimes you'll want to repeat a certain keystroke a specific number of times. For example, you may want to place a dotted line across the screen or move the insertion point a specific number of spaces. You also might need to repeat a certain command more than once—to delete the next five words or seven lines, for instance.

You can use the Repeat command to perform repeated actions easily and quickly.

Repeat dialog box

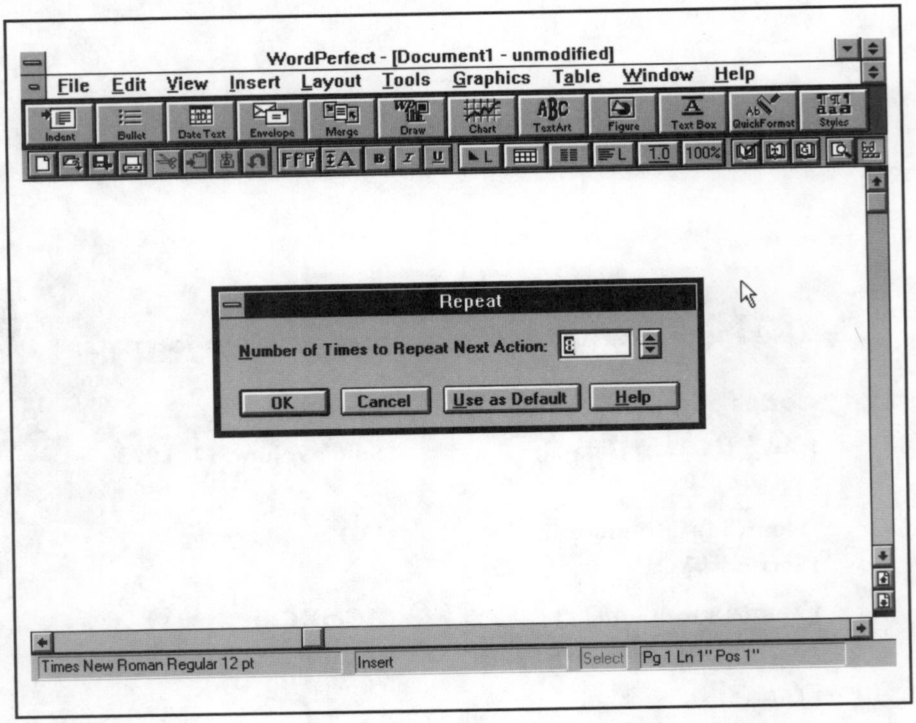

To repeat characters or commands:

1 Select Edit ➤ Repeat to display the Repeat dialog box, as shown in the figure. The default value of 8 indicates that the keystroke or command you use will be repeated eight times.

2 If you want a different number of repetitions, type a new number.

3 Select OK or press Enter.

4 Type the keystroke or press the command to be repeated. You can repeat any single character or keyboard command.

oops!

Cancel a repeat

If you change your mind about repeating an action while the Repeat dialog box is on the screen, select Cancel. If you change your mind after selecting OK, press Esc. If you already repeated the keystroke, select Edit ➤ Undo.

tip

Using Repeat to delete

Use the Repeat function to delete a specific number of words. For example, to quickly delete the next ten words, press select Edit ➤ Repeat, type 10, press Enter, then press Ctrl+End.

tip

Changing the default repeat

Select Edit ➤ Repeat, type the new repeat number, then select Use as Default. Choose OK to repeat a keystroke, or Cancel.

INSERTING PAGE BREAKS

As you type, WordPerfect will divide your document into pages automatically. When a new page starts, a single line appears across the screen and the Pg indicator in the status bar increases by one. (In Page View, page break lines are two-tone.) Automatic page breaks are called *soft page breaks*, and they are marked with [SPg] codes. The position of a soft page break can change as you insert or delete text.

But there might be times when you'll want to end a page yourself, such as for a short memo or title page. This calls for a

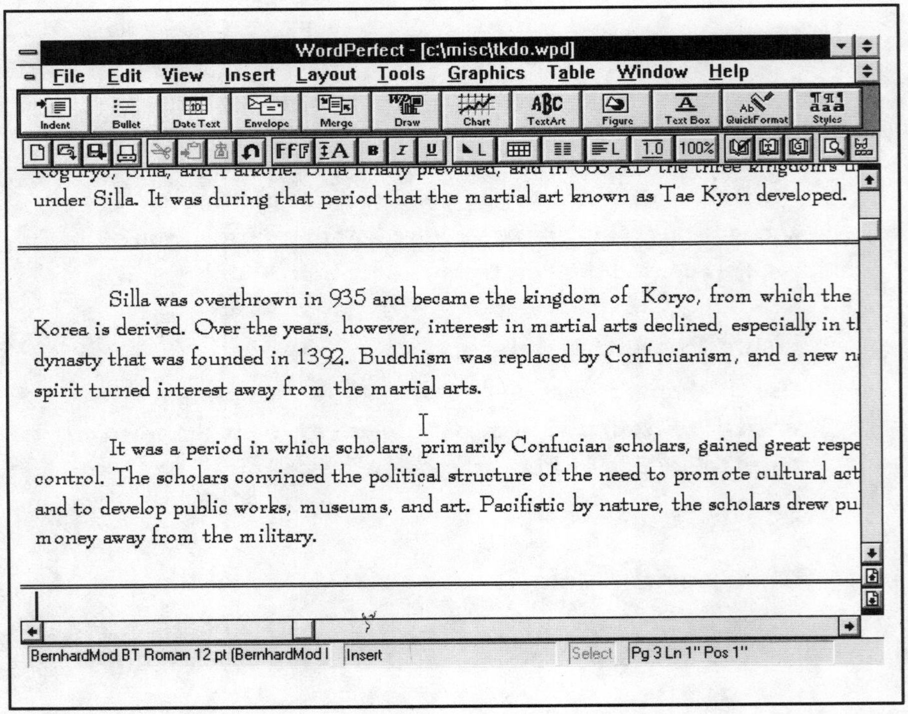

WordPerfect - [c:\misc\tkdo.wpd]
File Edit View Insert Layout Tools Graphics Table Window Help
Indent Bullet Date Text Envelope Merge Draw Chart TextArt Figure Text Box QuickFormat Styles
under Silla. It was during that period that the martial art known as Tae Kyon developed.
Silla was overthrown in 935 and became the kingdom of Koryo, from which the
Korea is derived. Over the years, however, interest in martial arts declined, especially in t
dynasty that was founded in 1392. Buddhism was replaced by Confucianism, and a new n
spirit turned interest away from the martial arts.
It was a period in which scholars, primarily Confucian scholars, gained great respe
control. The scholars convinced the political structure of the need to promote cultural act
and to develop public works, museums, and art. Pacifistic by nature, the scholars drew pu
money away from the military.
BernhardMod BT Roman 12 pt (BernhardMod I
Insert
Select
Pg 3 Ln 1" Pos 1"

Document showing two hard page breaks

hard page break, which is indicated by a double line across the page in draft view and the [HPg] code.

To insert a page break:

- Press Ctrl+Enter or select Insert ➤ Page Break.

WordPerfect will insert a double line like the ones shown in the figure.

tip ▶ **Beware of redundant page breaks**

If you add enough text above a hard page break, WordPerfect may insert a soft page break when the page becomes full. When you print the document, a blank page will be output—between the soft and hard page breaks. To avoid this, before printing a document, scroll through it to check the position of page breaks.

tip ▶ **Deleting hard page breaks**

Place the insertion point just above the page break line and press Del, or place the insertion point just after the page break line and press Backspace.

tip ▶ **Do not paginate with blank lines**

Use hard page breaks when you want to end a page (instead of pressing Enter until a soft page break occurs). The blank lines make it more time-consuming to scroll through a document, and will create havoc if you later add text to the page.

CREATING A TEMPLATE

Suppose you have a document that contains just the headings for a memo. You open the document and type the specifics of the memo in the appropriate locations. However, if you save the document without changing the name, the document now contains the text of an actual memo, not just the headings. The next time you want to type a memo, you have to retype the headings in a new document.

A WordPerfect template is a special type of document that contains only standard text and formats. Once you create a template, you can open it to enter text but you must save it with a

Create Document Template dialog box

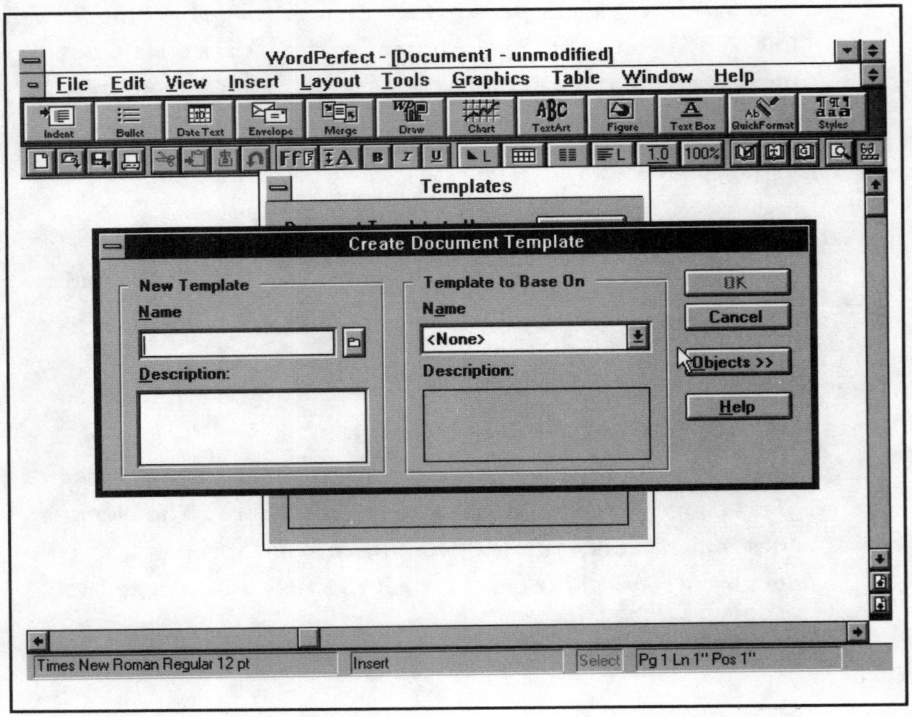

different name. The original template will remain unchanged unless you specifically want to edit it.

To create a template:

1. Select File ➤ Template (Ctrl+T) to display the Template dialog box.
2. Select Options ➤ Create Template to display the dialog box shown in the figure.
3. Type a name for the template, then select OK.
4. Type the standard text that you want in the template, then select File ➤ Save. WordPerfect saves templates with the WPT extension.
5. Click on the Exit Template button.

tip

Other Create Template options

In the Create Template Document dialog box, enter a brief description of the template's function. You'll be able to use the description to help select the correct template later on. The Template to Base On option lets you select an existing template to use as the base for a new template.

tip

Editing a template

To edit a template, select its name in the Template dialog box, then select Options ➤ Edit Template. Make your changes to the template then select File ➤ Save and click on the Exit Template button.

USING A TEMPLATE

When you want to type a document using a template, you open the template using the File menu. WordPerfect opens the template into a blank new document window. You add the specific text you want, then save the document with a new name. Because the template is opened in a new document window, selecting File ➤ Save will not overwrite the template with the edited document.

Templates dialog box

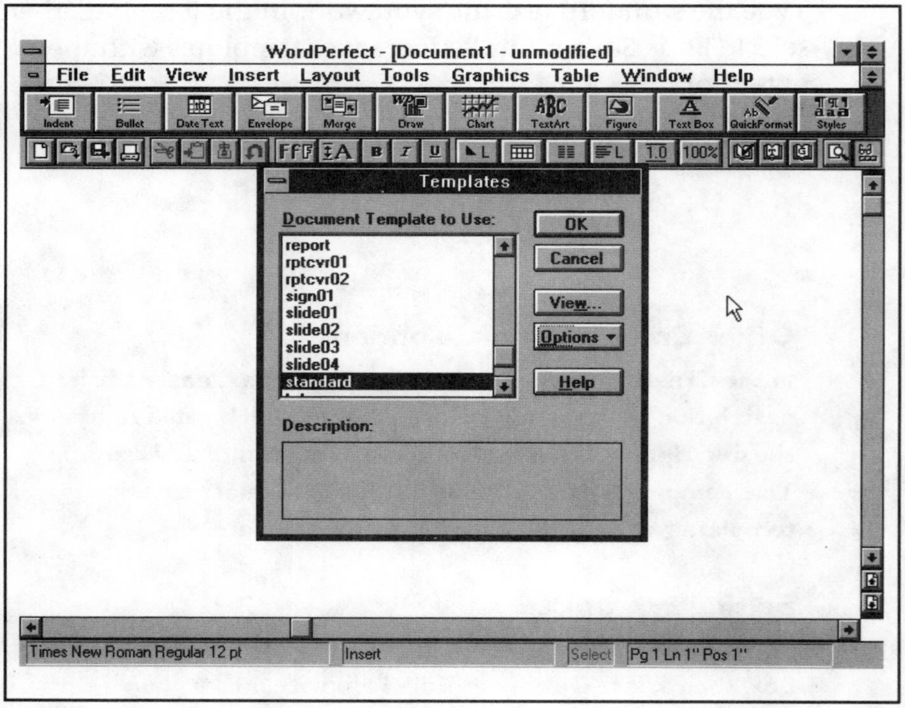

To use a template:

1. Select File ➤ Template (or Ctrl+T) to display the Template dialog box shown in the figure.
2. Double-click on the template you want to use, or select the template and click on OK.
3. Type the specific text for the document.
4. Select File ➤ Save As, enter a document name, then select OK.

tip

Previewing templates

Before you open a template, you can make certain it is the one you want to use. Highlight its name in the Template dialog box, then read the description that appears. If you are still not certain, select View to display the template in a Viewer window.

tip

WordPerfect templates

WordPerfect provides a number of useful templates to get you started. When you select certain ones, a dialog box will appear asking for information that WordPerfect needs to automatically fill in sections of the document (such as your name and telephone number to insert in a fax cover page). Enter the information requested in the dialog box, then select OK. Try the templates out to see how useful they can be!

It's So Easy

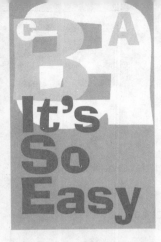

lesson 7

Using Multiple Documents and Windows

You can open and work on up to nine different documents at the same time in WordPerfect. This can be a great convenience if, say, you're typing a report and you need to refer back to a document you typed last week. Instead of having to print out the document, you can open it in its own window and refer to it while you are typing your current report. Or you can look at an outline of a document in one window while writing it in another, referring to the outline as needed.

You can also use windows to copy or move text from one document to another, just as easily as you can move from one location to another in the same document. In this lesson, you'll learn how to take best advantage of WordPerfect windows.

OPENING MULTIPLE DOCUMENTS

Working with multiple documents vastly increases your productivity and efficiency. You can write or edit one document while using others for reference. When you open a second document the one originally displayed is not erased, it is just moved into the background.

To open another document, do one of the following:

- When one document is on the screen, use File ➤ Open or the open button in the Power Bar to open another.

Several documents selected for opening

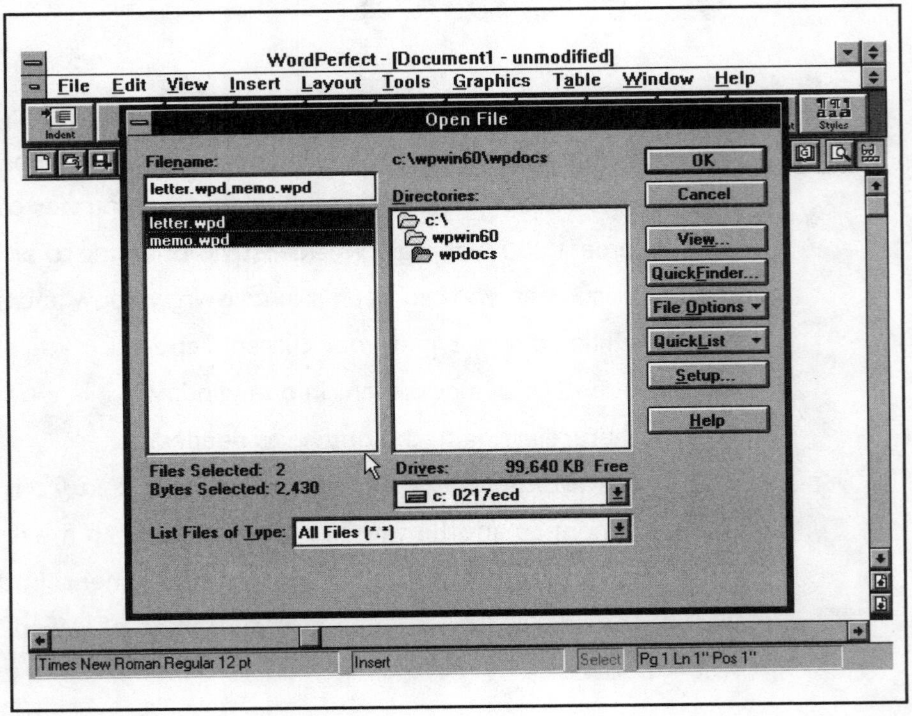

- Select File ➤ New to open a blank document window. You can then type a new document or open another document to be placed in the blank window.

To open several documents at one time:

1. Select File ➤ Open.
2. Hold down the Ctrl key and click on each of the documents you want to open.
3. Click on OK.

Saving one document individually will not save other opened documents. Before exiting WordPerfect, make sure you save all the documents that you changed.

oops!

Where did that document go?

If you select File ➤ New, you may then open an existing document to be placed in the empty window. However, if you add any text to the blank window and later open a document, the new document will open yet another window.

tip

Combining documents

To insert the text of a file on disk into a displayed document, place the insertion point where you want the text to appear, then select Insert ➤ File. Select the file from the Filename list, then select Insert. When the dialog box appears, select Yes.

SWITCHING BETWEEN DOCUMENTS

While you can have up to nine documents open at a time, only one is active. That is, you can only actually edit or format one document at a time. However, you can quickly switch from document to document.

Window menu

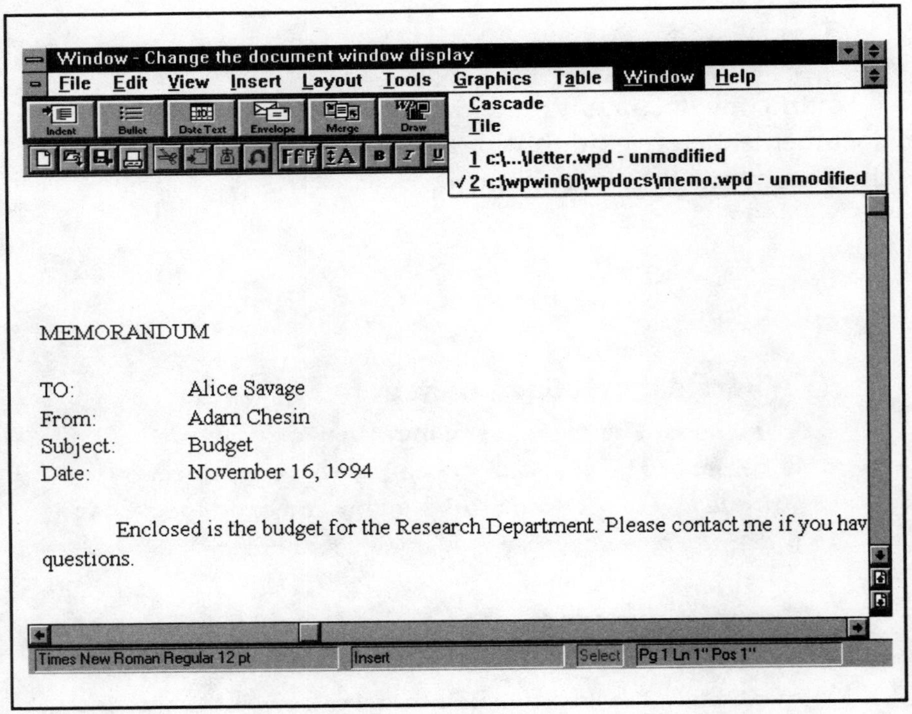

To switch between documents, do one of the following:

- Pull down the Window menu and click on the name of the document you want to display from the list of open documents.
- Press Ctrl+F6.

tip **Independent windows**

Changing views (from Page to Draft, for example) or magnification in one document will not affect the other documents.

tip **Position unchanged**

When you switch back to a document, the position of the insertion point will be unchanged.

tip **Prying eyes?**

If you have a document whose contents you'd rather not share with others in your office, try this trick. Select File ➤ New to open a blank window, then press Ctrl+F6 to select your document window. If someone who should not see your work approaches, press Ctrl+F6 to display the blank window.

DISPLAYING MULTIPLE WINDOWS

If you are working on several complex documents, you can move and copy text between them more efficiently if you display all of them on the screen. You can divide the screen into as many as nine windows at one time, and move from window to window using the mouse or keyboard.

There are two ways to display multiple windows. When you *tile* windows, the documents appear in separate non-overlapping windows. When you *cascade* windows, the windows are

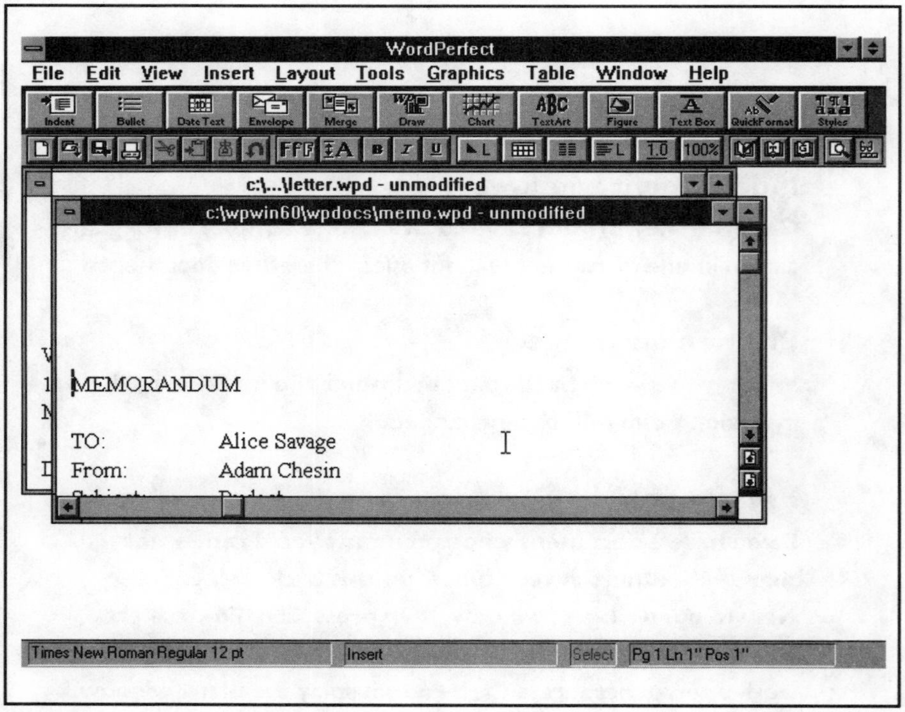

Cascaded windows

stacked on one another. The top window occupies most of the screen, but you can still see the Title Bars of other open windows.

To tile windows:

- Select Window ➤ Tile.

To cascade windows:

- Select Window ➤ Cascade.

To switch between displayed windows:

- Click on the window you want to make active. You can also press Ctrl+F6.

tip **Overlapping windows**

When windows overlap, making one active will bring it into the foreground.

Only one document window can be active at a time.

tip **Window construction**

Each window has its own Title Bar. The active window will contain Scroll Bars and a ruler, if it is turned on. The Title Bars of inactive windows are grayed and the Scroll Bars are hidden. When you select a window, its Scroll Bars will reappear.

CHANGING THE SIZE AND POSITION OF WINDOWS

You can quickly make the active window full-size by maximizing it, or change it to an icon by minimizing it. You can also customize the size and position of windows using the mouse.

Windows moved side-by-side

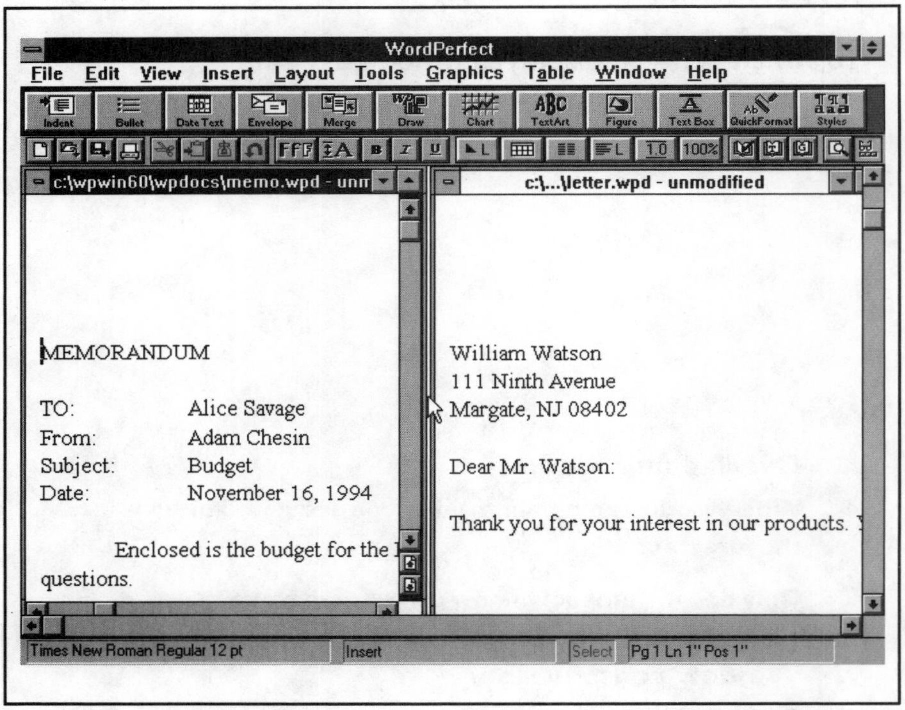

To change the size of a window, do one of the following:

- Drag one of the corners to change both the height and width of a window at one time.
- Drag the left or right border to change the width.
- Drag the top or bottom border to change the height.

To move a window:

- Point to the Title Bar and drag the mouse in the direction you want to move the window.

tip

Getting the correct size and position

As you drag the mouse, an outline of the window moves along with it. When the outline is the size you want, or in the correct location, release the mouse button. You can not move a window beyond the edge of the screen.

tip

Minimizing and maximizing

When you tile or cascade windows, the ▲ on the far right of the title bar is the maximize button. Click on this button to make the active window full size. The ▼ on the title bar is the minimize button. Click on this button to change the window into a small icon at the bottom of the screen. To re-display a minimized document, double-click on the icon. When a window is maximized, the combination ▲ and ▼ on the right of the Title Bar is the restore button. Click on this to return the window to its previous size.

MOVING TEXT BETWEEN DOCUMENTS

You can move and copy text from one open document to another whether or not they are displayed at the same time. The technique is similar to moving text within a document using Cut and Paste, or Copy and Paste.

To move or copy text between documents:

1 Switch to the document containing the text you want to move.

2 Select the text you want to move or copy.

Text about to be copied from one document to another

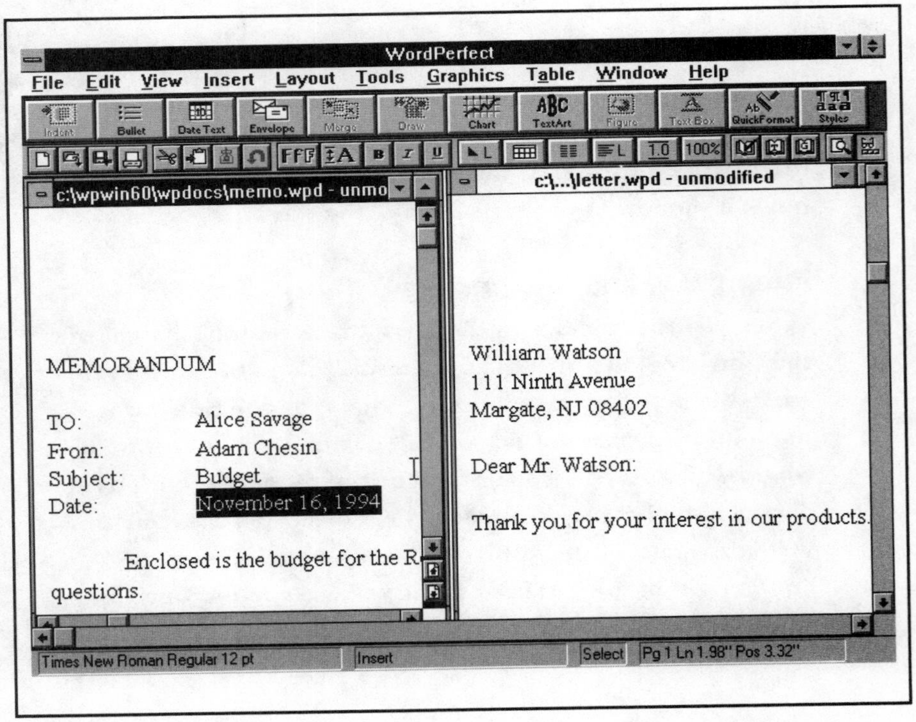

3 Select Edit ➤ Cut to move text (this deletes it from its original document), or Edit ➤ Copy to insert a duplicate of the text in another document.

4 Switch to the document you want to place the text in, or select File ➤ New to insert it into a new document.

5 Select Edit ➤ Paste or click on the Paste button in the Power Bar.

tip **Quick menus**

You can use the Quick menus to select Cut, Copy, and Paste.

tip **Moving text to unopened documents**

You can move and copy text from a open document to one not yet opened. Select the text you want to cut or copy, then select Edit ➤ Cut or Edit ➤ Copy. Open the other document, then select Edit ➤ Paste. Before opening the other document, you can also close the first.

tip **Dragging not allowed**

You cannot move text to another window using drag and drop.

Let's Do It!

PART TWO ▶ **Exercises**

You now know how easy it is to edit a document using WordPerfect. Let's practice your new editing skills.

Opening Documents

We'll start by creating and saving a small document. Then, we'll practice opening the document using the File menu and the Open dialog box.

1. Start Windows and WordPerfect.
2. Type the following text:

   Cholesterol is measured in a simple blood test that can be performed at your doctor's office, hospital, health clinic, or at special testing sites, such as health fairs. If your level is 240 mg/dl or higher, you are considered an increased risk for developing heart disease.

3. Select File ➤ Save (Ctrl+S), type CHOL, then select OK.
4. Select File ➤ Close to clear the window. Now let's practice opening the document.
5. Select File. The document CHOL.WPD is listed at the bottom of the File menu.

6 Click on the file name, CHOL.WPD. When you open a document, the insertion point is automatically at the top of the page.

7 Select File ➤ Close to clear the window.

Now let's use the Open dialog box.

8 Select File ➤ Open, or click on the Open button in the Power Bar. A list of files in the default directory appears.

9 Double-click on CHOL.WPD (scroll the list, if necessary). You can also highlight the document name, then click on OK.

10 Select File ➤ Close to clear the window.

11 Select File ➤ Exit if you're not ready to go on.

Inserting, Selecting, and Editing Text

Now let's add some text to the document, then practice selecting text and using the Undo and Undelete commands.

1 Open CHOL.WPD if it is not already on your screen.

2 Place the insertion point at the end of the last sentence in the document.

3 Press Enter twice to insert a blank line.

4 Press Tab to indent the paragraph, then type the following:

For patients with high levels, the physician may order an additional series of tests, called a lipid profile, which breaks down the type of cholesterol-carrying fat-protein chains (the lipoproteins) in your blood. The series reports LDL, HDL, triglyceride, as well as total cholesterol levels.

5 Place the insertion point in front of the first paragraph.

6 Hold down the left mouse button, then drag the mouse to the end of the paragraph. If you're not using the mouse, position the insertion point, press F8, then use the ↓ and → to select the text.

7 Press Del. Oops! We really don't want to delete all that text.

8 Select Edit ➤ Undelete (or press Ctrl+Shift+Z) to display the Undelete dialog box.

9 Select Restore.

10 Place the insertion point before the period at the end of the first paragraph.

11 Press the spacebar to insert a space.

12 Type **(and possibly death!)**. Well, that may be a little too morbid.

13 Select Edit ➤ Undo (or press Ctrl+Z) to delete the text.

14 Click on the Save button in the Power Bar, or select File ➤ Save. Since the document already has a name, it is saved immediately.

▶▶▶▶▶▶▶

15 Select File ➤ Exit if you're not ready to go on.

Moving and Copying Text

Now let's move and copy some text, and save a section of it as its own document. We'll start by copying text to make a title.

1 Open CHOL.WPD if it is not already on your screen.

2 Place the insertion point at the start of the document, at the far left in front of the first paragraph.

3 Press Enter twice to insert two blank lines.

4 Select the word Cholesterol in the first paragraph.

5 Place the mouse pointer on the selected word, click and hold down the left mouse button (do not release it until after the next step), then drag the pointer to the top of the document, in the first blank line.

6 Hold down the Ctrl key, release the mouse button, then release the Ctrl key.

If you do not have a mouse, select the text, then select Edit ➤ Copy. Move the insertion point to the top of the document, then select Edit ➤ Paste.

7 Select the entire first paragraph.

8 Click on the Save button in the Power Bar, or select File ➤ Save, to display the Save box.

9 Click on OK to accept the default setting, Selected Text. The Save As dialog box appears.

10 Type INTRO, then click on OK to save the text.

11 Click the mouse to deselect the text (or press F8).

12 Click on the Save button in the Power Bar or select File ➤ Save.

13 Select File ➤ Exit if you're not ready to go on.

Some Advanced Editing

Let's add the date to the document named CHOL.WPD, quickly insert a row of asterisks across the screen, then see how it looks enlarged and reduced.

1 Open CHOL.WPD if it is not already on your screen.

2 Place the insertion point at the start of the document.

3 Press Enter twice to insert a blank line.

4 Move the insertion point to the top of the document, at the left margin in the blank line.

5 Select Insert ➤ Date ➤ Date Code to insert the date as a code.

6 Move the insertion point in the blank line below the date.

7 Select Edit ➤ Repeat to display the repeat dialog box.

8 Type 65, then select OK.

9 Press * to draw the line.

▶▶▶▶▶▶▶

Now, take a look at your document in a different perspective.

10 Select View ➤ Zoom ➤ 200% ➤ OK to enlarge the document.

11 Select View ➤ Zoom ➤ 50% ➤ OK to reduce it.

12 Select View ➤ Zoom ➤ 100% ➤ OK to return to the default display.

13 Click on the Page Zoom Full button in the Power Bar to display the entire page.

14 Click on the button again to return to the previous view.

15 Select File ➤ Save.

16 Select File ➤ Exit if you're not ready to go on.

Working with Windows

Finally, we'll see how to work with more than one document.

1 Open CHOL.WPD if it is not already on your screen.

2 Select the last paragraph in the document.

3 Select Edit ➤ Copy.

4 Select File ➤ New to start a new document.

5 Select Edit ➤ Paste to insert the text you copied.

6 Select Window ➤ Tile to display both windows on the screen.

Figure 2.1: Tiled windows with copied text

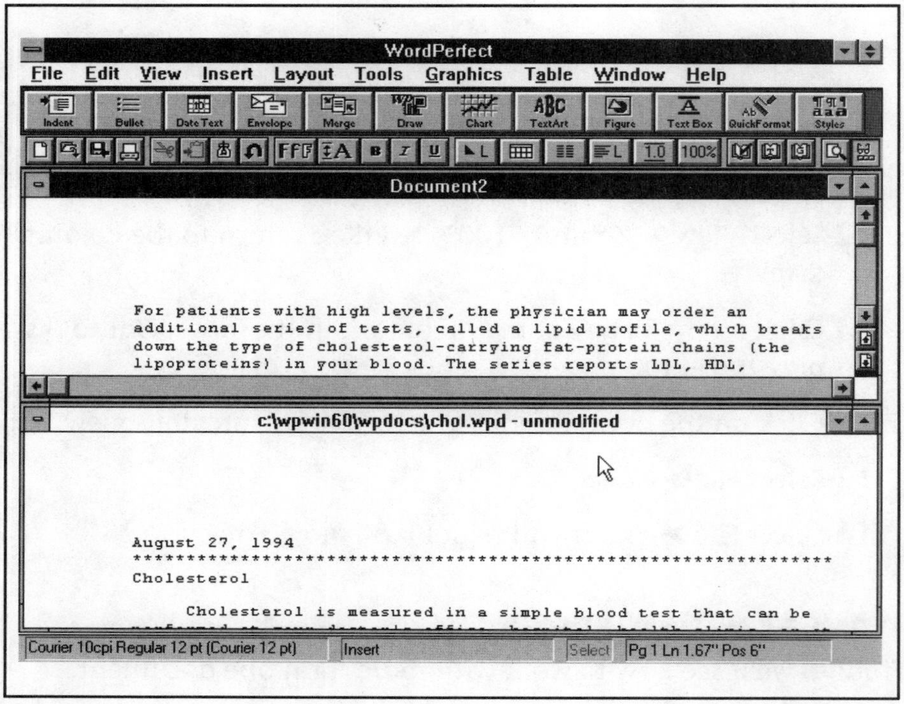
WordPerfect
File Edit View Insert Layout Tools Graphics Table Window Help
Indent Bullet Date Text Envelope Merge Draw Chart TextArt Figure Text Box QuickFormat Styles
Document2
For patients with high levels, the physician may order an
additional series of tests, called a lipid profile, which breaks
down the type of cholesterol-carrying fat-protein chains (the
lipoproteins) in your blood. The series reports LDL, HDL,
c:\wpwin60\wpdocs\chol.wpd - unmodified
August 27, 1994
Cholesterol
Cholesterol is measured in a simple blood test that can be
Courier 10cpi Regular 12 pt (Courier 12 pt)
Insert
Select
Pg 1 Ln 1.67" Pos 6"

7 Click on the Minimize button in the active window to change the window into an icon. The icon, however, is at the bottom of the screen under the other document window.

8 Point to the Title Bar of the remaining document window, and drag the window up beneath the Power Bar. The icon of the minimized window will now be displayed.

9 Click on the icon to display the control menu and select Maximize.

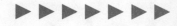

10 Press Ctrl+F6 to switch to the other window. It is also maximized.

Now exit WordPerfect without saving either document.

11 Select File ➤ Exit.

12 Select No in both dialog boxes that appear.

3 part three

FORMATTING YOUR DOCUMENTS

It's an unfortunate fact of life: no matter how new your concept, or how important your words, they have to be read to have any real impact. If it doesn't *look* worth reading, it probably won't be read.

In the lessons that follow, you will learn how to format your documents. You'll learn how to adjust the appearance of characters, lines, paragraphs, and pages so your words look as important as you know they are.

It's So Easy

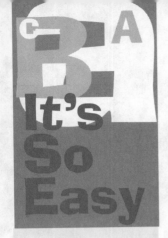

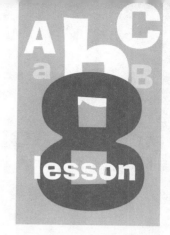

lesson 8

Changing the Appearance of Characters

WordPerfect can give your documents a desktop-published, professional look. But don't overdo it! Too many fonts and styles make text more difficult to read and not at all pleasing to the eye.

USING BOLD, UNDERLINE, ITALIC, AND MORE

The quickest way to format characters is by using the Power Bar. The Power Bar contains buttons for bold, italic, and underline.

To format characters:

1 Type until you are ready to format characters.

2 Click on the Power Bar button for the format you want.

- Click on the Bold button (or press Ctrl+B) to boldface.
- Click on the Italic button (or press Ctrl+I) to italicize.
- Click on the Underline button (or press Ctrl+U) to underline.

3 Type the characters.

4 When you've typed all the characters you want formatted, select the same style button (or press the Ctrl-key combination again) to turn the formatting off.

You can format characters in these and other styles using the Font menu, explained later in this lesson. The screen on the facing page shows the character formats.

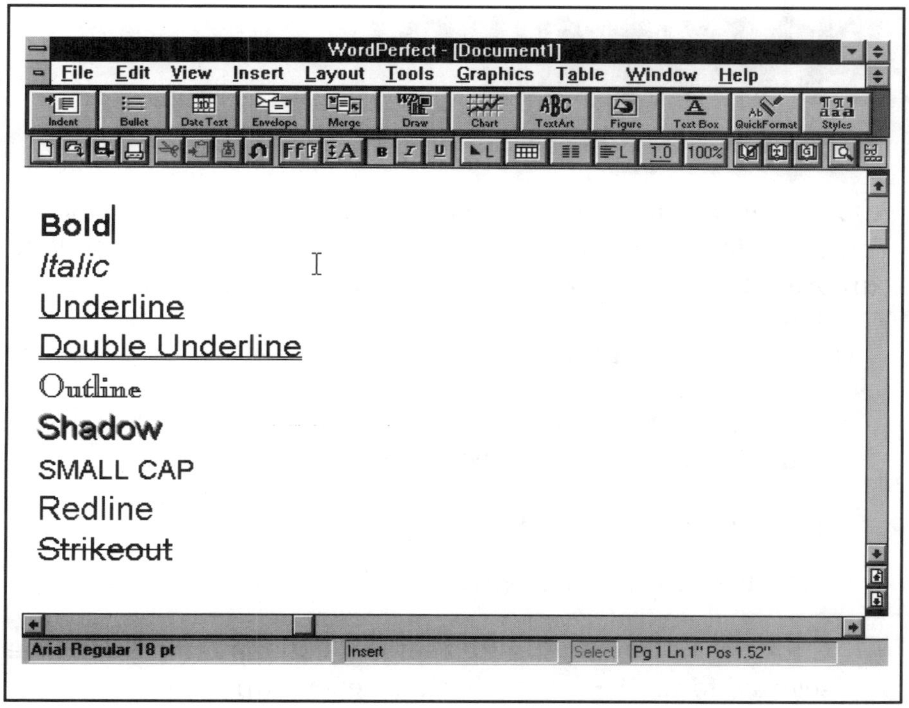

Character formats

tip

Changing your mind

To change the appearance of text after you've already typed it, you can select the text, then apply bold, italic, underline, or any other style. For more information on selecting text, see Lesson 4.

tip

Combining styles

To format in two styles, such as bold and underlined, select both formats before typing. Turn both off, in any order, when you are done.

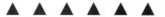

CHANGING TYPE FONTS AND SIZES WITH THE POWER BAR

A *font* refers to the general shape or design of the characters. You can select from all the fonts built into your printer, and you can use all the TrueType and other scalable fonts installed in Windows.

To change font with the Power Bar:

1. Click on the Font button on the Power Bar to display a list of available fonts, as shown in the figure.
2. Click on the desired font.

To change characters' size with the Power Bar:

1. Click on the Size button to display a list of point sizes for the selected font. The available sizes depend on the font.
2. Click on the desired size.
3. Type the text you want in that font and size.

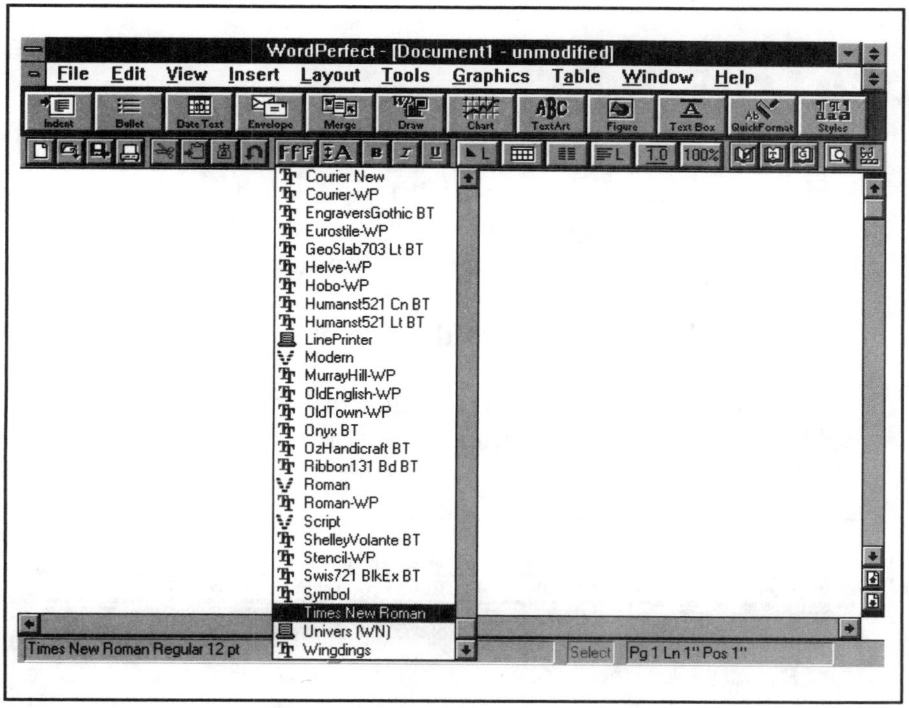

Font list from the Power Bar

tip ►

Changing the font of existing text

To change the font or size of text you've already typed, select the text first, then select a font and size. To enter a portion of text in a new font, type the text first, select it, then choose the font and size. If you choose a font or size without selecting text first, the code will affect all of the text from that location to the end of the document, or to the location of the next font change code.

Extra! Extra!

USING THE FONT DIALOG BOX

As an alternative to using the Power Bar, you can change character attributes, fonts, and sizes with the Font dialog box, shown in the figure. The Font dialog box lets you select special effects, such as outline and shadow, which are not available in the Power Bar.

To change character styles with the dialog box:

1. Select Layout ➤ Font, or click the right mouse button to display the Quick menu, then select Font.

Font dialog box

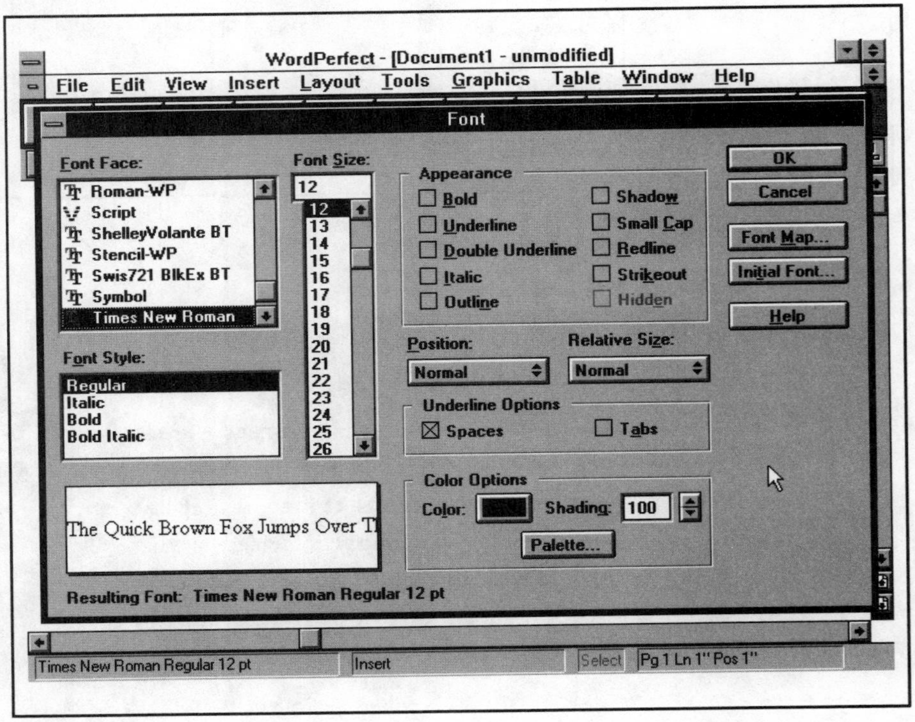

2 Pull down the Font Face list box to display available fonts.

3 Select a font from the list.

4 Pull down the Font Size list box to display available sizes.

5 Select the size and other font attributes or print colors.

6 Select OK.

7 Type the text you want in that font and size.

You can also display the Font dialog box by double-clicking on the Font button in the Power Bar.

tip

Changing underline styles

In the Font dialog box, toggle Spaces off to underline just words, not spaces between them. Toggle Tabs on to underline tab spaces.

tip

Changing the font of existing text

To change the font or size of text you've already typed, select the text first, then select options from the Font dialog box.

tip

Changing the document's default font

To quickly change the document's default font, select Initial Font in the Font dialog box. Select the font you want to use as the document's initial font.

CHANGING RELATIVE FONT SIZE

Normally, you select a specific font size using the Power Bar or the Font dialog box. However, there may be times when you'll want to change the size of characters *relative* to the current font. This size is expressed as a percentage of the current font, as shown in the figure. You can also select a relative position to create subscripts and superscripts.

To select a relative font size:

1 Select Layout ➤ Font ➤ Relative Size.

Percentages used for relative font sizes

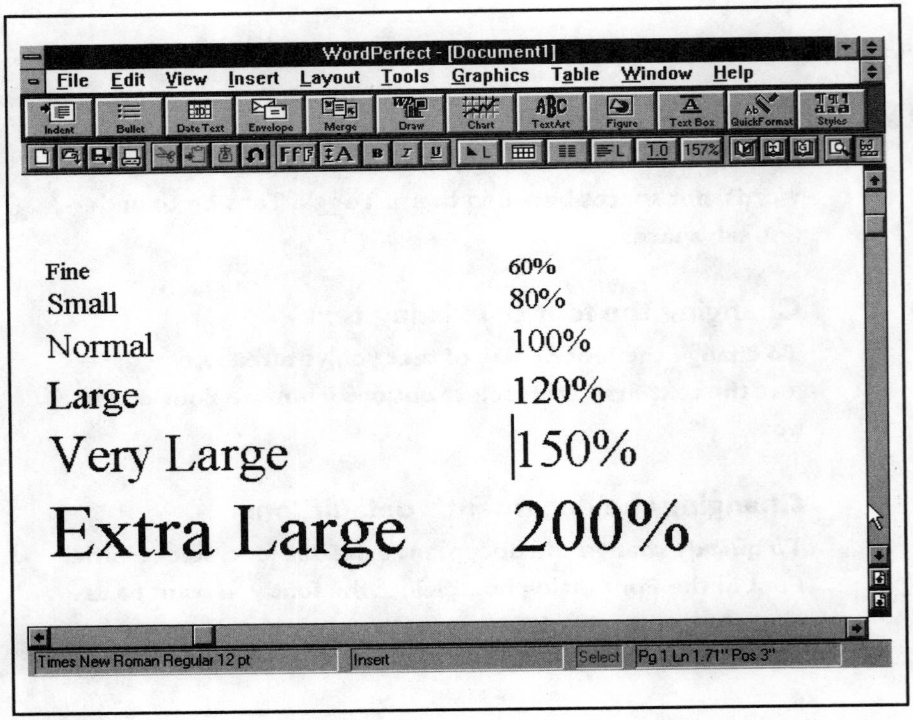

2 Select the size: Fine, Small, Normal, Large, Very Large, or Extra Large.

3 Type the text.

4 Select Layout ➤ Font ➤ Relative Size ➤ Normal to change back to normal size.

To create a subscript or superscript:

1 Select Layout ➤ Font ➤ Position.

2 Select Superscript or Subscript.

3 Type the text.

4 Select Layout ➤ Font ➤ Position ➤ Normal to change back to normal position.

tip **When it doesn't look correct**

If the selected sizes do not appear when printed, they are not available to your printer. In some cases, WordPerfect will automatically select an alternate font or size for you.

tip **How relative sizes work**

The size of the relative font depends on the current font being used. For example, if the current font is a 12-point font and you select Large, the resulting font will be 14.4-point. If the current font were 18-points, selecting Large would result in a 21.6-point font. Fonts are measured in points, and there are 72 points to an inch.

CHANGING FORMATS

You can change the format of new text as you type it, or change the appearance of existing text, by selecting it and then applying the format. Once text is formatted, you can remove the format or add other formats easily.

A selected check box indicates the format of text at the insertion point.

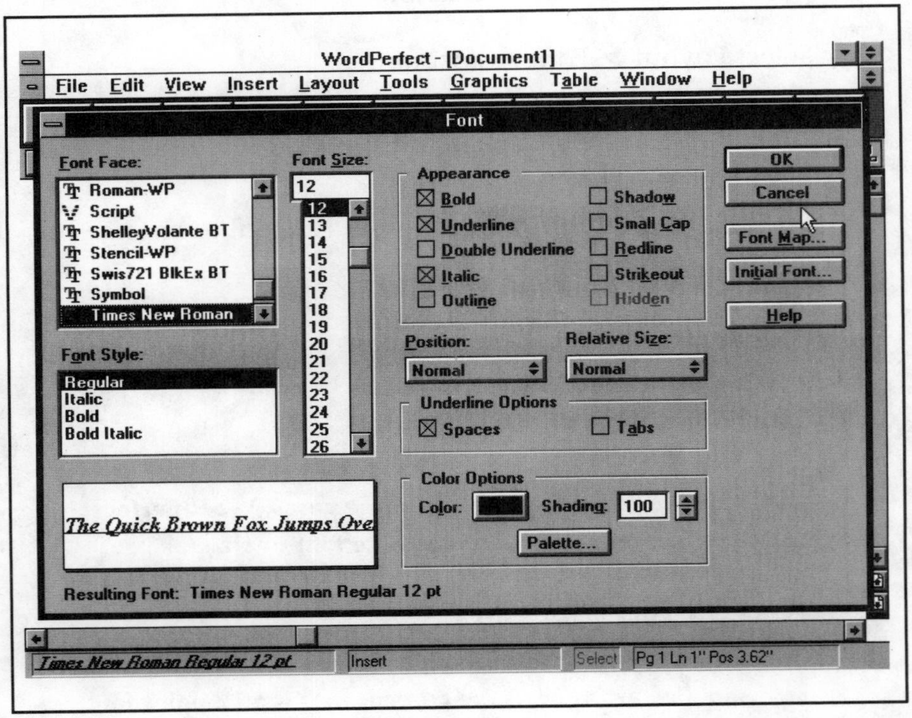

To remove formats from text:

- Reveal codes and delete the format code preceding the text, or select the formatted text, then select the format you want to remove from the Power Bar or Font dialog box.

To add additional formats:

- Select the text and choose a format from the Power Bar or Font dialog box.

tip

How is it formatted?

The Power Bar buttons and the Font dialog box will reflect the format of the text at the insertion point. If the insertion point is in underlined text, for example, the underline button will appear pressed down. In the dialog box, an X will appear at the underline checkbox. However, if you select a section of text that includes characters with no attributes as well as formatted characters, the Power Bar buttons will not appear pressed down. In the Font dialog box, WordPerfect will shade the checkboxes for all formats applied to characters in the selected text.

tip

Click twice

If clicking once on the Power Bar button does not remove the format, click again.

CHANGING THE CASE OF CHARACTERS

Normally, you enter uppercase characters from the keyboard by pressing the Shift key or the Caps Lock key. But have you ever accidentally pressed Caps Lock, only to notice the mistake after you've typed several paragraphs? Rather than retype the whole thing, you can quickly change the case of existing characters using the Edit menu.

To change the case of text:

1 Select the text you want to change.

Text in original and converted cases

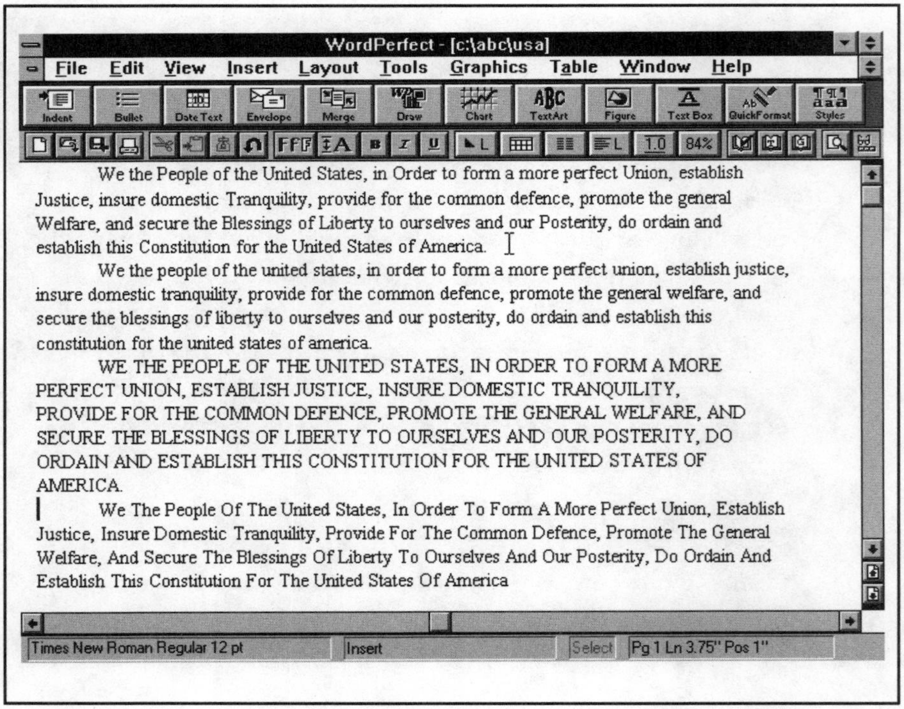

2 Select Edit ➤ Convert Case.

3 Select Uppercase, Lowercase, or Initial Capitals.

new feature

Initial caps is new to version 6.0

The Initial Caps option changes the first letter of every word (except for the article *a* that does not begin a sentence) to capital, not just the first letter of the sentence.

oops!

That's not what I wanted

If you select Initial Caps by mistake, select the text then select Lowercase. Only the first character of the sentence will remain uppercase.

tip

Lowercase

Selecting lowercase will convert every character in the sentence—except the first letter in the sentence, the pronoun I, and contractions starting with I such as I'd and I'll and I've.

INSERTING SPECIAL CHARACTERS

In this era of international business, it is no longer uncommon to need to print foreign-language characters, mathematical, scientific, or graphical symbols.

WordPerfect has 15 character sets, numbered 0 to 14, that allow you to add thousands of special characters to your documents: ASCII (0), Multinational (1), Phonetic (2), Box Drawing (3), Typographic Symbols (4), Iconic Symbols (5), Math/Scientific (6), Math/Scientific Extended (7), Greek (8), Hebrew (9), Cyrillic (10), Japanese (11), User-Defined (12), Arabic (13), and

WordPerfect Character box with special characters in the background document

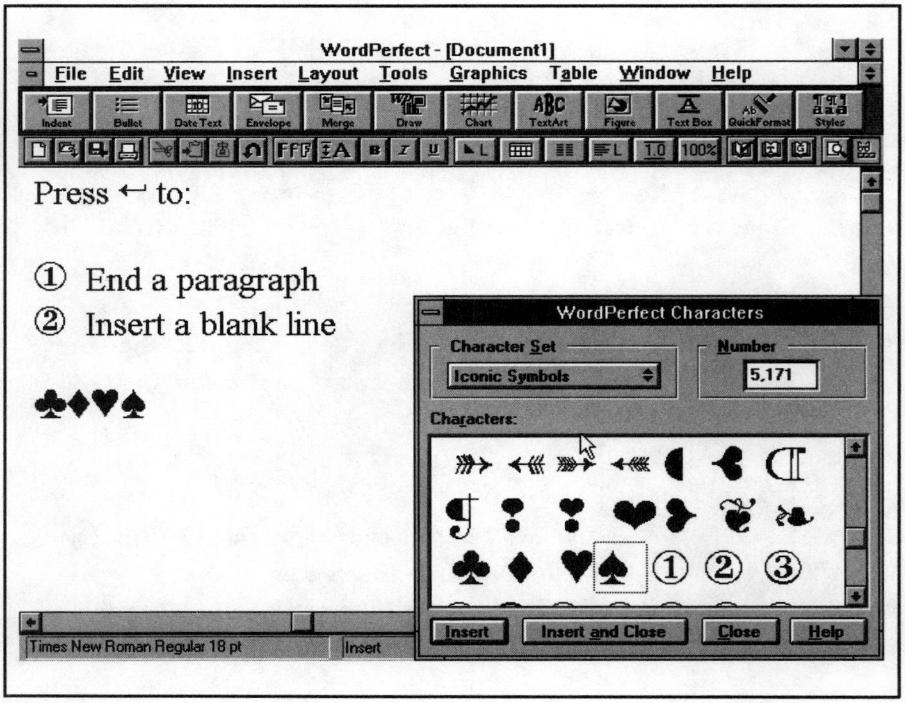

Arabic Script (14). If your printer does not have the characters you want to use available internally, WordPerfect prints them as graphic images closely matching the font being used.

To Insert special characters:

1 Select Insert ➤ Character (Ctrl-W) to see the WordPerfect Characters dialog box.

2 Pull down the Set list box and select the character set. The characters in that set are displayed in the Characters box.

3 Double-click on the character you want to insert, or choose the character, then select Insert and Close. Select Insert if you want to remain in the Characters dialog box.

The character will appear at the position of the insertion point, in the same size as the current font.

tip ▶ **Character size**

Once the character is displayed, you can change its size just as you do for any text. Select the character, then choose a point size from the Power Bar or Font dialog box. However, the only sizes available are those for the current font. If you are using a font that is not available in different sizes, select the character, choose a scalable font, then select a point size.

tip ▶ **Small boxes?**

If WordPerfect cannot display a graphic character on your screen, it will display a small box. The character, however, will still print correctly on graphic supported printers.

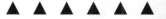

REMOVING REDLINE AND STRIKEOUT

You use redline and strikeout to make tentative changes to a document. You strikeout text to show you'd like to delete it, and you redline text you'd like to add.

When you are ready to make the final changes to the document, WordPerfect can do the final editing for you.

To remove redline and strikeout:

1 Select File ➤ Compare Documents ➤ Remove Markings. You'll see the Remove Markings dialog box, as shown in the figure.

Redline and strikeout options

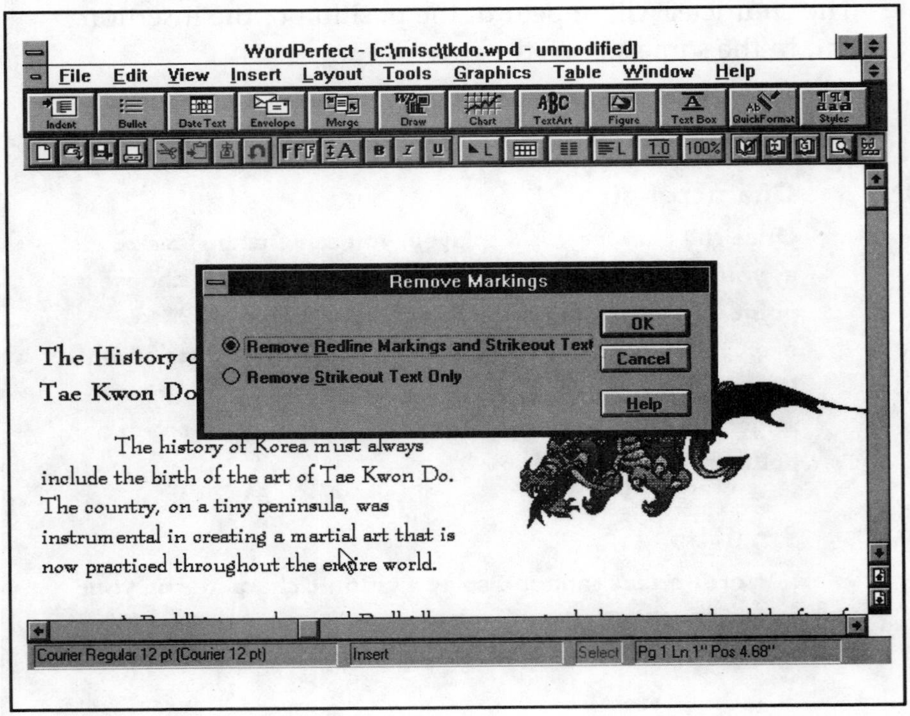

2 Select Remove Redline Markings and Strikeout Text. Text that has been formatted as strikeout will be deleted, and the redline markings will be removed from text formatted with redline codes.

3 Select Remove Strikeout Text Only to leave redline markings on text.

tip

Using redline and strikeout

When you want to add suggested text to a document, format it as Redline; select Layout ➤ Font, then click on the Redline checkbox. The text will appear on screen in a different color and print in reverse on a gray background. This informs other writers that the text is not part of the original document. When you want to suggest to other readers that certain text should be deleted, format that text as strikeout; select the text, then choose Layout ➤ Font, and click on the Strikeout checkbox. The text will appear on screen and print with a line through it. If all your suggestions are agreed upon, use the Remove Redline Margins and Strikeout Text option.

tip

Retaining strikeout text

If you choose *not* to delete some text formatted as strikeout, delete the strikeout codes manually ([StkOut]) or by using the Replace option on the Edit menu.

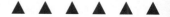

USING HIDDEN TEXT

Now you see it, now you don't. When you format text as *hidden*, you can choose whether or not it appears on screen and is printed with the document. Use hidden text to write reminders or notes that you want with the document but not printed with the final copy.

To format text as hidden:

1. Select Layout ➤ Font, then click on the Hidden checkbox.
2. Select OK.
3. Type the text you want to hide.

Hidden attribute selected

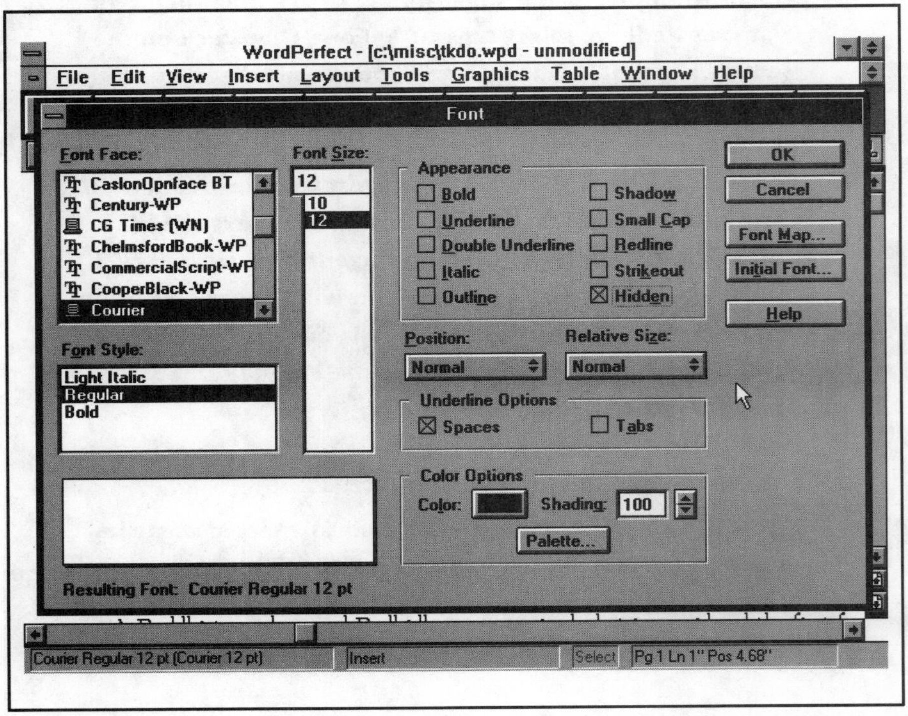

4 To begin typing normal text, select Layout ➤ Font and click on the Hidden checkbox to turn the feature off.

To hide or display hidden text:

- Select View ➤ Hidden Text.

To prevent hidden text from being printed, make sure the checkmark does *not* appear next to Hidden text in the View menu. If you forget to turn off the option, the text you wanted to hide will be printed.

tip

Hidden Text option may be grayed

If the Hidden option is grayed in the Font dialog box, select View ➤ Hidden Text. You cannot format text as hidden when the display of hidden text is turned off.

oops!

Check pagination before printing

Showing or hiding hidden text will affect the document's pagination. Before you print the document, make sure the Hidden Text option in the View menu is set as you want it to be for the print-out, then scan the document for proper pagination.

for more...

Converting hidden text

To format existing text as hidden, select the text, then select Layout ➤ Font, and click on the Hidden checkbox. Remove the hidden text format from a section of hidden text the same way.

COPYING STYLES WITH QUICK FORMAT

Once you format text the way you want it to appear, you can copy the format and apply it to other text. For example, if you select a character style, font, and point size for a heading, you can apply the same format to another heading without repeating all of the menu or Power Bar selections.

To copy a format:

1. Place the insertion point in the text that contains the formats you want to copy.

Quick Format dialog box

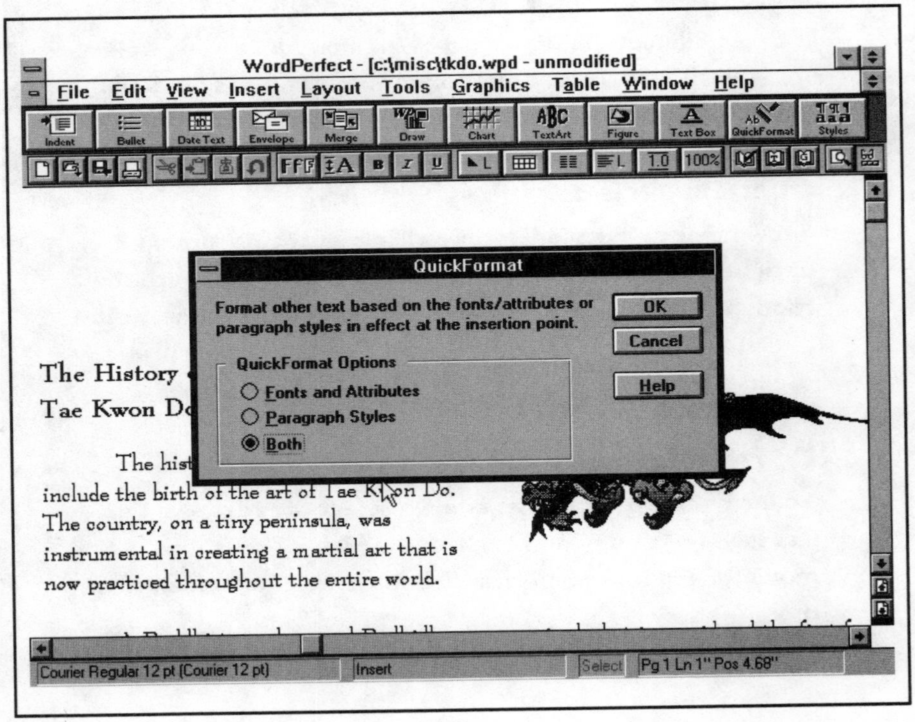

2 Click the right mouse button to display the Quick menu.

3 Select Quick Format to display the dialog box shown in the figure.

4 Click on Fonts and Attributes, then select OK. The mouse pointer will change shape to a large I-beam followed by an icon of a paint roller.

5 Select the text you want to apply the format to—use the Scroll Bars to scroll the screen if necessary. When you release the mouse button, WordPerfect will apply the format.

6 Copy the format to any other desired text.

7 When you are done copying the format, click right to display the Quick menu and select Quick Format.

button bar

Quick click quick format

Click on the Quick Format button to display the quick format dialog box.

tip

Keyboard format

To copy formats using the keyboard, select Layout ➤ Quick Format.

tip

Changing Your mind

If you decide not to apply the format, select Quick Format from the Quick Menu before selecting other text.

It's So Easy

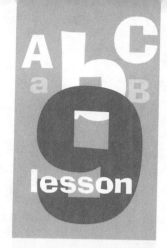

lesson 9

Formatting Lines

No matter how important your words, they have to be read to have any impact. And attractive line formatting can make your document easier and more interesting to read. By adjusting spacing and the alignment of text, you can help insure that your document has the maximum effect.

CHANGING LINE SPACING

Line spacing changes the overall appearance of the document. It can be set for the entire document, or just for sections within it. Spacing is allowed in decimal increments, such as 1.5 or 2.3.

To change line spacing:

1. Place the insertion point where you want the new line spacing to take effect.
2. Select Layout ➤ Line ➤ Spacing to display the Line Spacing dialog box, as shown in the figure.

Line Spacing dialog box

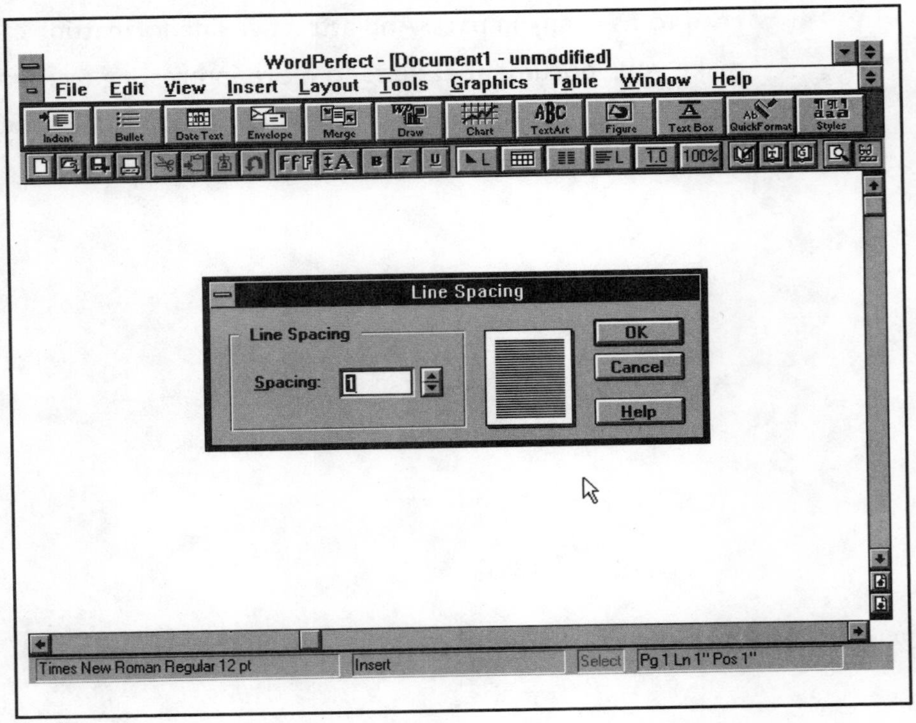

3 Enter the desired line spacing, or click on the up or down pointers to increase or decrease the spacing in one-tenth increments.

4 Select OK.

power bar

All mouse line spacing

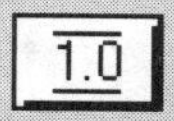

To change line spacing with the Power Bar, click on the Line Spacing button (marked 1.0) and hold down the mouse button. Select 1.0, 1.5, 2.0, or select Other to display the Line Spacing dialog box.

tip

Position the insertion point

Line spacing affects the text from the beginning of the paragraph in which the insertion point is located, to the end of the document unless another code is inserted. If you change line spacing and some text does not appear to change, there may be a spacing code already inserted. To change the spacing of the entire document, select the entire document first.

CENTERING TEXT

Titles and subtitles often look best when centered on the page. They provide a break in the text and call attention to a change in subject or purpose. You can center *single lines* of text as you type them, or as many lines of existing text as you want.

To center a title or line of text:

1 Place the insertion point at the start of the line.

2 Select Layout ➤ Line ➤ Center (Shift+F7). The insertion point moves to the center of the screen. You can also select Center from the Quick menu.

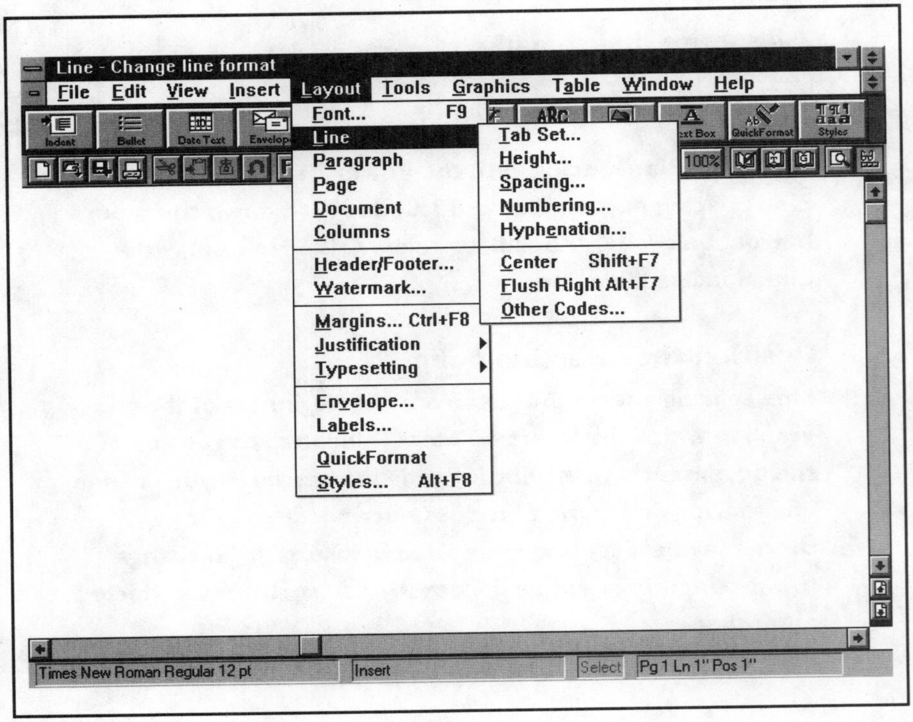

Layout Line menu

3 Type the text you want centered.

4 Press Enter. Centering affects text up to the carriage return that ends the line.

To decenter centered text, reveal the codes and delete the [Hd Center on Mar] or [Just: Center] code.

power bar

Using the Power Bar

To center text with the Power Bar, click on the Justification button and select Center.

tip

Justification formats

When you format text using the Justification button in the Power Bar (or by selecting Layout ➤ Justification, or by pressing the Ctrl-key combination), the format does not end when you press Enter. To end the format, select Left from the Power Bar justification button, or select Layout ➤ Justification ➤ Left.

tip

To center existing text

Place the insertion point at the start of the line and select Layout ➤ Line ➤ Center (Shift+F7), or select Center from the quick menu. To center a large section of text, select the text, then use any method of centering.

ALIGNING TEXT FLUSH RIGHT

Flush right text is aligned on the right margin with an uneven margin on the left—just the opposite of regular, unjustified text. This format is most commonly used in business announcements and programs.

To align a line of text on the right:

1. Select Layout ➤ Line ➤ Flush Right (or press Alt+F7). The insertion point will move to the right margin. You can also select Flush Right from the quick menu.

Right-aligned text

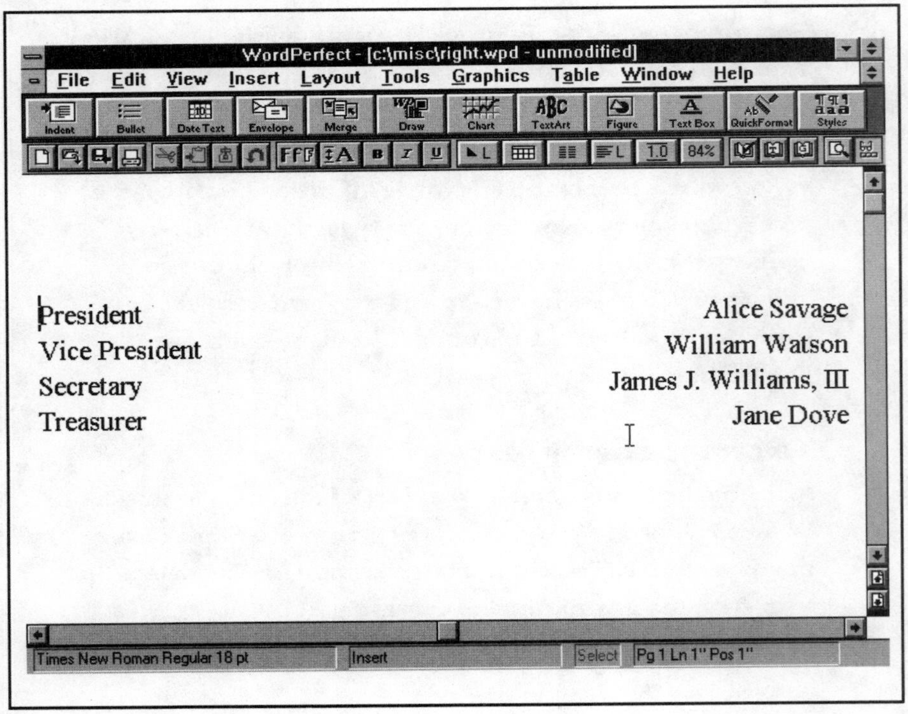

2 Type the text. Characters entered will move to the left, and the [Hd Flush Right] code is inserted at the start of the text.

3 Press Enter.

To return flush right text to normal, reveal codes and delete [Hd Flush Right] or the [Just:Right] codes.

power bar

Flush right made simple

To justify text on the right using the Power Bar, pull down the Justification button and select Right.

tip

To align existing text on the right

Place the insertion point *at the start* of the line and select Layout ➤ Line ➤ Flush Right (Alt+F7). To right-align multiple lines, select them, then use any method of right aligning.

tip

Combining left- and right-alignment

To format text as shown in the figure, type the text you want to appear at the left of the page, select Layout ➤ Line ➤ Flush Right (Alt+F7), then type the text aligned on the right.

CREATING FULL JUSTIFICATION

When you fully justify text, WordPerfect aligns the text between the left and right margins by increasing or decreasing the space between words as necessary. You can select to justify only lines that were ended by word wrap, or every line of the paragraph, including the last.

To justify text:

1. Place the insertion point where you want justification to begin.

Full justification and All justification

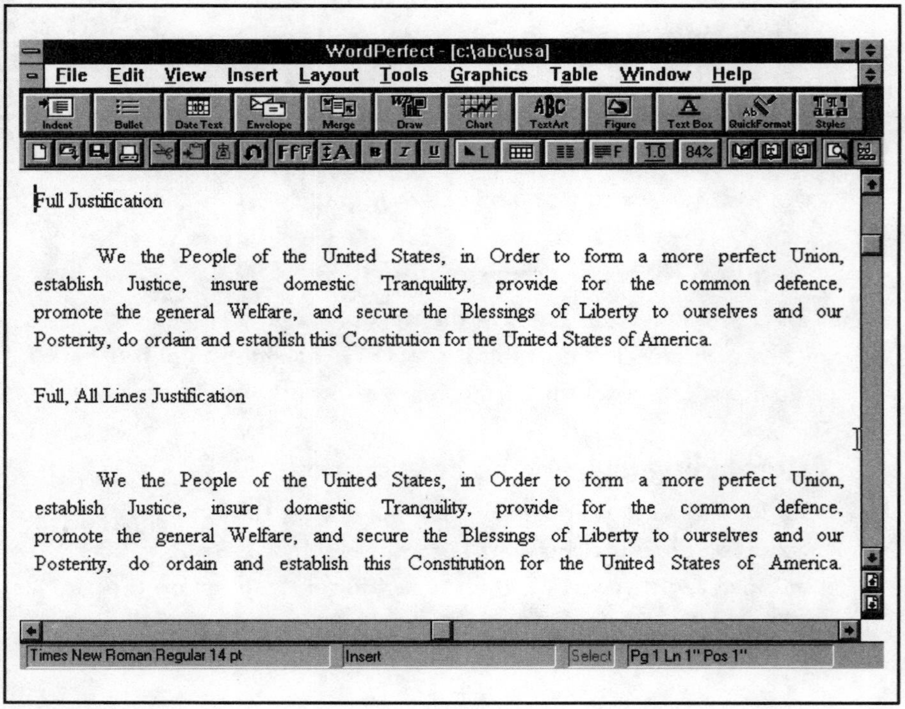
WordPerfect - [c:\abc\usa]
File Edit View Insert Layout Tools Graphics Table Window Help
Indent
Bullet
Date Text
Envelope
Merge
Draw
Chart
TextArt
Figure
Text Box
QuickFormat
Styles
Full Justification
We the People of the United States, in Order to form a more perfect Union, establish Justice, insure domestic Tranquility, provide for the common defence, promote the general Welfare, and secure the Blessings of Liberty to ourselves and our Posterity, do ordain and establish this Constitution for the United States of America.
Full, All Lines Justification
We the People of the United States, in Order to form a more perfect Union, establish Justice, insure domestic Tranquility, provide for the common defence, promote the general Welfare, and secure the Blessings of Liberty to ourselves and our Posterity, do ordain and establish this Constitution for the United States of America.
Times New Roman Regular 14 pt
Insert
Select
Pg 1 Ln 1" Pos 1"

2 Select Layout ➤ Justification.

3 Select Full or All. The figure shows both types of justification.

oops! **Too many spaces!**

As shown in the figure, unless the last line of the paragraph is nearly full, selecting All can result in unsightly spaces. There are times when selecting Full will also result in unsightly extra spaces. Hyphenation can alleviate this problem; see "Hyphenating Text Automatically" in Lesson 10 to learn more.

power bar **Easier justification**

To justify text with the Power Bar, pull down the Justification button and select Full or All.

tip **Canceling justification**

To cancel justification, position the insertion point at the start of the text and select Layout ➤ Justification ➤ Left.

SETTING TABS WITH THE RULER BAR

With WordPerfect, you can create four types of tab stops. With a default Left tab, columns are aligned on the left. A Right tab aligns columns on the right, a Center tab centers text around the tab stops, and a Decimal tab aligns numbers on the decimal point.

To set tabs with the ruler:

1. Select View ➤ Ruler Bar (or press Alt+Shift+F3) to display the ruler. The default tab stops are indicated by the triangles set every half inch.

Ruler and Tab Set options on the Power Bar

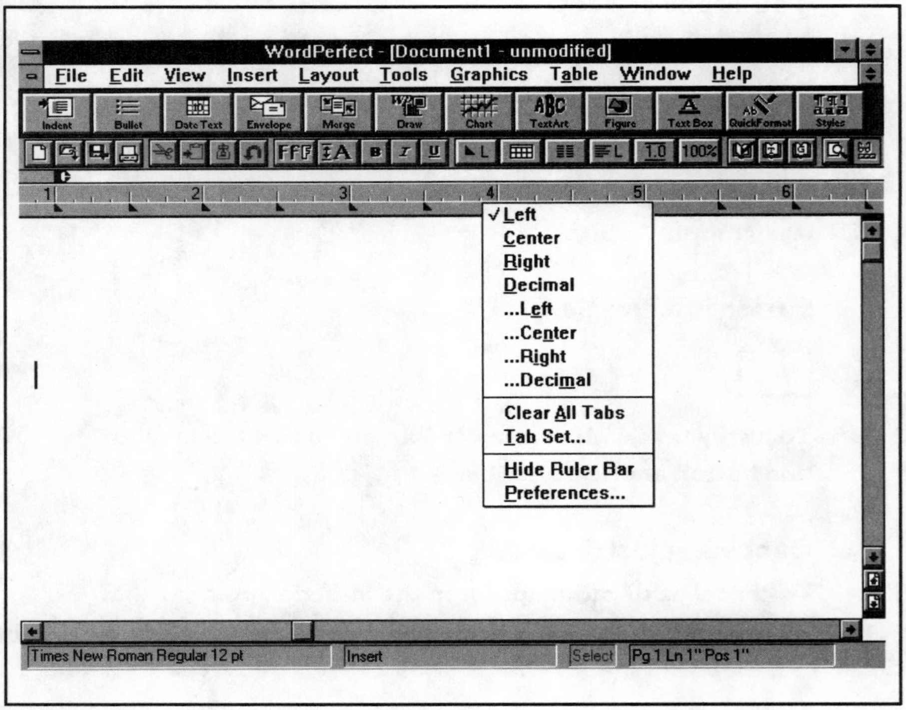

2 Click the *right* mouse button on the bottom part of the ruler (below the numbered line) to display the tab set Quick menu.

3 Select a tab type from the Quick menu.

4 Click at the position on the ruler where you want to set the tab. The triangular tab stop indicator shows the tab type.

tip

Deleting and moving tabs

To delete all the tab stops, display the Tab Set Quick menu and select Clear All Tabs. To delete one tab, drag the tab indicator down into the document window, then release the mouse button. To move a tab, drag its indicator to a new position on the ruler.

power bar

Setting tabs with the Power Bar

To display the Ruler Bar with the Power Bar, pull down the Tab Set button and select Set Tabs. Pull down the Tab Set button and select a tab type, then click on the ruler to set a tab. The tab type options from the Power Bar will be unselectable until you display the ruler.

SETTING TABS WITH THE DIALOG BOX

While you can set tabs quickly with the Ruler and Power Bar, you have greater control over tabs using the Tab Set dialog box.

To set tabs with the dialog box:

1 Select Layout ➤ Line ➤ Tab Set to display the Tab Set dialog box. The ruler will appear if it was not already displayed.

2 Select Clear All to delete all of the preset tabs.

Tab Set window

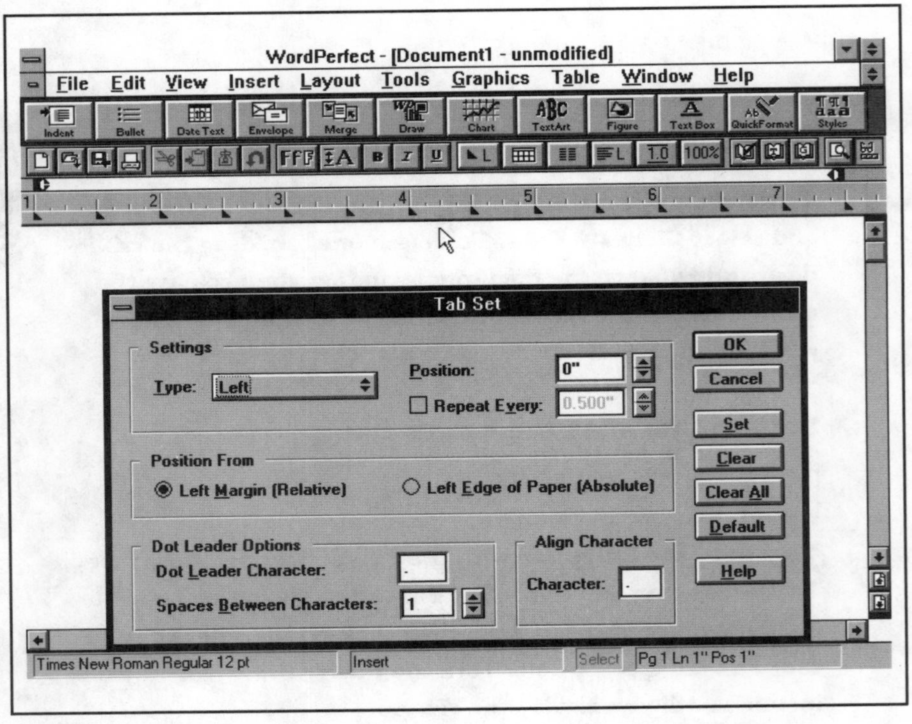

3 In the Position text box, type the position where you want to set a tab.

4 Pull down the Type list box and select the tab type.

5 Click on Set.

6 Select OK when done.

power bar

Double-click to display the dialog box

To quickly display the Tab Set dialog box, double-click on the Tab Set button on the Power Bar, or select Set Tabs from the ruler's Tab Set Quick Menu.

tip

To delete a tab

To delete a tab stop from the Set Tab dialog box, type the location of the tab stop in the Position Text box, then select Clear. To return the default tab stop positions, select Default.

tip

Relative versus Absolute tabs

WordPerfect uses relative tabs—the default Left Margin (Relative) setting in the Tab Set dialog box. If you change the left margin, the tabs will shift to maintain the same relative distance. You can also select Left Edge of Paper to create Absolute tab stops which will remain where you set them even if you change margins.

It's So Easy

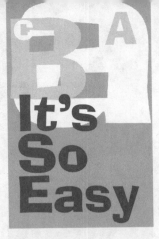

lesson 10

Formatting Paragraphs

The default paragraph format used by WordPerfect is the *block style*. This means that every line—including the first one in a paragraph—starts at the left margin. In this lesson, you'll learn how to change the way paragraphs are arranged—by indenting them on the left or right, and by adding hyphens to even out lines on the right. You'll also learn how to automatically number paragraphs and highlight them with graphic symbols.

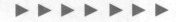

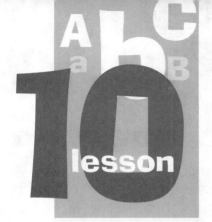

INDENTING PARAGRAPHS

If you want to indent the first line of a paragraph, just press the Tab key. You might, however, want to indent an entire paragraph from the left margin, or from the right *and* left margins as for a long quotation.

To indent a paragraph from the left margin:

1. Select Layout ➤ Paragraph ➤ Indent (F7), or select Indent from the Quick menu.
2. Type the text.
3. Press Enter.

Indented paragraphs

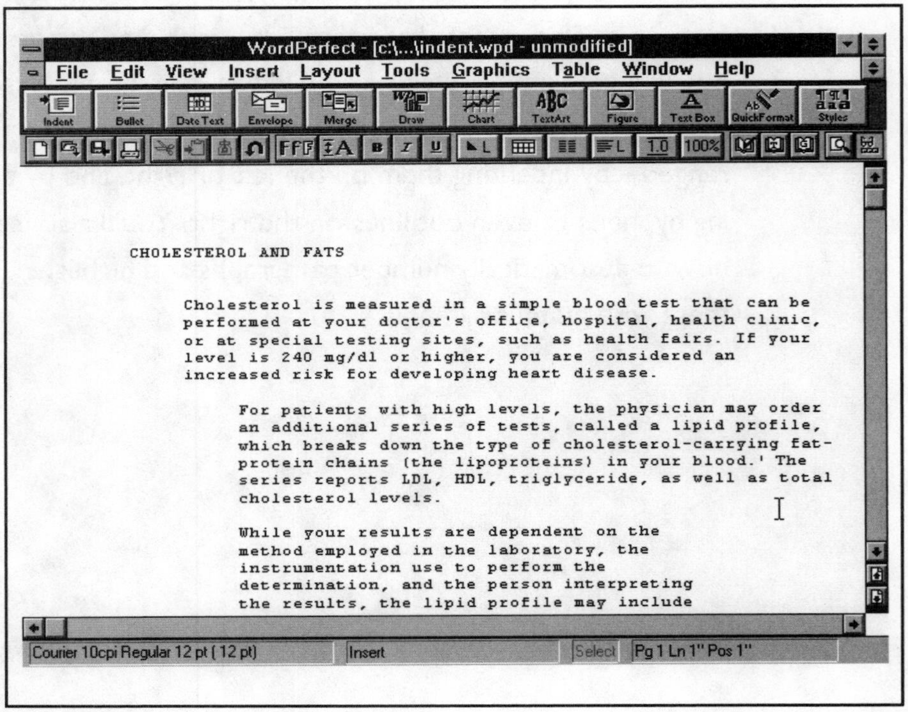
WordPerfect - [c:\...\indent.wpd - unmodified]
File Edit View Insert Layout Tools Graphics Table Window Help
Indent
Bullet
Date Text
Envelope
Merge
Draw
Chart
TextArt
Figure
Text Box
QuickFormat
Styles
CHOLESTEROL AND FATS
Cholesterol is measured in a simple blood test that can be performed at your doctor's office, hospital, health clinic, or at special testing sites, such as health fairs. If your level is 240 mg/dl or higher, you are considered an increased risk for developing heart disease.
For patients with high levels, the physician may order an additional series of tests, called a lipid profile, which breaks down the type of cholesterol-carrying fat-protein chains (the lipoproteins) in your blood.' The series reports LDL, HDL, triglyceride, as well as total cholesterol levels.
While your results are dependent on the method employed in the laboratory, the instrumentation use to perform the determination, and the person interpreting the results, the lipid profile may include
Courier 10cpi Regular 12 pt (12 pt)
Insert
Select
Pg 1 Ln 1" Pos 1"

To indent a paragraph from both margins:

1. Select Layout ➤ Paragraph ➤ Double Indent (or press Ctrl+Shift+F7).
2. Type the text, then press Enter.

tip ▶ **How indent works**

Each time you select Indent, the left margin moves to the next tab stop to the right. Select Indent once to indent a paragraph ½ inch (the first tab by default), twice for a 1-inch indentation, and so on. At the end of the line, WordPerfect moves the insertion point to the indented position, not the original margin, until you press Enter. To indent an existing paragraph, place the insertion point *at the start of the paragraph* then select Indent. Other paragraphs will not be affected. Double Indent functions the same way but changes both the left and right margins.

tip ▶ **Indentations versus margins**

You can indent a paragraph by changing the left margin. However, margin changes affect the entire document, so you'd have to reset the margin following the indented text. Change margins when you want the entire document, or a large portion of it, indented. See "Setting Margins" in Lesson 11 for more information.

CREATING HANGING INDENTATION

Standard paragraphs have only the first line indented with remaining text flush on the left. *Hanging indentations* are just the opposite; the first line starts to the left of the rest of the paragraph. Use hanging indentations when you want paragraphs to stand out from each other, as with numbered paragraphs and outlines.

To create a hanging indent:

1. Select Layout ➤ Paragraph ➤ Hanging Indent (or press Ctrl+F7).

An outline using hanging indentation

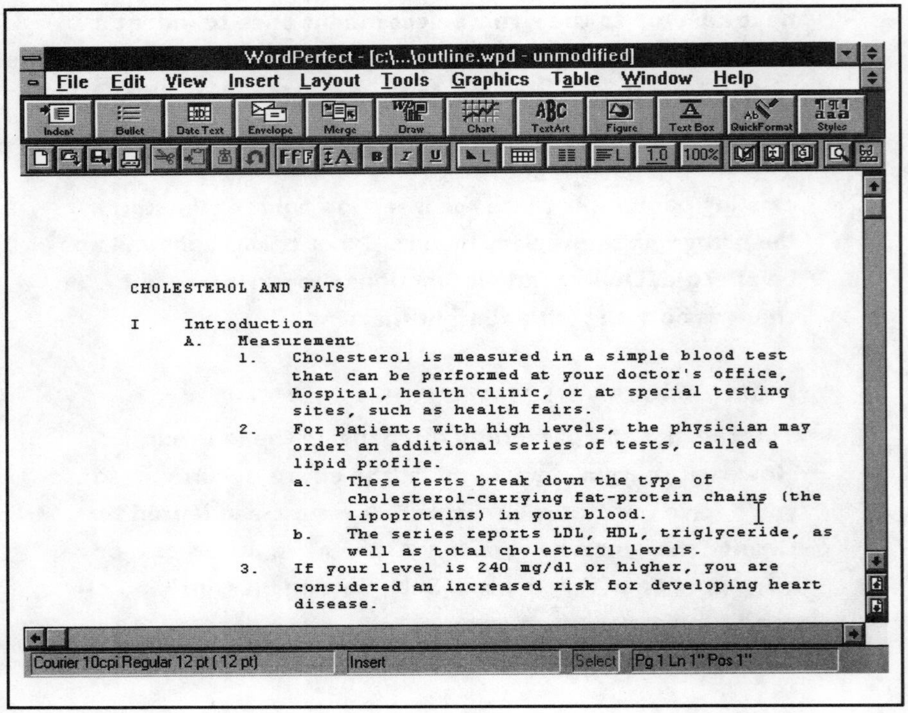
WordPerfect - [c:\...\outline.wpd - unmodified]
File Edit View Insert Layout Tools Graphics Table Window Help
Indent Bullet Date Text Envelope Merge Draw Chart TextArt Figure Text Box QuickFormat Styles
CHOLESTEROL AND FATS
I Introduction
A. Measurement
1. Cholesterol is measured in a simple blood test that can be performed at your doctor's office, hospital, health clinic, or at special testing sites, such as health fairs.
2. For patients with high levels, the physician may order an additional series of tests, called a lipid profile.
a. These tests break down the type of cholesterol-carrying fat-protein chains (the lipoproteins) in your blood.
b. The series reports LDL, HDL, triglyceride, as well as total cholesterol levels.
3. If your level is 240 mg/dl or higher, you are considered an increased risk for developing heart disease.
Courier 10cpi Regular 12 pt (12 pt)
Insert
Select
Pg 1 Ln 1" Pos 1"

2 Type the paragraph number, followed by a period if desired.

3 Press Tab.

4 Type the text.

5 Press Enter to end the paragraph and return the insertion point to the left margin. The figure shows an outline that uses numbered and lettered paragraphs.

tip

How hanging indentation works

Hanging indentation actually inserts two codes, a left indentation and a backtab (margin release). The backtab moves the insertion point to the left margin of the first line. Subsequent lines start at the indent position until you press Enter.

tip

Hanging indentation from the keyboard

To create numbered paragraphs without using the Layout menu, type the paragraph number, then press F7. WordPerfect will continue lines at the indented position. To create indented positions more to the right—for lower outline levels, for example—press Tab to reach the location where you want the paragraph number.

tip

Hanging text

Hanging indentations can also be used for text. For this format, just select Layout ➤ Paragraph ➤ Hanging Indent, then type the paragraph. To format this manually, press F7, then Shift+Tab, the backtab command.

CREATING BULLETED AND NUMBERED LISTS

If you are writing a list with only one level of hanging indentation, you can have WordPerfect insert the paragraph numbers and create the hanging indentation for you in one step.

To create a bulleted or numbered list:

1 Select Insert ➤ Bullets & Numbers to display the dialog box shown in the figure.

2 Click on the style of bullet or number you want to insert.

Bullets & Numbers dialog box

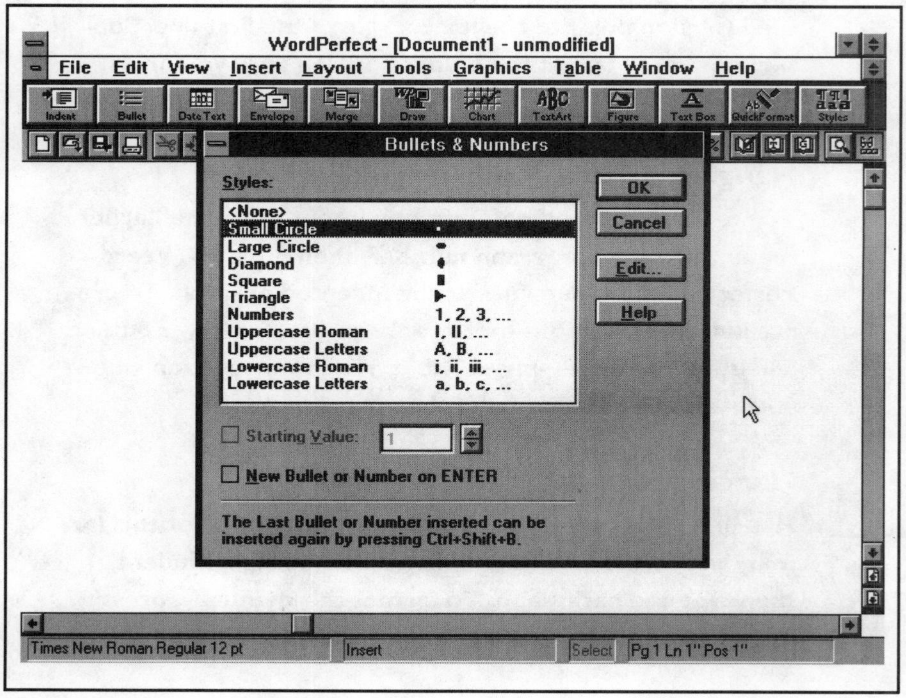

3 Select New Bullet or Number on ENTER.

4 Select OK. WordPerfect will insert the selected symbol, starting number or letter, and create a hanging indentation.

5 Type the text of the list. Each time you press Enter, WordPerfect inserts the symbol or the next highest number or letter. If you did not select New Bullet or Number on Enter, only one paragraph would be bulleted or numbered.

6 To stop inserting bullets or numbers, select Insert ➤ Bullets & Numbers ➤ None ➤ OK.

button bar

Bullets in a click

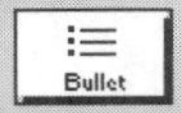

Click on the Bullet button to display the Bullets and Numbers dialog box.

tip

Starting over

If you later select a number or letter option you've used before, WordPerfect will continue numbering where it left off earlier. To start over, or to select a different starting number or letter, select Starting Value and enter the starting number. If you are using letters, type the corresponding numbers—1 for A, 2 for B, 3 for C, etc.

HYPHENATING TEXT AUTOMATICALLY

WordPerfect lets you type without pressing Enter at the end of each line. But at times, such as when long words wrap to the next line, a justified paragraph can have too many extra spaces between words.

Ordinary manual hyphenation slows down your typing by making you pause at the end of lines to make hyphenation decisions. When you use automatic hyphenation, however, WordPerfect actually divides words for you and adds hyphens at the appropriate places.

Line Hyphenation dialog box

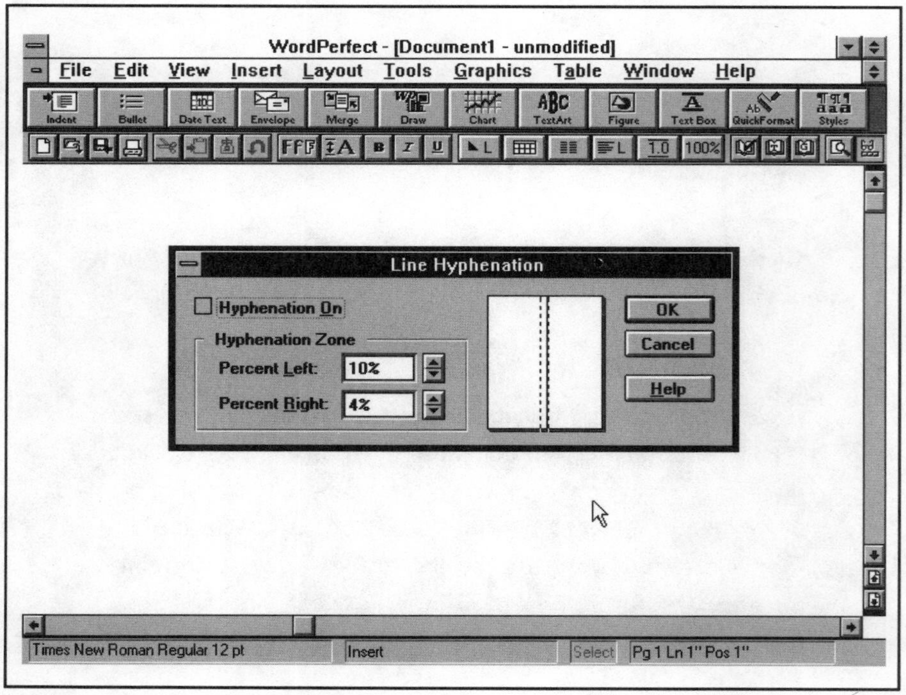

1 Place where you want to begin hyphenation.

2 Select Layout ➤ Line ➤ Hyphenation to display the dialog box shown in the figure.

3 Click on Hyphenation On, then select OK.

4 WordPerfect will automatically insert a hyphen where appropriate. If WordPerfect's rules of hyphenation don't apply, a dialog box will appear asking you to confirm the hyphen position. Press the → and ← keys to move the hyphen to an appropriate place, then select Insert Hyphen.

tip ▶ How automatic hyphenation works

When WordPerfect hyphenates a word automatically, it inserts an [Auto Hyphen EOL] code in the document but displays a hyphen character on screen. If you later insert or delete text and the word no longer needs to be hyphenated, WordPerfect deletes the hyphen and the code automatically.

tip ▶ Hyphenating existing text

Turn on hyphenation either before you type or at the beginning of existing text. As you scroll through text, WordPerfect will hyphenate for you.

tip ▶ Deleting hyphens

To remove all of the automatic hyphenations, reveal codes and delete the [Hyph: On] code.

ENTERING HYPHENS YOURSELF

Automatic hyphenation is useful but it cannot handle every situation, such as telephone numbers, or words like son-in-law. The figure shows some text that contains several hyphens.

To create manual hyphens:

- Press the – key by itself (for words such as mother-in-law).
- Press Ctrl+– to prevent WordPerfect from dividing items such as telephone and social security numbers.

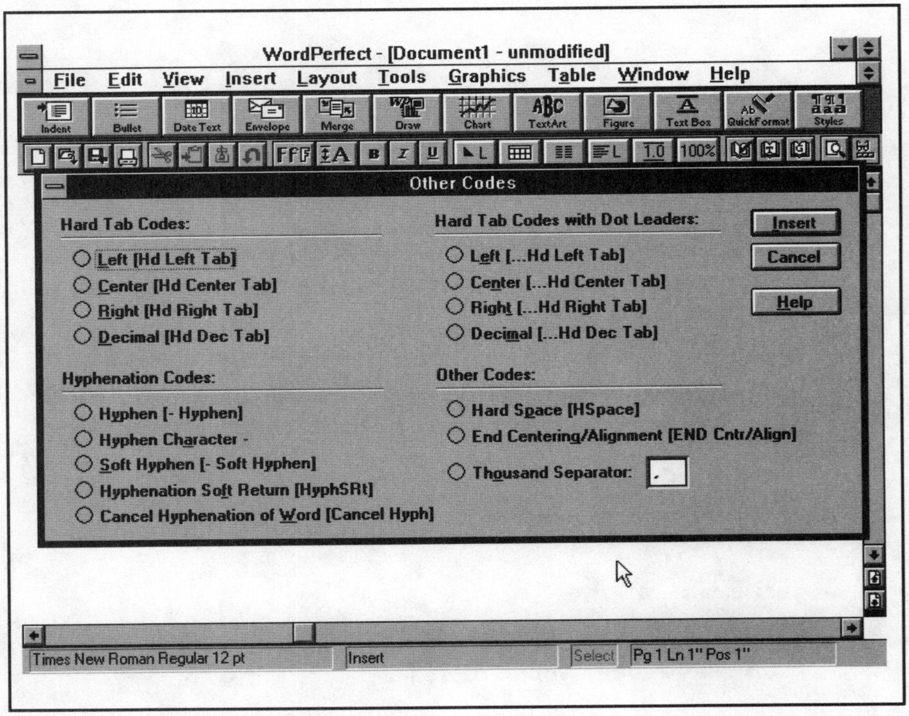

Other Codes dialog box

- Select Layout ➤ Line ➤ Other Codes ➤ Hyphenation Soft Return to enter an *invisible soft hyphen*. WordPerfect will divide the word at that position, without displaying a hyphen, if later editing requires the word to break at the end of the line.
- Select Layout ➤ Line ➤ Other Codes ➤ Soft Hyphen to enter a *soft hyphen*, to break a word between lines without a hyphen.

tip

How WordPerfect divides words with manual hyphenation

When you press – by itself, WordPerfect inserts a [-Hyphen] code. If you later add or delete text from the paragraph, WordPerfect will divide the word between lines at the hyphen. WordPerfect will not divide a formula at the position of the minus sign, entered with Ctrl+-.

tip

Soft hyphens—semi-automatic hyphenation

When you insert a Soft Hyphen from the Other Codes dialog box, no hyphen will appear on screen unless WordPerfect needs to word-wrap the word between lines. If later editing forces the word to be wrapped, it will be hyphenated at that point even with hyphenation turned off. An invisible soft hyphen (Hyphen Soft Return from the Other Codes dialog box) never appears on screen. WordPerfect will use that position to divide the word if later editing requires the word to be divided at the end of a line—but no hyphen will appear.

C B A

It's So Easy

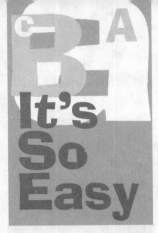

lesson 11

Formatting Pages

Each time you start WordPerfect, standard default settings are provided automatically to let you type and print documents without worrying about how big the page is. The default margins result in a page with 54 lines of text, each $6\frac{1}{2}$ inches wide. The text will appear neatly arranged when printed on standard business stationery, with text aligned flush with the left margin.

You don't have to change a thing if you like these settings and want to use them for every page of your document. But you can change these settings easily if you want other formats.

SETTING THE MARGINS

The page margins determine how much text will fit on each page. The right and left margins, for example, set the length of the printed line and can be adjusted for different widths of paper. To make a document appear longer, make the margins a little wider. Make them smaller to fit as much text as possible on a page.

To set the left and right margins with the ruler:

- Drag the left or right margin indicators (above the ruled line) to the desired left or right margin position.

Margins dialog box

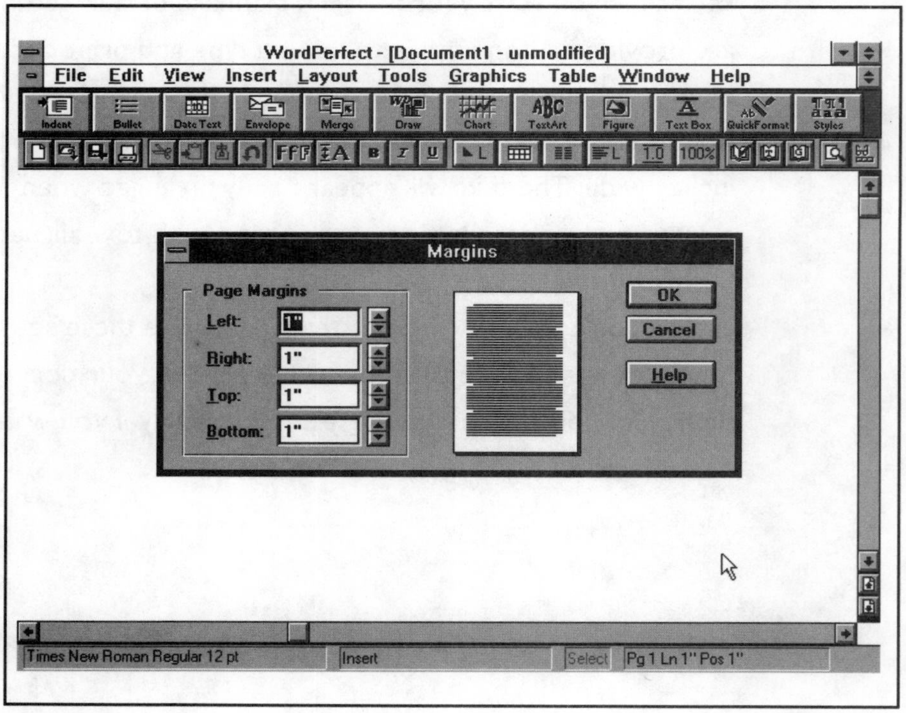

To set the margins with the dialog box:

1. Select Layout ➤ Margins (Ctrl+F8) to display the Margins dialog box, as shown in the figure. You can also display the dialog box by clicking the right mouse button in the left margin, then selecting Margins from the Quick menu.
2. Set the left, right, top, and bottom margins as desired.
3. Select OK to close the dialog box.

warning!

Beware of your position!

When you change the left or right margins, WordPerfect inserts a code at the beginning of the paragraph in which the cursor is located. The change affects every paragraph from that position to the end of the document—or until the next margin size code. WordPerfect places the Top and Bottom margin code at the start of the page in which the cursor is located. So, be sure to place the insertion point on the first page you want to format.

Extra! Extra!

tip

Margins versus Indent

Use Indent to change the margins of an individual paragraph or selection of text. Use margins to change the margins for the entire document.

tip

Why did the margins change?

Some printers have minimum required margins. If you set smaller ones, WordPerfect automatically changes the settings to the printer's minimum.

CREATING TITLE PAGES

Title pages usually contain several lines of text centered both horizontally and vertically on the page. To get this effect, you could type the text, then set the top, left, and right margins so the text appears in the proper location. However, it's easier to take advantage of WordPerfect's automatic center page options.

To create a title page:

1. Select Layout ➤ Page ➤ Center to display the dialog box shown in the figure.
2. Select Current Page.

Center Page(s) dialog box

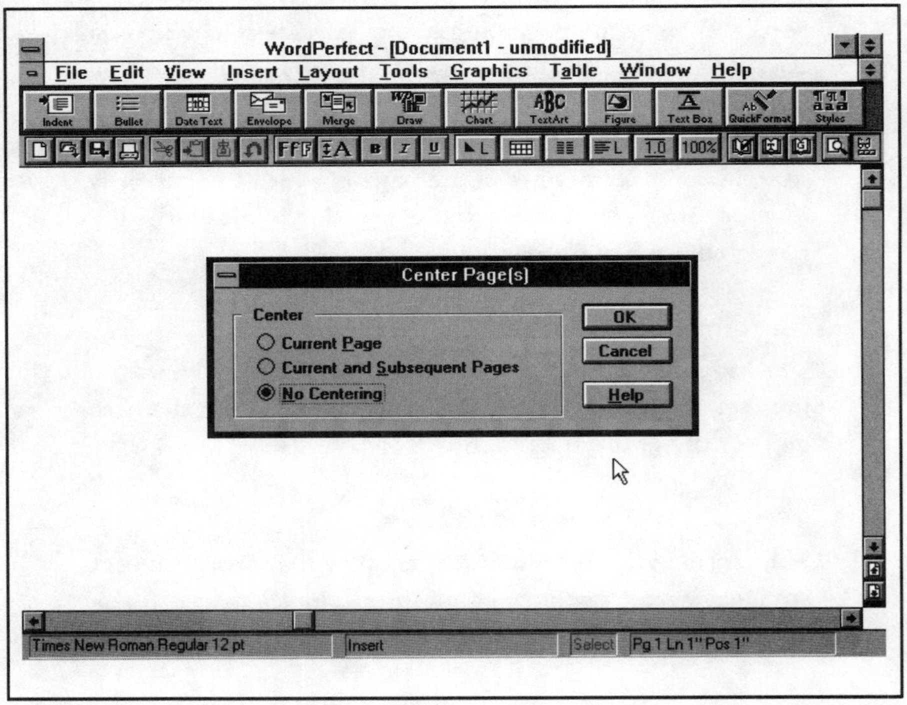

3 Select OK.

4 Type the text to be centered.

5 Press Ctrl+Enter.

To center every page from the insertion point to the end of the document:

- Select Layout ➤ Page ➤ Center ➤ Current and Subsequent Pages ➤ OK.

tip

Text on center

The center page options only center text between the top and bottom margins—not between the left and right margins. To center text across the page, use Shift+F7 or select Layout ➤ Justification ➤ Center.

tip

Watch those blank lines

If you want the text slightly higher than center, just add a few blank lines with the Enter key after typing the text. To print it slightly lower than center, add the lines above the text, but after the [Cntr Cur Pg: On] code.

tip

Canceling centered pages

Select Layout ➤ Page ➤ Center ➤ No Centering ➤ OK. Alternatively, reveal codes, then delete the [Cntr Cur Pg:On] or [Cntr Pgs: On] code.

SELECTING A PRESET PAGE SIZE

WordPerfect includes several *paper definitions* along with the information it stores for your printer. Each definition includes the width and length of the paper, as well as its orientation and method of feeding through the printer.

To change page sizes:

1. Place the insertion point on the first page of your document.

Paper Size dialog box

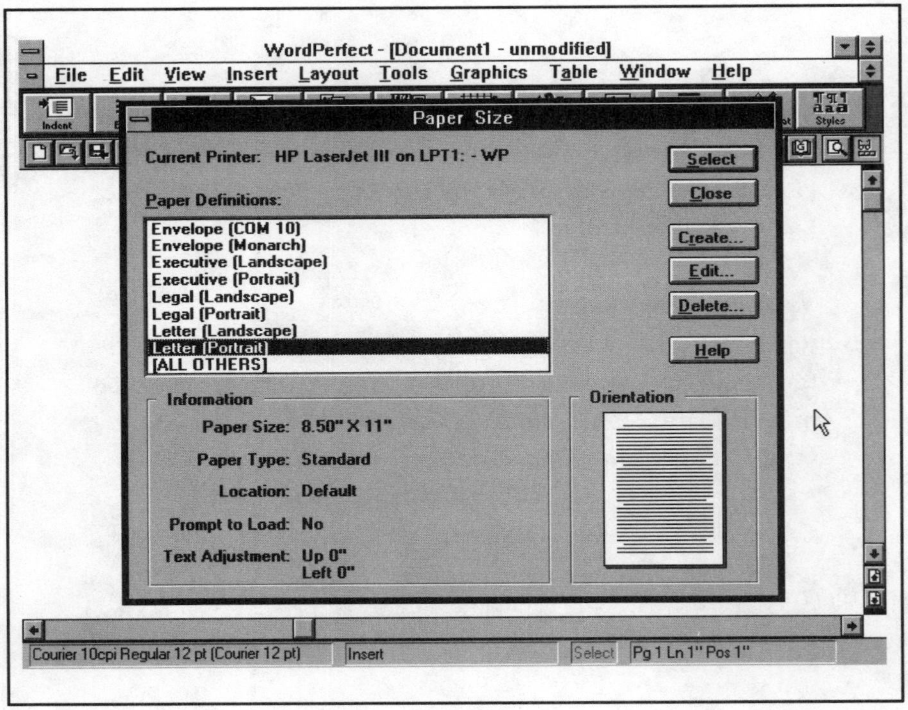

2 Select Layout ➤ Page ➤ Paper Size to display the dialog box shown in the figure. The definitions listed depend on your printer.

3 Scroll the Paper Definitions list box and select from the available options. The illustration of the page will change to reflect the selected definition.

4 Click on Select to accept the selected size.

arning!

Watch your position!

When you change page sizes, WordPerfect inserts a page size code at the beginning of the page in which the insertion point is located. If your document is more than one page long, make sure you are on the first page you want to format.

tip

Changing individual pages

To change the size of just one page in a document, place the cursor on that page, then select a new size. If you want following pages to print on the default size, place the cursor on the next page, then select Letter (Portrait) in the Page Size dialog box.

PRINTING AN ENVELOPE WITH A LETTER

In a few keystrokes, you can format and print an envelope using an address you've already typed on screen.

1 Type the letter, including the inside address.

2 Select Layout ➤ Envelope to display the Envelope dialog box.

3 Check the mailing address. If it is incorrect, select the Mailing Address box and edit the address.

Envelope dialog box

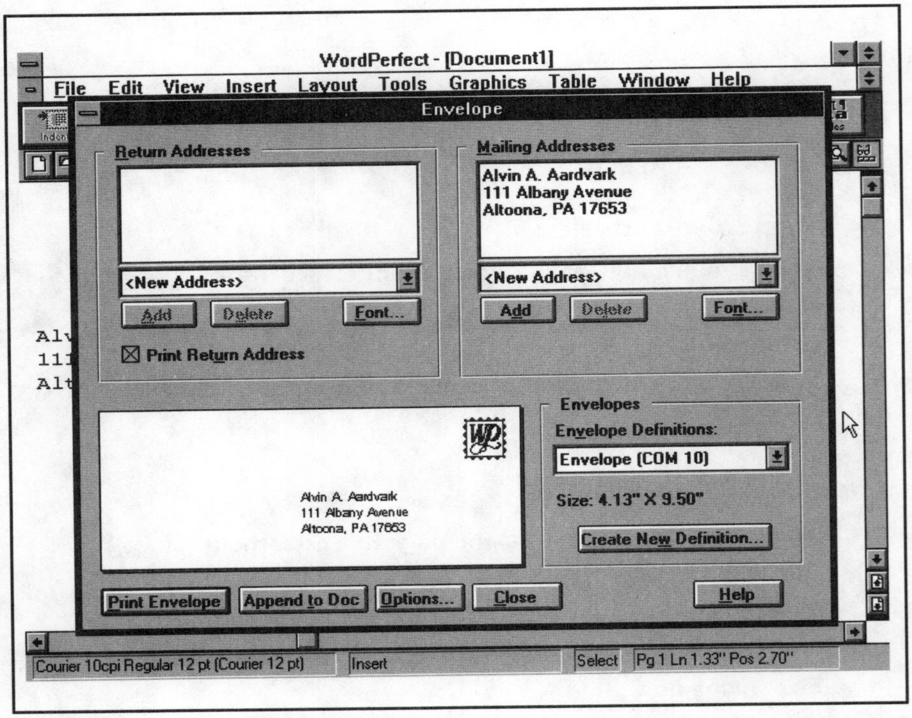

4 To include your return address, select the Return Address box and type your address.

5 Check the envelope size. If it is incorrect, pull down the Envelope Definitions list box and select from defined envelope forms for your printer.

6 Select Append to Doc to place the envelope at the end of your document, separated from the text with a page break, or select Print Envelope to print the envelope immediately.

button bar

Do it fast

To display the Envelope dialog box, click on the Envelope button.

tip

POSTNET bar codes

To insert a bar code, select Options in the Envelope dialog box to display the Envelope Options box. Click on Include USPS POSTNET Bar Code, then select OK. WordPerfect will add a POSTNET Bar Code text box to the Envelope dialog box. If the correct zip code does not appear in the text box, select the box and enter the zip code. Other Envelope options allow you to change the position of the addresses.

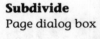

CREATING BOOKLETS

A booklet is a document printed with four pages on one sheet of paper, in landscape orientation. When you fold the sheet in half, you have a four-page booklet. WordPerfect will organize the pages for you and print them on the appropriate side of the page.

1 Open the document you want to print as a booklet.

2 Select Layout ➤ Page ➤ Paper Size ➤ Letter (Landscape), then click on Select.

3 Select Layout ➤ Page ➤ Subdivide Page to display the dialog box shown in the figure.

Subdivide Page dialog box

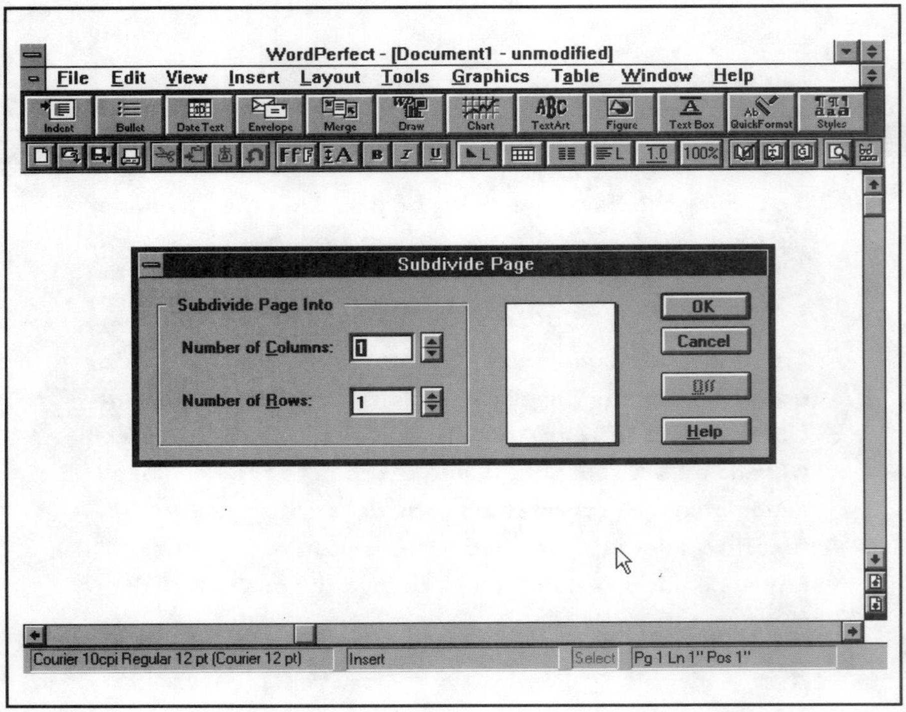

4 Type 2, then select OK.

5 Select File ➤ Print ➤ Options.

6 Click on Booklet Printing, then select OK.

7 Select Print to print one side of each sheet of paper.

8 Remove the printed pages.

9 Press Alt+Tab until you see a box with the name Print Manager. A dialog box will appear telling you to insert page 1.

10 Starting with the first page that came out of your printer, reinsert each page so the blank side will be printed on, and select OK. WordPerfect will print the other side of the pages.

11 Fold the printed pages in half.

tip ▶ Paper feed

It may take you some trial and error to feed the pages correctly for the second pass through the printer. You must insert the pages so they print on the blank side, with the top of the page in first.

tip ▶ Set the margins

When you subdivide the page, WordPerfect retains the default one inch margins which may be too large for a $5\frac{1}{2}$ inch folded size. Reduce the margins to fit more text on the page.

It's So Easy

lesson 12

Enhancing Your Pages

This lesson will show you how to add some finishing touches to your documents to make them even more effective. You'll learn how to use headers, footers, and page numbers to identify the document. That way, if individual pages get separated from the document, the reader will be able to figure out where they came from. You'll also learn how to use *watermarks* for extra impact and to identify documents as your own.

CREATING HEADERS AND FOOTERS

A *header* prints specified lines of text at the top of every page. *Footers* do the same, but at the bottom. Headers and footers will appear on the screen in Page and Two-Page views, but not in draft.

1 Place the insertion point on the first page you want to contain the header or footer.

2 Select Layout ➤ Header/Footer. You can have two different headers and two different footers, known as *A* and *B*.

Header/Footer window

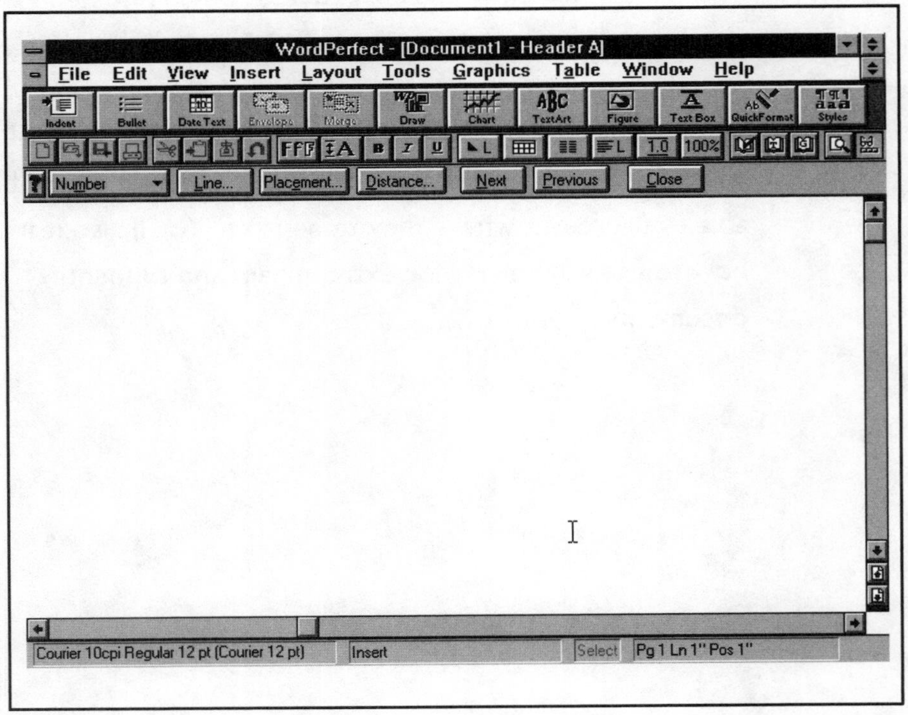

3 Select Header A, Header B, Footer A, or Footer B.

4 Select Create to display the Header/Footer window, as shown in the figure. Use the Feature Bar under the Power Bar to customize the header or footer.

5 Type the text of the header and footer.

6 Select Close.

tip

Customizing headers and footers

To number pages in a header or footer, place the insertion point where you want the number to appear, select Number in the Feature Bar, then select Page Number. Pages will be numbered consecutively. To alternate headers or footers, select Placement, then choose Odd Pages, Even Pages, or Every Page. Coordinate A and B to print them on alternating pages—select Odd Pages for one, Even Pages for the other.

tip

To edit a header or footer

To edit a header or footer, select Layout ➤ Header/Footer, select the header or footer (A or B), then Edit. To stop a header from printing on the current and subsequent pages, place the insertion point on the page, then select Layout ➤ Header/Footer, select the header or footer, then click on Discontinue.

INSERTING WATERMARKS

If you hold a fine sheet of paper up to the light, you may see a watermark in the background. Watermarks usually contain the paper's manufacturer or brand name. You can use watermarks yourself to subtly promote your company name, logo, or special message.

A WordPerfect watermark prints as a 25% shade. Like headers and footers, you can print watermarks on every page, or alternating pages. Watermarks will not appear in Draft view.

To insert a watermark:

1 Place the insertion point at the start of the line where you want the watermark to appear.

Watermark containing a graphic image

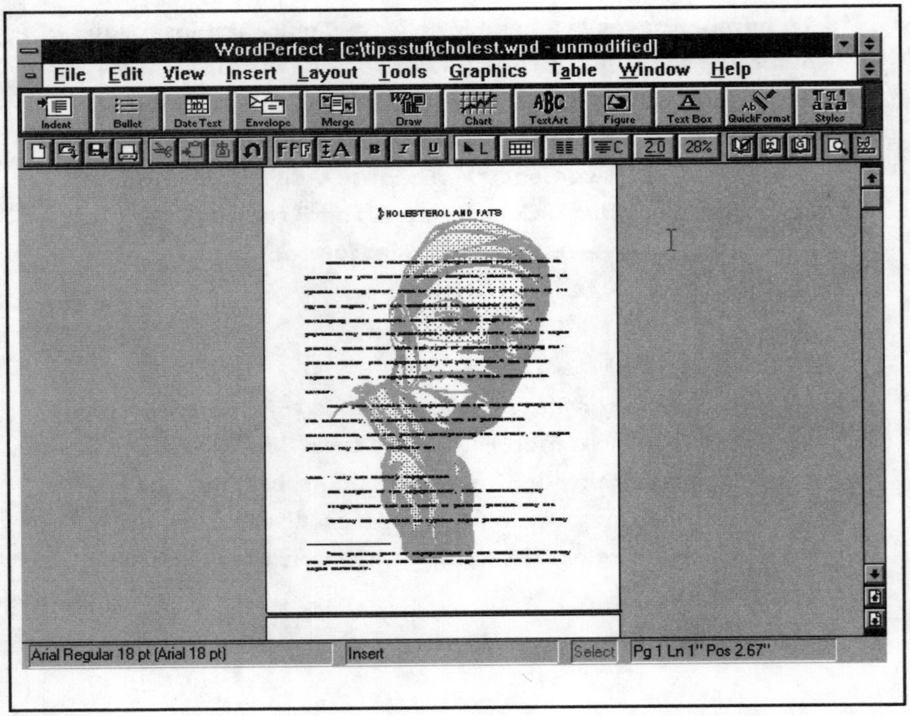

2 Select Layout ➤ Watermark.

3 Select Watermark A or Watermark B.

4 Select Create.

5 Select Placement, then choose Even Pages, Odd Pages, or Every Page.

6 Select Layout ➤ Justification ➤ Center.

7 Type the text of the watermark. It will appear in gray print.

8 Select Close. The figure shows a graphic watermark.

tip ▶ **How watermarks work**

A watermark prints in gray, "behind" the other text on the page. Unless you have a color printer, you can only print one color at a time. So, the watermark is actually printed in the same color ink as the text but in a 25% tone—a series of dots only one quarter as dense as the dots that make up other characters.

tip ▶ **Sudden impact**

Format the text of the watermark using a large font size. Select Figure to insert a graphic—once you learn how to use WordPerfect's powerful graphics, you can add drawings, pictures, and other graphic elements to your watermarks for dramatic effects. Select File to insert the text of a file on your disk.

PAGE NUMBERS

A page number can be printed by itself on every page even without including it in a header or footer. You can select the position of the number and even change the number that will be printed. Like headers and footers, the page number will not appear on the screen in draft view.

To number pages:

1 Place the insertion point on the first page you want to contain the page number.

Page Numbering dialog box

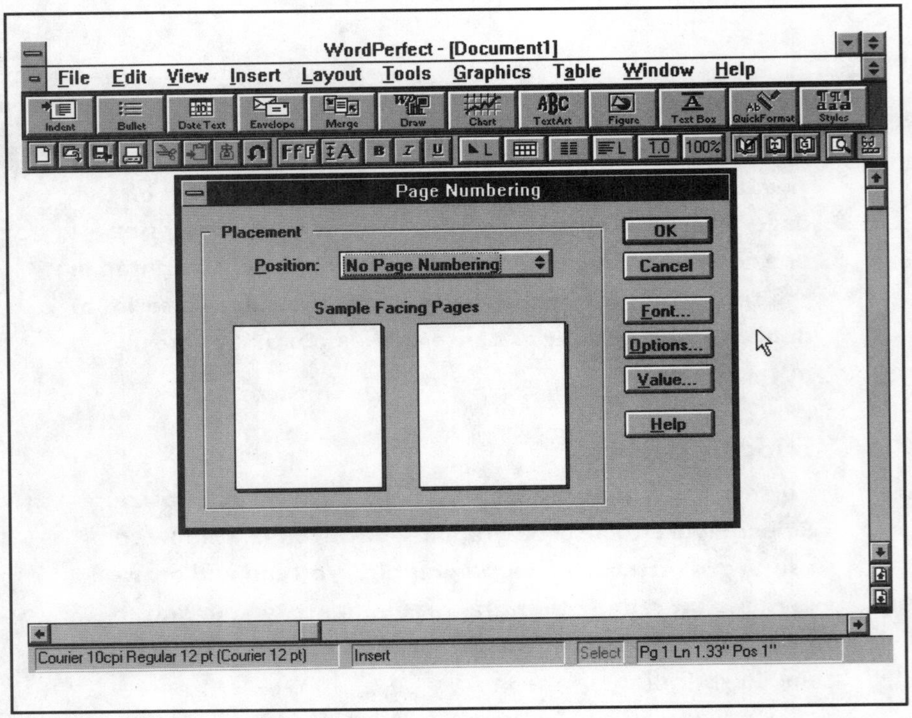

2 Select Layout ➤ Page ➤ Numbering to display the dialog box shown in the figure.

3 Pull down the Position list box and select a position. The options are No Page Numbering, Top Left, Top Center, Top Right, Alternating Top, Bottom Left, Bottom Center, Bottom Right, and Alternating Bottom.

4 Select Font to choose a font for the page numbers.

5 Select OK.

warning! ▶ **Headers versus page numbers**

A page number set for the top of the page will print on the same line as a header. A number set for the bottom will print on the same line as a footer. Be careful if you set both.

tip ▶ **Changing page numbers**

Suppose you have a 50 page document, followed by an appendix. If you turn on page numbers at the start of the document, the first page of the appendix will be numbered 51. To number the appendix separately, place the insertion point on its first page, select Layout ➤ Page ➤ Numbering ➤ Value, enter 1 in the New Page Number Text dialog box, then select OK.

CUSTOMIZING PAGE NUMBERS

You can enhance page numbering by adding text, such as *This is Page 2*, or by numbering pages in letters or Roman numerals. Lower case Roman numerals, for example, are often used for front matter, such as a table of contents or introduction.

1 Select Layout ➤ Page ➤ Numbering ➤ Options to display the dialog box shown in the figure.

2 Enter text before the [Pg #] code, such as Page [Pg #].

Page Numbering Options dialog box

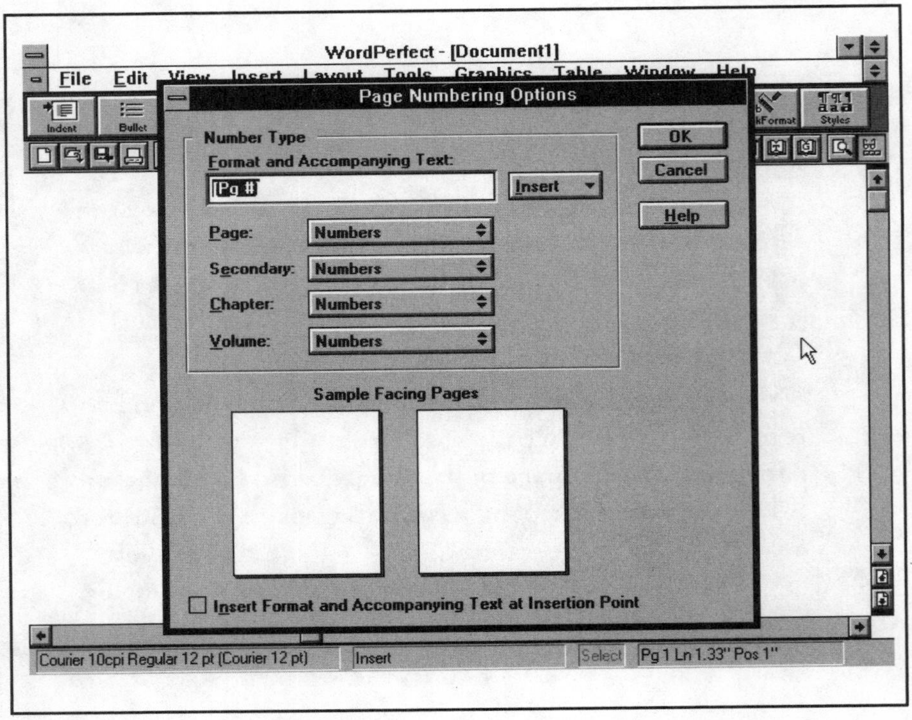

3 Pull down the Page list and select Numbers, Lower Case Letters, Upper Case Letters, Lower Case Roman, or Upper Case Roman.

4 Select OK.

tip **The numbering position must be set**

Selecting custom number options does not turn on page numbering. You must still select a number position.

tip **Location, location, location**

WordPerfect inserts page number and format codes at the start of the page in which the insertion point is located. Before selecting custom options, place the insertion point on the first page you want to customize. For example, to number the appendix using Roman numerals, place the insertion point on the first page of the appendix before selecting options.

SUPPRESSING PAGE ELEMENTS

We usually do not place headers and footers on cover letters and title pages. Luckily, WordPerfect lets you *suppress* headers, footers, and page numbers on specific pages.

1 Place the insertion point on the page where you wish to suppress headers, footers, or page numbers.

2 Select Layout ➤ Page ➤ Suppress to show the Suppress dialog box, as shown in the figure.

Suppress dialog box

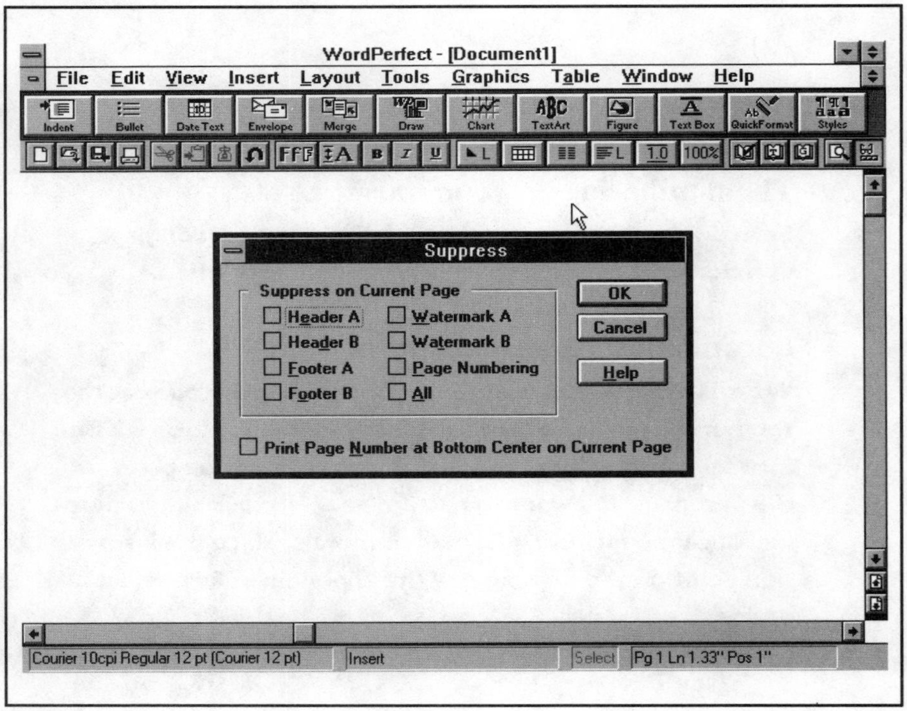

3 Select each of the items you want to suppress.

4 Click on OK.

tip **How Suppress works**

Selecting an item to suppress temporarily suspends it from printing on the current page. Other pages are not affected.

tip **All or nothing**

Select All to suppress all of the listed elements—headers, footers, watermarks, and page numbers.

tip **Retaining a page number**

The Print Page Number at Bottom Center on Current Page option prints just a page number at the bottom center even if headers, footers, and other page numbering have been suppressed. Use this option if your header or footer contains a page number and you want to suppress the item but still number the page.

Good formatting can add impact to even the simplest document. By adjusting the appearance of characters, lines, paragraphs, and pages, you make your document easy and enjoyable to read.

Changing the Appearance of Characters

Let's practice formatting now. We'll type some text, use underlining, change fonts and point size, and add a graphic symbol.

1 Start WordPerfect and type the following text:

The History of Tae Kwon Do

While modern Tae Kwon Do can trace some of its style to Chaun Fa, its history goes back over 2000 years.

Ruins of the Koguryo dynasty from 37 BC were discovered in Korea with figures positioned in poses resembling Tae Kwon Do movements.

In 668 AD the three kingdoms of Koguryo, Silla, and Paikche united to become Korea. It was during that period that the martial art known as Tae Kyon developed.

2 Select the words Tae Kwon Do in the first sentence of the first paragraph.

3 Click on the Underline button in the Power Bar (or press Ctrl+U).

4 Place the insertion point at the start of the document.

5 Pull down the Font list in the Power Bar. (As an alternative to using the Power Bar in these steps, select Layout ➤ Font and use the Font dialog box.)

6 Select one of the available fonts—preferably a TrueType scalable font.

7 Pull down the Size list.

8 Select 14, if it is available.

Now we'll change the relative size of the title.

9 Select the title, The History of Tae Kwon Do.

10 Select Layout ➤ Font ➤ Relative Size ➤ Very Large, then click on OK. If the title word-wraps to a second line, select it again and choose the Large relative size.

11 Place the insertion point at the end of the document.

12 Press Enter twice.

Finally, we'll insert a graphic character, a star represented by character number 80 in the fifth character set.

13 Select Insert ➤ Character to display the WordPerfect Characters dialog box.

14 Type **5,80**, for the fifth character set, the 80th character. The star will appear selected in the dialog box.

15 Select Insert and Close to insert a graphic star.

16 Select the star character.

17 Select Layout ➤ Font ➤ Relative Size ➤ Extra Large, then click on OK. Your document should now look like Figure 3.1.

18 Select File ➤ Print ➤ Print to print the document.

19 Select File ➤ Save.

20 Type **TKD**, then click on OK.

21 Select File ➤ Exit if you're not ready to go on.

Formatting Lines

Now let's change the line spacing, center the title, and justify the text. Here's how.

1 Open TKD.WPD if it is not already on your screen.

2 Place the insertion point at the start of the document.

3 Select Layout ➤ Line ➤ Spacing.

4 Type **2**.

5 Click on OK.

6 Place the insertion point at the start of the title.

▶▶▶▶▶▶▶

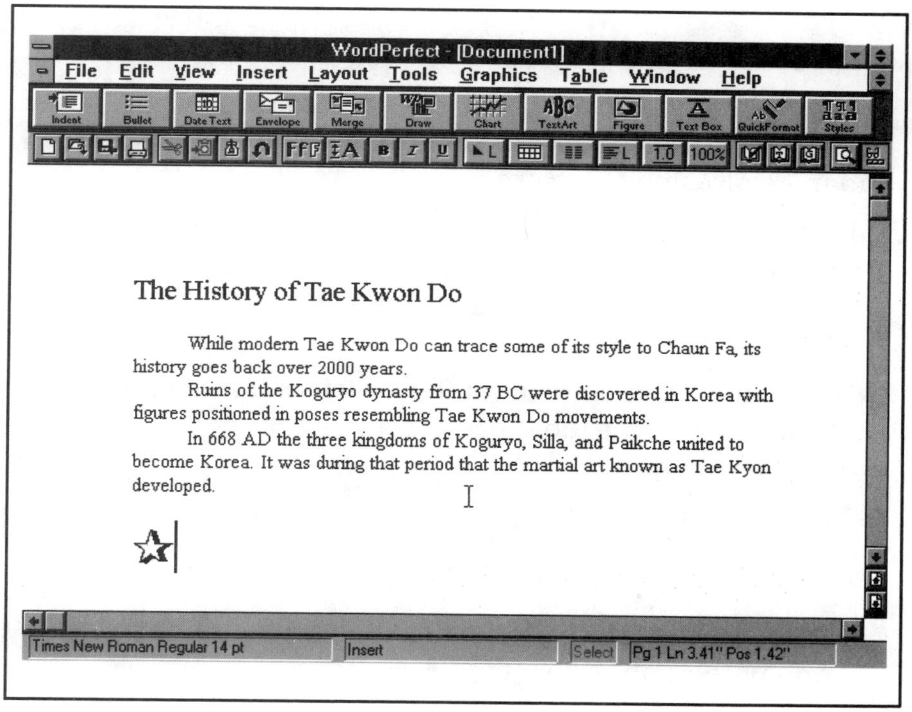
WordPerfect - [Document1]
File Edit View Insert Layout Tools Graphics Table Window Help
Indent Bullet Date Text Envelope Merge Draw Chart TextArt Figure Text Box QuickFormat Styles
The History of Tae Kwon Do
While modern Tae Kwon Do can trace some of its style to Chaun Fa, its history goes back over 2000 years.
Ruins of the Koguryo dynasty from 37 BC were discovered in Korea with figures positioned in poses resembling Tae Kwon Do movements.
In 668 AD the three kingdoms of Koguryo, Silla, and Paikche united to become Korea. It was during that period that the martial art known as Tae Kyon developed.
Times New Roman Regular 14 pt
Insert
Select
Pg 1 Ln 3.41" Pos 1.42"

Figure 3.1: The TKD document

7 Select Layout ➤ Line ➤ Center (or press Shift+F7).

8 Place the insertion point in front of the first paragraph.

9 Select Layout ➤ Justification ➤ Full.

10 Select File ➤ Save.

11 Select File ➤ Exit if you're not ready to go on.

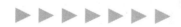

Formatting Paragraphs

Indenting paragraphs helps call attention to specific portions of text. It also breaks up long sections, making things easy to read and more pleasing to the eye.

Try formatting paragraphs now by creating three different indentation styles, starting with a hanging indentation.

1. Open TKD.WPD if it is not already on your screen.
2. Place the insertion point at the far left in front of first paragraph, before the tab space.
3. Select Layout ➤ Paragraph ➤ Hanging Indent (or press Ctrl+F7). The text shifts to the $^1/_2$-inch position.
4. Type **1.** to number the paragraph.
5. Place the insertion point at the left margin in front of second paragraph, before the tab space.
6. Select Layout ➤ Paragraph ➤ Indent (or press F7).
7. Press Del to remove the tab space.
8. Place the insertion point in front of the last paragraph, this time after the tab space.
9. Select Layout ➤ Paragraph ➤ Double Indent (or press Ctrl+Shift+F7). The paragraph is indented one inch on the left (because of the tab stop) and $^1/_2$-inch on the right.
10. Select the entire document.
11. Select Insert ➤ Bullets & Numbers.

▶▶▶▶▶▶▶

12 Choose Diamond, then click on OK. Diamonds appear in front of each paragraph, which shift to a second level of indentation.

13 Select File ➤ Close ➤ No to clear the window without saving the document.

14 Select File ➤ Exit if you're not ready to go on.

Formatting Pages

Page formats affect the entire page. You can set margins to change the amount of text that fits on the page, and change page sizes to print in different sized paper or envelopes.

Let's widen the left and right margins, and print the document on legal-sized paper.

1 Open TKD.WPD if it is not already on your screen.

2 Select Layout ➤ Margins.

3 Type **2** for the left margin, then press Tab.

4 Type **2** for the right margin, then select OK or press Enter.

5 Select Layout ➤ Page ➤ Paper Size.

6 Scroll the list and select Legal (Portrait), if it is available. (If you are using a Windows printer driver, select Legal.)

7 Choose Select.

Let's zoom in to see the entire page.

8 Click on the Page Zoom Full button in the Power Bar. Your document should look like Figure 3.2.

9 Click on the button again to return to the previous magnification and mode.

10 Select File ➤ Close ➤ No to clear the window without saving the document.

11 Select File ➤ Exit if you're not ready to go on.

Figure 3.2: Reformatted document showing wide margins and legal-size paper

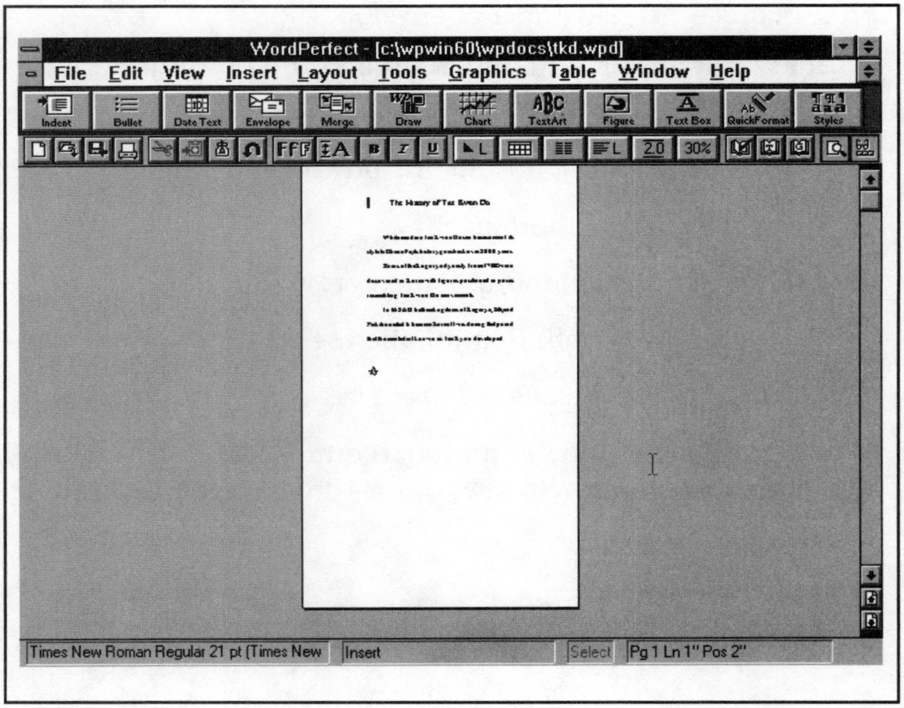

►►►►►►►

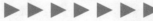

Adding Headers, Footers, and Page Numbers

You can add some finishing touches to your documents with headers, footers and page numbers. But don't overdo it! Make them simple so they don't distract from the text.

Follow these steps to add a header and page number to the TKD document.

1. Open the document named TKD.WPD if it is not already on your screen.
2. Select Layout ➤ Header/Footer.
3. Select Header A.
4. Select Create.
5. Type your name.
6. Select Layout ➤ Line ➤ Flush Right (or press Alt+F7).
7. Select Insert ➤ Date ➤ Date Text.
8. Select Close to return to the document. Remember, you will not see headers in Draft view.
9. Select Layout ➤ Page ➤ Numbering.
10. Pull down the Position list and select Bottom Center, then click on OK.
11. Click on the Page Zoom Full button to see the entire page, including the header and page number. Your document should look like Figure 3.3.

▶▶▶▶▶▶▶

12 Click on the button again to return to the previous magnification and mode.

13 Select File ➤ Save.

14 Select File ➤ Close to clear the window.

15 Select File ➤ Exit.

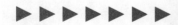

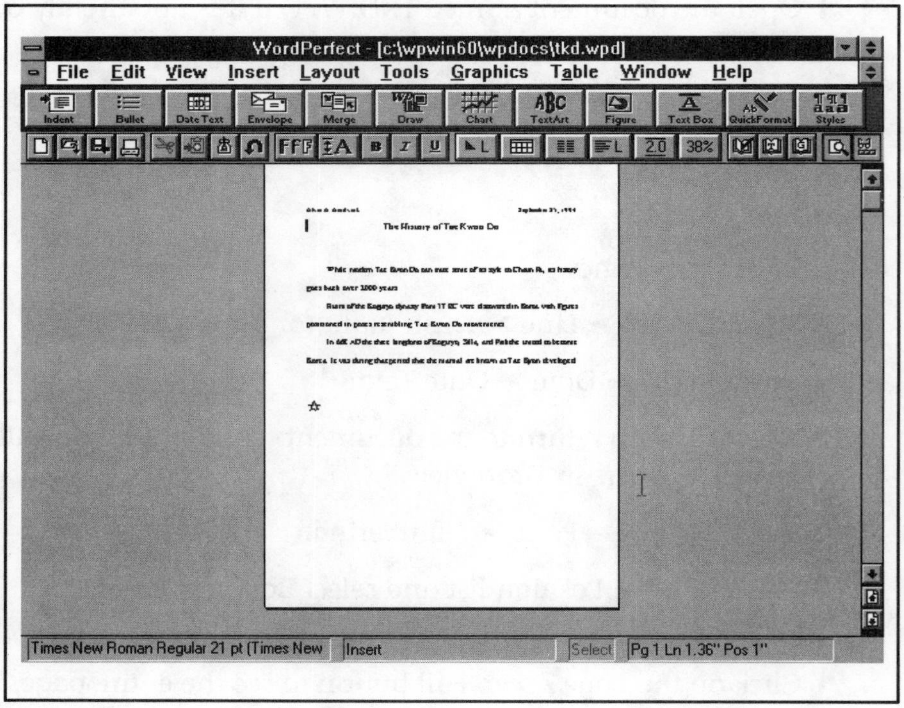

Figure 3.3: The TKD document with a header and page number

4 part four

SPECIAL WORDPERFECT FEATURES

You've made it to next plateau in word processing. You know how to write, edit, and format documents of all types. Now it's time to have fun and learn the powerful features that have made WordPerfect famous.

Desktop publishing, form letters, and automating with macros are just a few of the features awaiting you when you turn the page. Hold on tight and enjoy the ride!

It's So Easy

lesson 13

Working with Tables and Columns

WordPerfect has several features for creating documents in columnar and tabular format. To create spreadsheets and other neatly ordered rows and columns of words or numbers, use WordPerfect's automatic table feature. Use the column feature to produce newsletters, resumes, and other documents with multiple columns across the page. To create charts and graphs, use WordPerfect's powerful Chart command, explained in Lesson 17.

CREATING A TABLE

Before creating a table, plan the number of rows and columns that you'll need. You'll be able to insert and delete rows and columns—just like in a spreadsheet program—but you'll need a number to start with.

To create a table:

1. Display the Power Bar if it is not on the screen (View ➤ Power Bar.)
2. Point to the Table button (the one with a small icon of a table) on the Power Bar and hold down the left mouse button. A miniature grid appears, representing the rows and columns of a table.
3. Drag the mouse down and to the right. As you drag the mouse, squares in the grid become selected and the number of rows and columns is indicated on the top of the grid.
4. Drag the mouse until you've selected the number of rows and columns you want in the table, then release the mouse button.

WordPerfect will display a blank table on the screen.

Each cell of the table is referenced by its row and column numbers. The top left cell is A1. The cell to its right is B1, the cell below it is A2, and so forth, as shown below.

	A	**B**	**C**	**D**
1	A1	B1	C1	D1
2	A2	B2	C2	D2

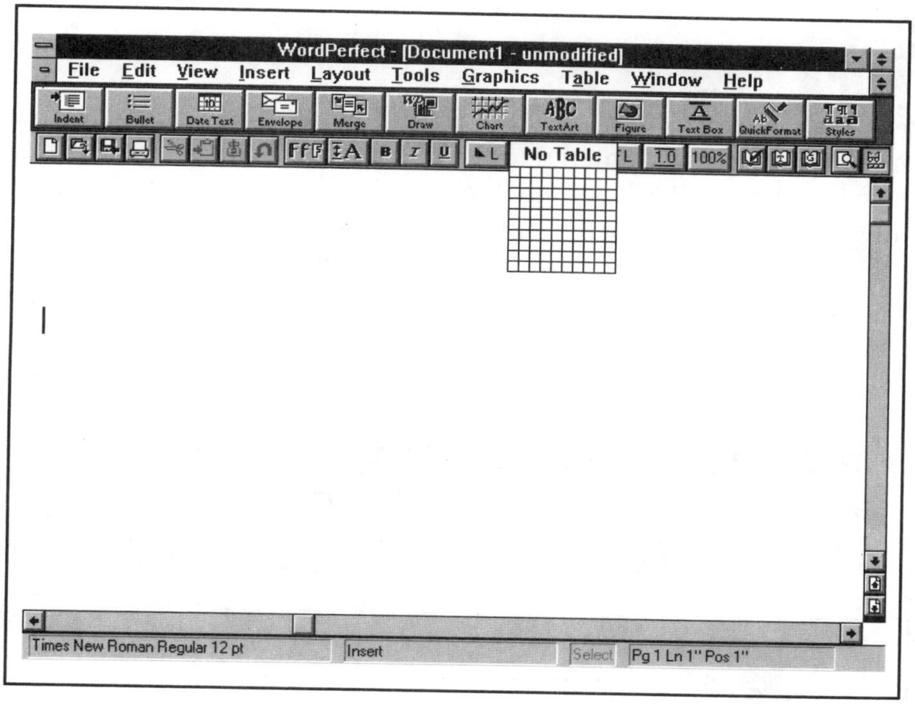

Table Power Bar button

tip ▶ **Watch the status line**

The center section of the status line will indicate the location of the insertion point.

tip ▶ **Using the menu**

To create a table with the keyboard, select Table ➤ Create, enter the number of columns and rows desired, then select OK.

ENTERING DATA INTO TABLES

As soon as you've created a table, you are ready to enter data into it. Many tables have *labels* along the top row and in the left-most column. The labels identify or explain the information in the other rows and columns. Don't worry about how your entry aligns in a cell, or in rows and columns. You'll be able to format the table using the Table menu.

Table complete with cell entries

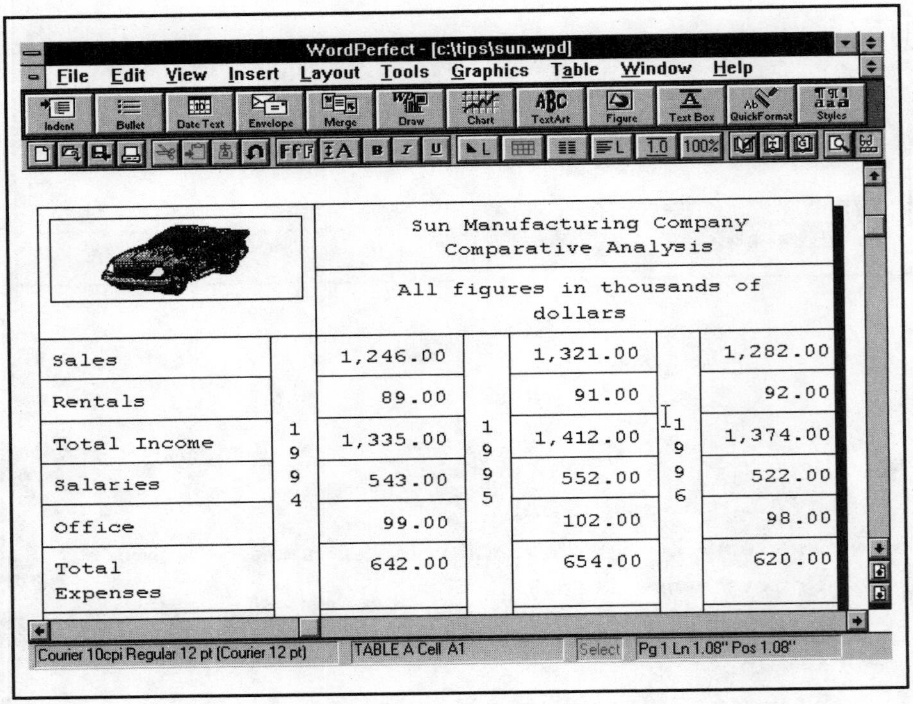

To enter data in cells:

1 Move to the cell into which you want to enter data, by using any of the following methods:

- Click on the cell with the mouse.
- Press ↑ and ↓ to move up and down columns.
- Press ←, →, Tab, and Shift+Tab to move across rows.

2 Type the data for the cell. The cell height will adjust automatically to the amount of text. *Do not press Enter to move to the next cell.* If you do, the cell height will increase by one line. Press the Backspace key to delete the accidentally entered blank line.

tip

Word-wrap in narrow cells

WordPerfect does not automatically adjust cell width to accommodate text. Widen a cell as explained in "Formatting Tables" later in this lesson.

new feature

Formatting cells

Use the options in the Power Bar and Layout menu (or their equivalent shortcut keys) to format text in cells. For example, to underline the text in a cell, select the text and press Ctrl+U or click on the Underline button. To center text, place the insertion point anywhere in the cell and press Ctrl+E. Using the Table menu, however, you can format cells, columns, and rows without selecting text. See "Formatting Tables" later in this lesson.

EDITING TABLES

Once you create a table, you can change its size, divide it into multiple tables, and even combine two tables into one. Using the Table menu, you can even change the table's lines, colors, and other formats.

To change the table:

1 Place the insertion point in any cell of the table.

2 Select Table to display the Table pull down menu, as shown in the figure.

Table menu

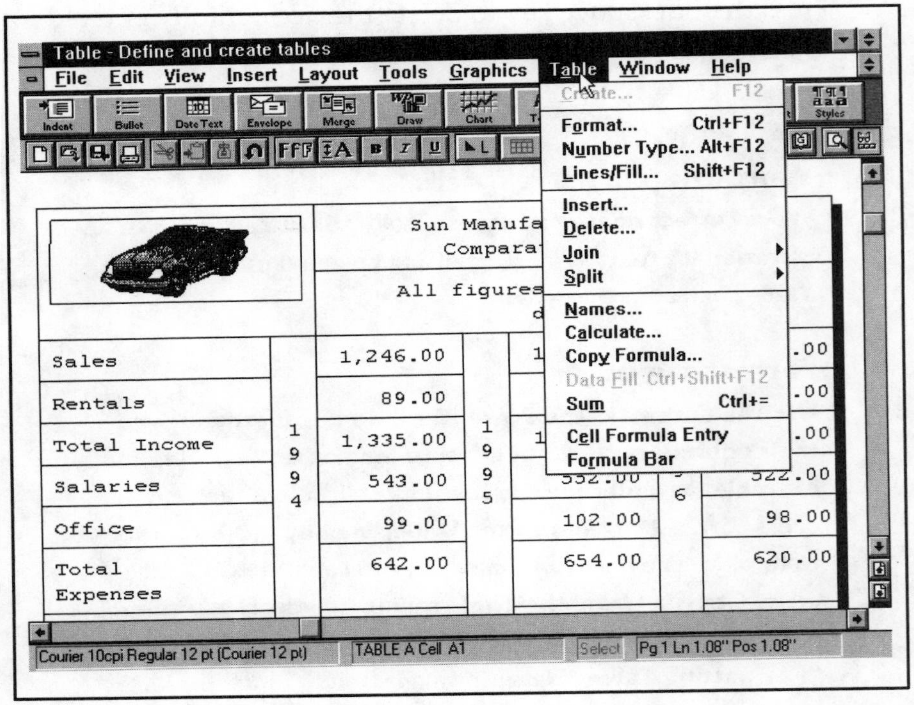

3 Select the option you want to perform from the following list:

Insert: Adds rows or columns

Delete: Deletes rows or columns

Join: Combines adjacent cells or tables. To join two tables, they must have the same number of columns.

Split: Splits a cell or table into two.

Calculate: Recalculates formula and functions.

Sum: Displays the total of the numeric values in the cells above the current cell.

oops!

Trouble splitting and joining tables?

In order to combine two tables using the Join command, there must be no blank lines or text between them. If you split a table into two, they appear with no blank space between them. To insert a blank line between tables, place the insertion point at the start of cell A1 in the second table, select View ➤ Reveal Codes (or press Alt+F3), then press ← to move the insertion point outside of the table. Press Enter to insert a blank line, then select View ➤ Reveal Codes (or press Alt+F3) to remove the code display.

FORMATTING TABLES

While you can format a table using the Font dialog box and the Power Bar, options on the Table menu give you complete control over the table's format. Using the Table menu, you can quickly format selected cells, or entire rows and columns.

To format a table:

1 Place the insertion point in the cell, row, or column you want to format.

2 Select Table ➤ Format to display the dialog box shown in the figure.

Table Format dialog box

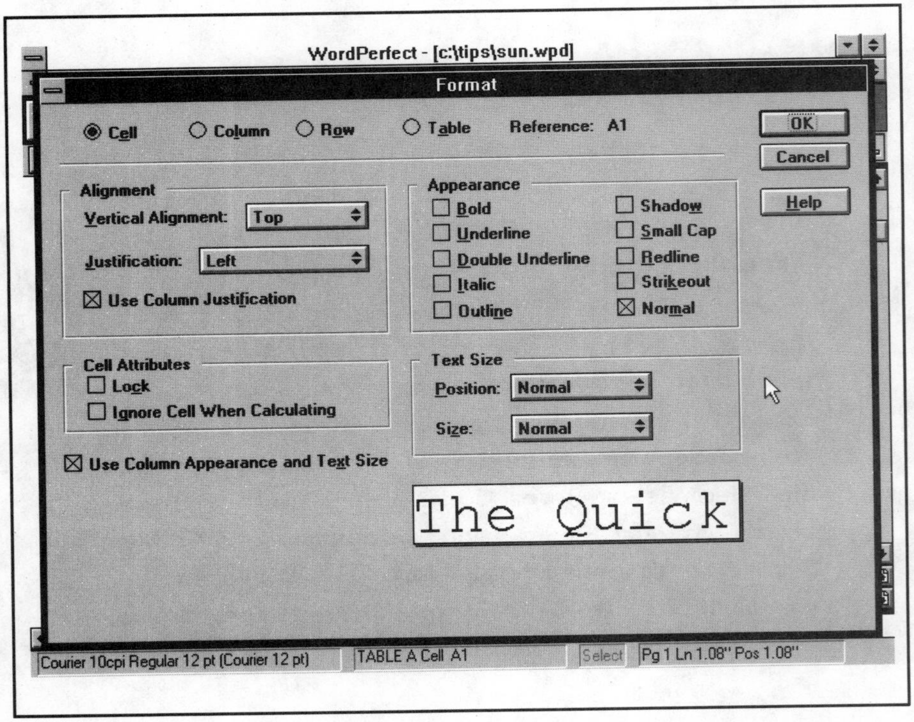

3 Select an option button to indicate the section of the table you want to format—a cell, column, row, or the entire table.

4 Select settings and options in the other sections of the dialog box. The options will vary with the type of section you are formatting.

5 Select OK.

Using WordPerfect's Table feature, you can create effective tables and forms of all types. A full discussion of these capabilities will not fit in an ABCs book, so experiment with the Format, Number Type, and Lines/Fill dialog boxes to discover their full potential.

tip ▶ **Save your work**

Save your table before making extensive changes to it. You can always cancel your changes by closing the window, or you can save the edited table under a new name to retain the original version.

tip ▶ **Other options**

To change the way numbers are displayed, select Table ➤ Number Type, select options in the dialog box, then click on OK. To change the shape of table lines, or to add a shaded fill or color to cells, select Table ➤ Lines/Fill, choose options from the dialog box, then click on OK.

PERFORMING MATH WITH FORMULAS

If you want to include totals, averages, or other mathematical results in a table, you can use *formulas* to compute the numbers for you. Formulas can make your table a full-fledged spreadsheet.

Suppose you have a table showing your income and expenses for the year. You can use some formulas to total the entries in those categories, and other formulas to subtract total expenses from total income to obtain your net profit.

Calculate dialog box

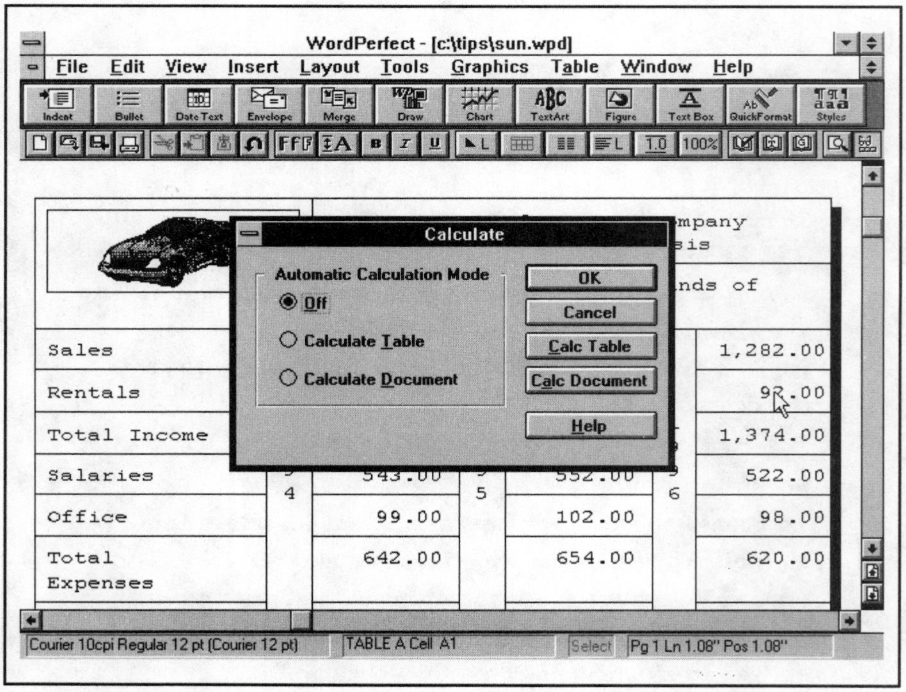

To enter a formula into a cell:

1. Pull down the Table menu and confirm that a check mark appears next to the Cell Formula Entry option. Select the option if no check mark appears.
2. Place the insertion point in the cell in which you want to insert the formula.
3. Type the formula. (See the Tip on this page for the proper way to write your formulas).
4. Select Table ➤ Calculate to display the dialog box shown in the figure.
5. Select Calc Table. The results of the formula will appear in the cell.

If you later change the value in a cell referenced in the formula, you must calculate the results again.

tip ► **Operators and cell references**

A formula can include mathematical operators, numeric values, and cell references. If you are writing a simple equation, just type in the equation as you would on a calculator, using + for addition, – for subtraction, * for multiplication, and / for division. To create a more flexible formula, you can reference a cell by its location in the table. For example, entering B2-B3 in cell B4 will calculate and display the difference between cells B2 and B3 in cell B4.

tip ► **Quick sum**

You can quickly calculate the sum of cells in a column by selecting Table ➤ Sum (or pressing Ctrl+=).

CREATING NEWSPAPER COLUMNS

If you're responsible for producing a newsletter or other multi-column document, take advantage of WordPerfect's built-in Newspaper Column feature. *Newspaper columns* automatically run from one column on a page to the next one—from left to right. When the far right column is filled, text moves to the far left column on the next page.

Columns button

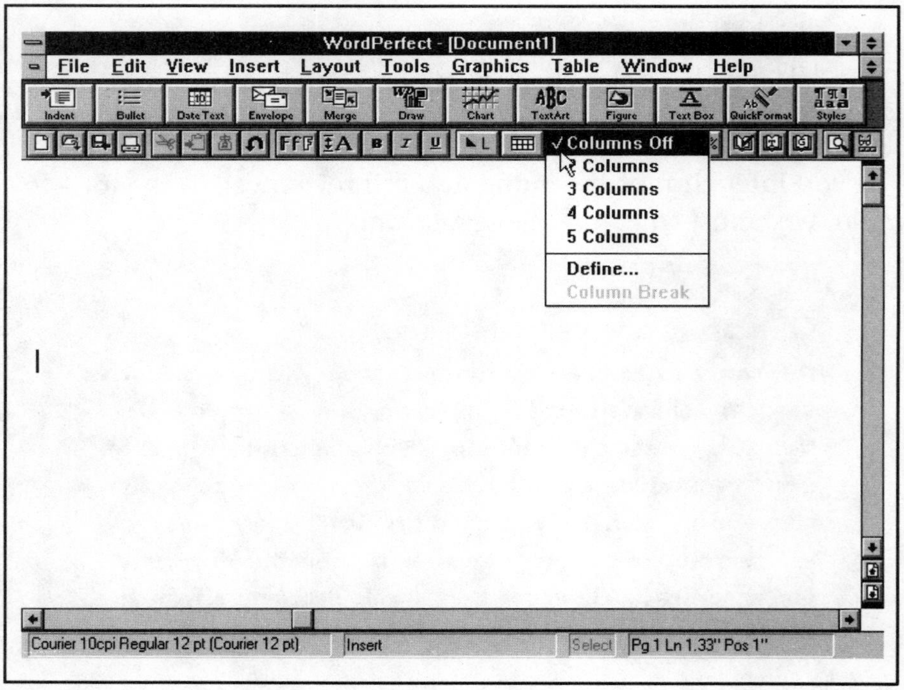

To type newspaper columns:

1 Pull down the Columns button on the Power Bar (the button next to the Table button.) The figure shows the button options.

2 Select the number of columns desired.

3 Type your text. Text will flow from column to column. To manually end one column and begin another, press Ctrl+Enter.

Before creating multiple columns, you may want to type your document using the default single column format and save it to your disk. Then place the cursor where you want the columns to begin, and experiment! You can always start over by revealing codes, deleting the column definition code, and trying another format.

tip **Keyboard columns**

To create columns with the keyboard, select Layout ➤ Columns ➤ Define to display the Columns dialog box. Type the number of columns desired, then click on OK. You can change the distance between columns by entering the measurement in the Spacing Between Columns text box.

tip **Mixing single and multiple columns**

Before typing columns, type any desired single-column text, such as a title or introductory paragraph, then turn on Columns and type the rest of the text. To type single-column text again, press Ctrl-Enter to end the last column, then pull down the Column button and select Columns Off, or select Layout ➤ Columns ➤ Off.

CREATING PARALLEL ALIGNED COLUMNS

In some cases you don't want text to flow freely from column to column because text on the left refers directly to text on the right. These are called *parallel columns*. With parallel columns, you enter text in blocks: first on the left, then the corresponding text on the right. Press Ctrl+Enter to end a block and move to the other column.

To create parallel columns:

1. Select Layout ➤ Columns ➤ Define to display the dialog box shown in the figure.

Columns dialog box showing parallel columns selected

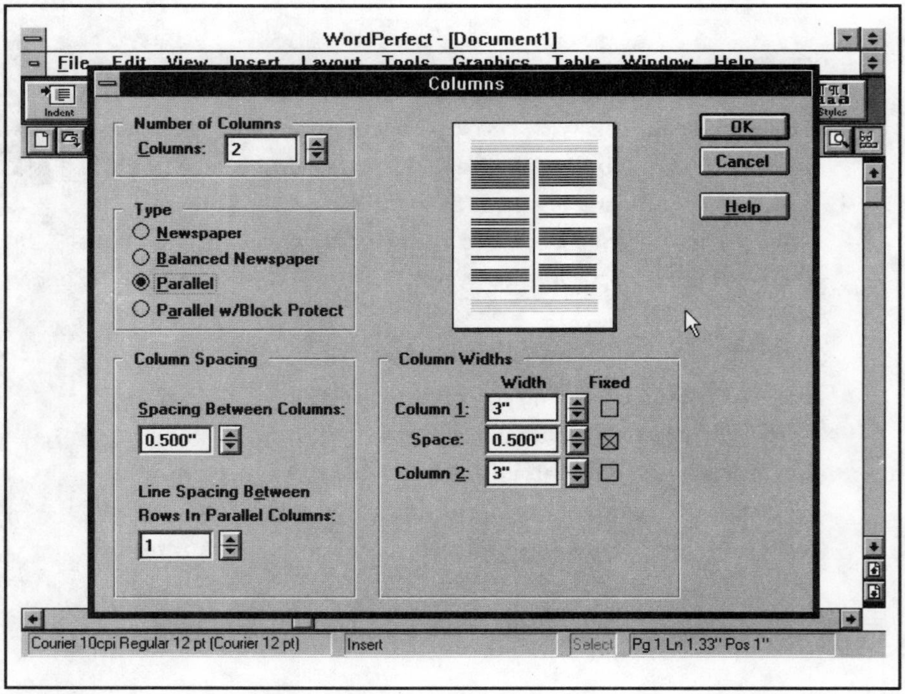

2 Select Number of Columns and enter the number of columns desired.

3 Click on Parallel in the Type section.

4 For unequal columns, enter the width of the column in the Custom Width section. The graphic of a page will illustrate the layout.

5 Click on OK.

6 Type a left-hand column, then press Ctrl+Enter.

7 Type a right-hand column, then press Ctrl+Enter.

tip ▶ **Block protection**

Parallel columns can be regular or block-protected. In block-protected parallel columns, if the text in one column extends into the new page, both columns will be carried over so they start on that page. Regular parallel columns, on the other hand, will span a page break.

tip ▶ **Distance between rows**

WordPerfect inserts a blank line when you press Ctrl+Enter to end the right-most parallel column. To change the spacing, enter a number in the Line Spacing Between Rows in Parallel Columns text box. For example, enter 0 for no spacing or 2 for two blank lines.

It's So Easy

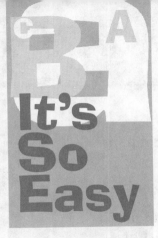

14 lesson

Enhancing Text with Lines and Boxes

Sometimes it takes more than just words to capture a reader's attention. You can make documents visually attractive by adding lines, borders, and boxes. With a bit of practice, you'll be able to create truly dazzling documents. In this lesson, you will learn how to add lines and boxes. In Lesson 17 you'll learn how to use graphics and create free-hand drawings.

ADDING VERTICAL AND HORIZONTAL LINES

Horizontal and vertical lines are great for separating text or adding some visual perspective. Use the Graphics menu to insert lines before or after text, or along the margins. To really set off a page, add a horizontal line to a header or footer.

To create a graphic line:

1. Place the insertion point where you want to insert the line.
2. Select Graphics ➤ Horizontal Line, or select Graphics ➤ Vertical Line to display the line in the default shape and size.

Create Graphic Line dialog box

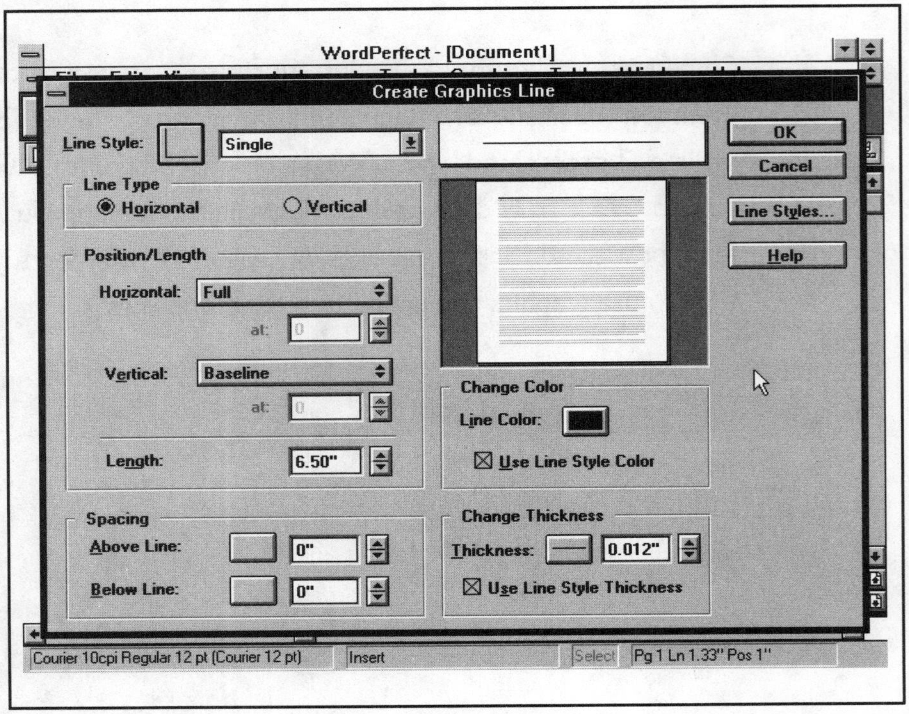

The default horizontal line is 6 $^1/_2$-inches long, centered between the left and right margins. The default vertical line is 9 inches long down the left side of the page.

tip

Creating a custom line

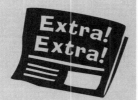

You can create a custom line by selecting Graphics ➤ Custom Line to display the dialog box shown in the figure. Select options from the dialog box, as follows:

Line Style **sets the shape of the line or selects multiple lines.**

Line Type **sets the direction of the line.**

Position/Length **determines a line's length and its position on the page. The horizontal setting determines the position in relation to the left and right margins. The vertical position determines the position in relation to the text line at the insertion point.**

Spacing **sets the distance of text above and below a horizontal line, and the distance from the margin for a vertical line.**

Change Color **changes the color of the line.**

Change Thickness **sets the thickness of the line in inches or points.**

CHANGING THE SIZE AND POSITION OF LINES

Once you insert a line in your document, you can use the mouse to change its size, shape, and position. (Using the keyboard, you have to move and size lines using the Edit Line dialog box.)

To change a graphic line:

1. Place the mouse pointer on the line.
2. Click the left mouse button. The line will be surrounded by small black squares, called *handles*, as shown in the figure.
3. To move the line, point to the line so the pointer appears as a four-directional arrow, then drag the mouse.
4. To change the size of the line, move the mouse to a handle, so the pointer is a two-directional arrow:
   - Drag the center handle on top or bottom to change the height of the graphic.
   - Drag the center handle on the left or right to change the width of the graphic.
   - Drag a handle on a corner to change both the width and height at the same time.

As you drag the mouse, a dotted representation of the line moves with it. Release the mouse button when the line is the desired size or at the desired location.

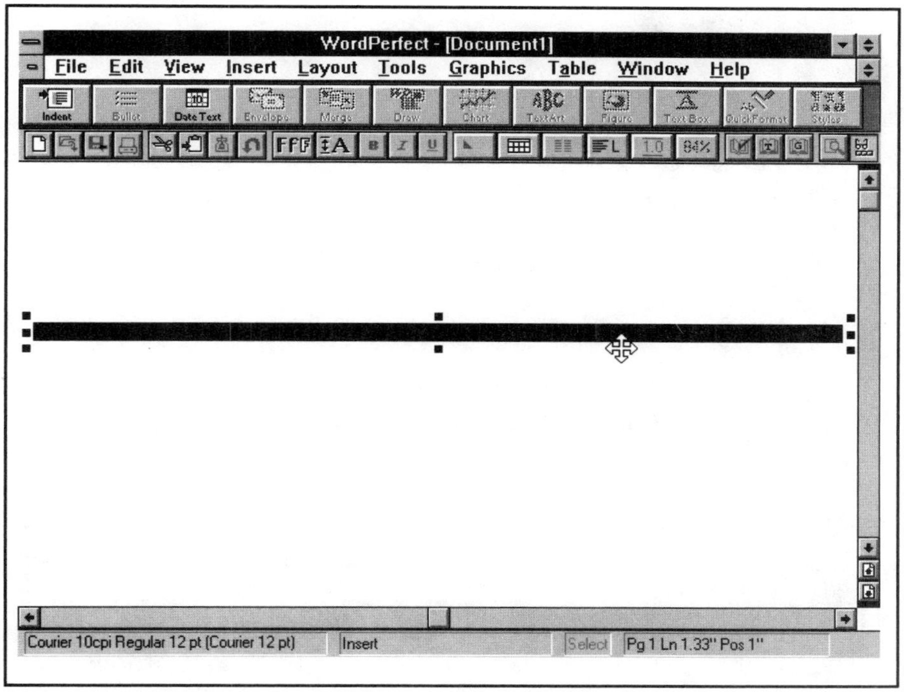

Selected line

tip **When you select a thin line, you may only see six handles. Once you widen the line, eight handles will appear.**

tip

To delete a line

To delete a line, select it, then press Del.

tip

Editing lines

Double-click on the line to display the Edit Graphic Line dialog box (or select Graphics ➤ Edit Line). Change the orientation, position, and other settings, then select OK.

SURROUNDING TEXT IN A BOX

Make a section of text stand out by placing it in a box. Box an entire paragraph, or just a title or headline to draw the reader's attention.

To surround text in a box:

1. Select the text you wish to surround in a box.
2. Select Layout ➤ Paragraph ➤ Border/Fill to display the Paragraph Border dialog box, shown in the figure.

Paragraph Border dialog box

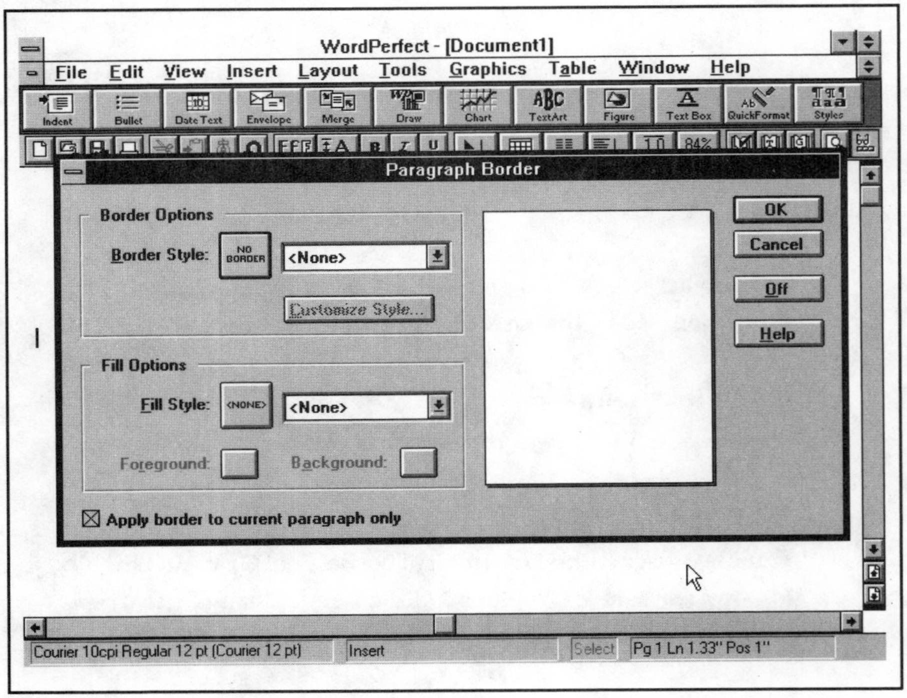

3 Select Border Style to select from preset line types.

4 Select Fill Style to select a gray shade or patterns to print in the background of the page.

5 Select Customize Style to set the line thickness, corner type, color, and shadow of the border.

6 Select OK.

oops!

Don't forget to select

If you do not select text first, the box will surround all of the text on the page starting with the paragraph in which the insertion point is located. Place the insertion point where you want the box to stop, select Layout ➤ Paragraph ➤ Border/Fill, pull down the Border Style list and select None.

tip

Box width

WordPerfect extends the box from the right to left margin, even if you selected a one-word title centered on the page. To make a narrower box, change the page margins for the text. Just remember to reset the margins following the box.

CREATING A PAGE BORDER

Create eye-catching announcements, certificates, and other documents by surrounding the page with a border. Place a border around a single page, or around every page in your document with a few clicks of the mouse!

To create a page border:

1. Select Layout ➤ Page ➤ Border/Fill to display the Border/Fill dialog box. The dialog box has the same options as the Paragraph Border dialog box.

Custom border options

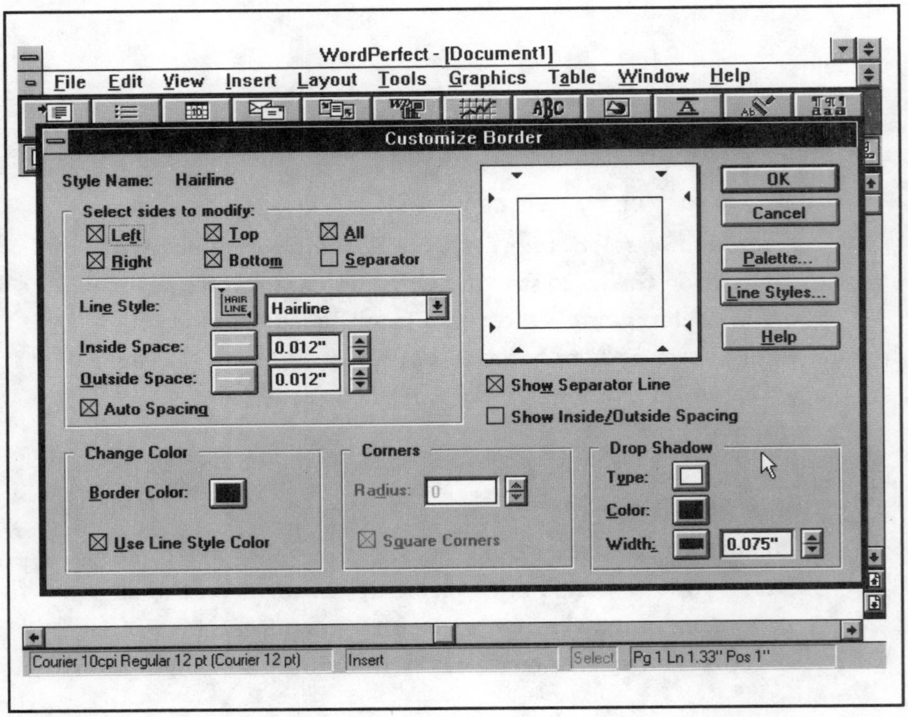

2 Select Border Style to select from preset line types.

3 Select Fill Style to select a gray shade or pattern to print in the background of the page.

4 Select Customize Style to set the line thickness, corner type, color, and shadow of the border.

5 Select OK.

The Custom Border dialog box is shown in the figure. It is the same box that is displayed for customizing paragraph boxes.

tip ▶ **Repeating borders**

The page border appears on every page of the document, starting with the page in which the insertion point is located. To turn off the border on a subsequent page, select Layout ➤ Page ➤ Border/Fill, then select None in the Border Style option.

tip ▶ **Borders and columns**

If your document uses multiple columns, you can create a page border that also includes lines between columns. Select Layout ➤ Page ➤ Border/Fill, pull down the Border Style option and select Column All.

It's So Easy

15 lesson

Creating Form Letters

If you work in a business office, you already know the importance of form letters. A well-designed form letter allows you to send the same information to many different people, but with a personal touch—so the greeting reads *Dear Ms. Apple* or *Dear Mr. Jones* rather than the cold *Dear Sir or Madam.*

But you don't need a business to take advantage of form letters. How about responses to classified ads, requests for information, or letters of complaint? Perhaps you are sending notes, thank-you letters, or invitations to family members or friends. Except for some personalized text, such as the name and address, each letter has the same words. So, save time and use a form letter!

CREATING A DATA FILE FOR FORM DOCUMENTS

The first task in creating a form letter is to write the data file. Picture the data file as an electronic version of an index card file. Every card, called a *record,* contains all the data about one person or item. Each record has several pieces of information, such as the name, address, and other information about clients or employees. Each piece of information is called a *field.*

To create a data file:

1. Open a new document window, select Tools ➤ Merge, click on Place Records in a Table, then select Data.

Quick Data Entry dialog box

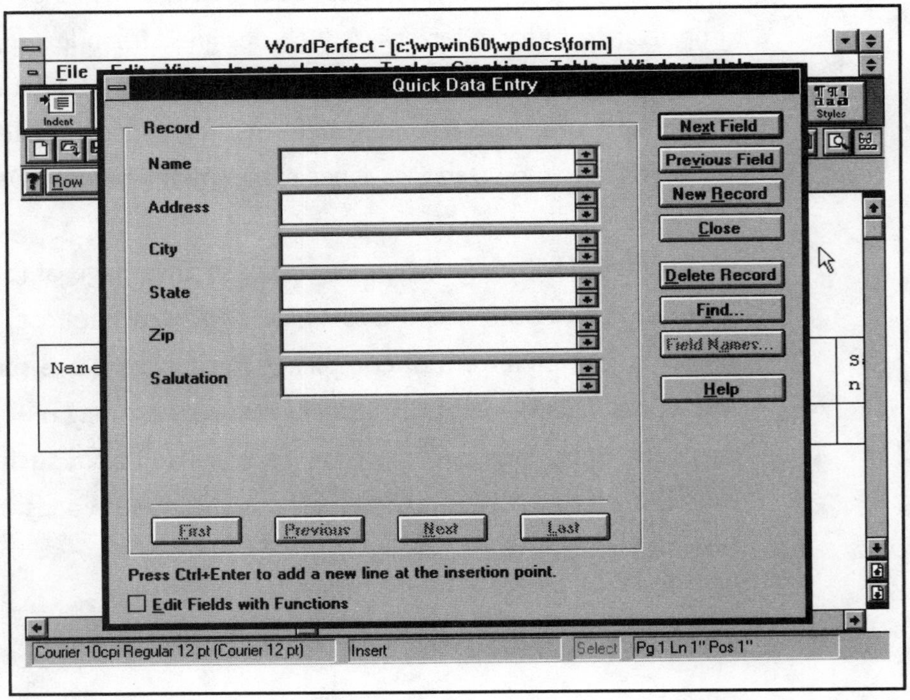

2 For each field, type a field name, such as Client Name, then press Enter.

3 Select OK. The Quick Data Entry dialog box appears.

4 Type the contents of each field, then press Enter. When you press Enter after the last field, WordPerfect will clear the text boxes and start a new record.

5 Select Close, then select Yes to save the data.

6 Enter a filename, then select OK.

A table will appear with the field names in the first row, and your records in the following rows.

tip **Working with data tables**

You can use all of the Table menu commands to edit the data table, or to enter data manually.

tip **Data files as text**

Do not select Place Records in a Table to create a data file similar to the ones in earlier WordPerfect versions. When you complete the Quick Entry dialog box, each field will end with the ENDFIELD code, each record with the ENDRECORD code. To enter data manually, press Alt+Enter for the ENDFIELD code, and Alt+Shift+Enter for the ENDRECORD code.

WRITING A FORM LETTER

Now that you have a database, you can create the document that contains the form letter. When you come to a place where you want the variable information to appear, you have to enter a field code giving the name of the field that you want inserted at that location. WordPerfect will insert variable information during the merge process.

To write a form letter:

1. Select Tools ➤ Merge. If the active window contains any text, a dialog box will appear asking if you want to create the form letter in the active window or a new document window. Select New Document window. A dialog box will appear asking for the name of the data file to use for the merge.
2. Type the name of the data file, or pull down the folder icon, select the file, and click on OK.
3. Type the letter.
4. When you reach the spot where you want to enter a field, select Insert Field from the Feature Bar, then double-click on the field name in the list that appears.
5. Save the completed form document.

Once you click on Insert Field, the Insert Field Name or Number dialog box will remain on the screen. To insert other fields, just double-click on their names. Click on Close in the dialog box to remove it from the screen when you are done.

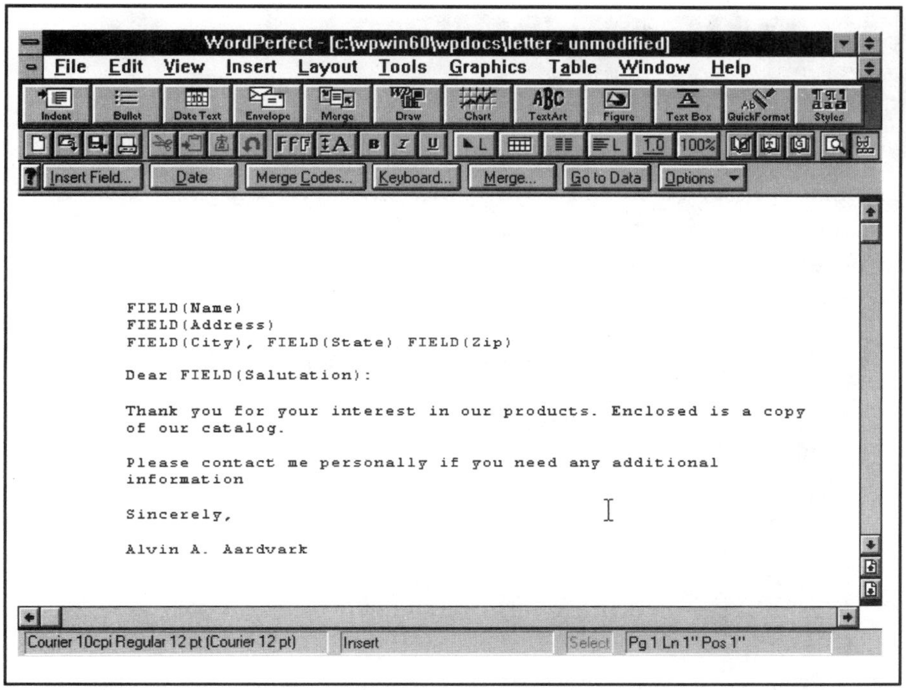

Completed form document showing Merge feature bar

tip

Merge codes

Unlike other codes used by WordPerfect, the field and Merge codes are displayed on the screen along with other text.

warning!

Watch out!

As long as you print the documents using the Merge feature, only the variable information will be printed. If you print using File ➤ Print, the codes will print as displayed and the variable information will not be inserted.

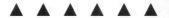

MERGING AND PRINTING FORM DOCUMENTS

When you perform a merge, the variable information from a record is inserted in the appropriate place in a form letter. A page break is inserted and another letter is created, until all of the records have been used.

To merge form letters:

1. Select File ➤ New to clear the document window.
2. Select Tools ➤ Merge ➤ Merge to display the Perform Merge dialog box.
3. Type the name of the form file. To select the file from a list, click on the triangle to the left of the Form File text box, then choose Select File. Choose the file from the Select Form File dialog box, then select OK.
4. Press Tab. If the form file is associated with a data file, the name of the data file will automatically appear. If not, type the name of the data file (or click on the triangle to the left of the Data File text box), choose Select File, then select a file from the Select Data File dialog box.
5. Press Enter or click on OK to begin the merge.

A message box with the words *Merging Record* and the number of each record will appear as the letters are generated. The letters will be displayed on the screen only after all of the merging is completed. Newly merged documents can be printed immediately, saved on disk, or edited.

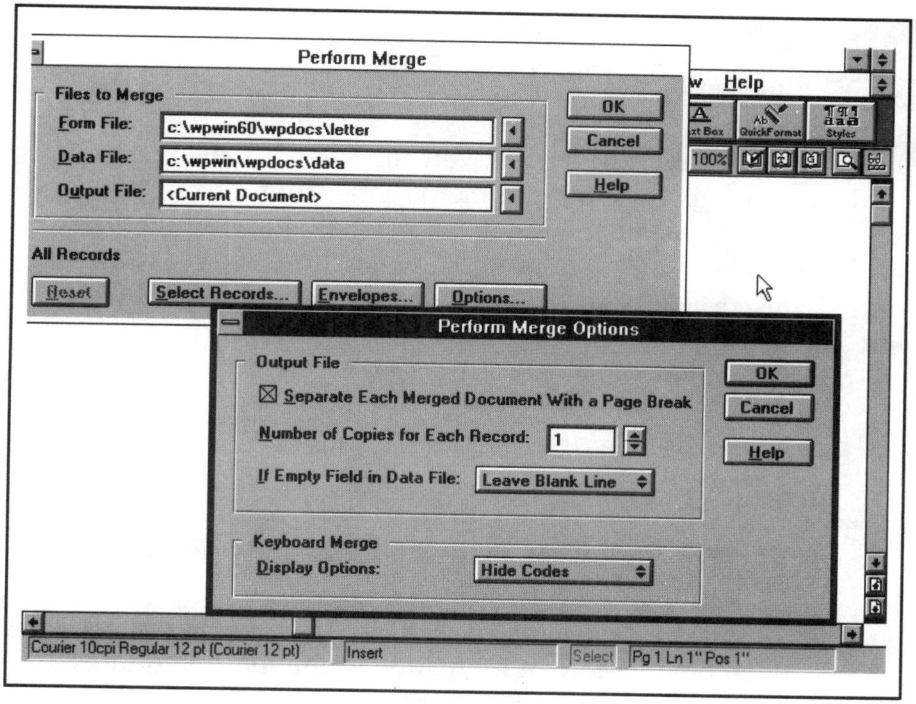

Merge Options dialog box with the Perform Merge dialog box in the background

tip

Merging form documents to the printer

Pull down the Output File list in the Perform Merge dialog box and select Printer.

tip

Skipping blank address lines

To avoid printing blank lines for empty fields, in the Perform Merge dialog box, select Options, pull down the If Empty Field In Data File list, and select Remove Blank Lines.

PRINTING ENVELOPES FOR FORM LETTERS

If you are printing form letters, you can generate the envelopes at the same time by using the merge codes that make up the inside address. The envelopes will be inserted in a group following all of the form letters. Just be sure to keep the letters in order after they are printed so you can match them to the appropriate envelope!

To print form envelopes:

1. Select Tools ➤ Merge ➤ Merge.
2. Enter the form file and data file names.
3. Click on Envelopes to display the Envelope window.
4. Select the Mailing Address box.
5. For each field you want to include in the mailing address, click on the Field button to display a list of fields in the data file, then double click on the field name. After inserting a field, if necessary, press Enter to move the insertion point to the next line in the mailing address box.
6. Select OK twice.

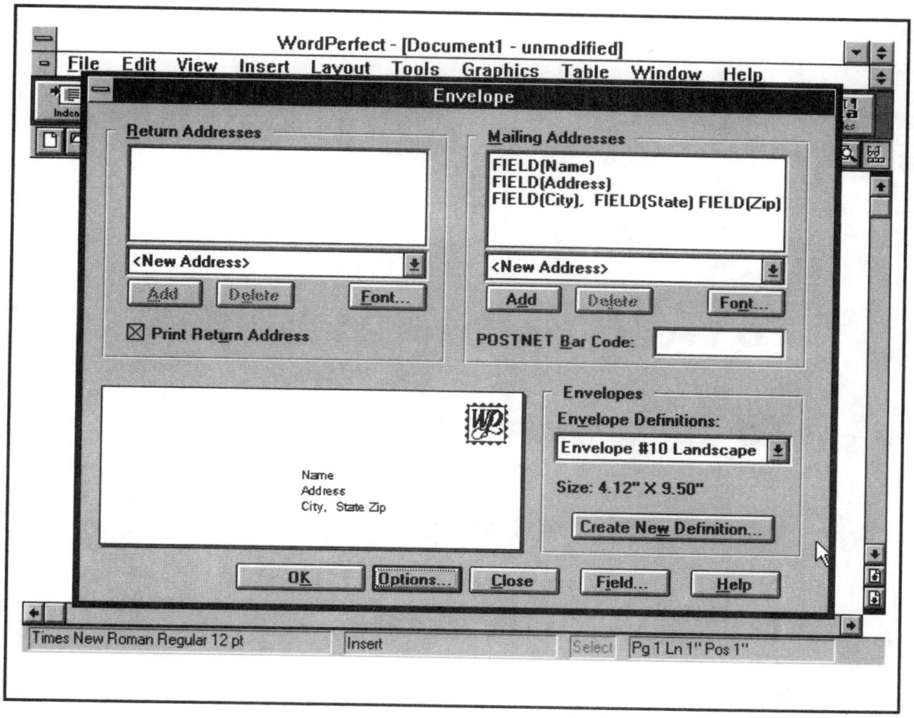

Merge codes for printing envelopes

new feature

Automatic envelopes

This handy feature is new to WordPerfect 6.0 for Windows.

tip

POSTNET bar codes in envelopes

If the POSTNET Bar Code text box does not appear in the envelope dialog box, click on Options, then select Include USPS POSTNET Bar Code. In the Postnet text box, type the name of the field containing the zip code.

It's So Easy

lesson 16

WordPerfect Tools

WordPerfect provides a number of tools that go far beyond basic word processing functions. No matter what the task, these tools make your work easier and faster. You can create macros to speed typing and menu selections, customize the Power and Button Bars to suit your tastes, check your spelling, or use the thesaurus and grammar checker to improve your vocabulary and writing technique.

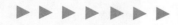

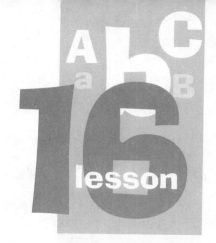

RECORDING AND PLAYING MACROS

A *macro* is a special command that you create to automate repetitive tasks such as formatting your page for each business letter you write. You can create a macro that records the keystrokes, then replay the macro anytime in the future by simply typing its name. Macros can be used to repeat text, commands, or any menu or dialog box selections.

To record a macro:

1. Select Tools ➤ Macro ➤ Record (Ctrl+F10) to display the Record Macro dialog box, as shown in the figure.

Record Macro dialog box

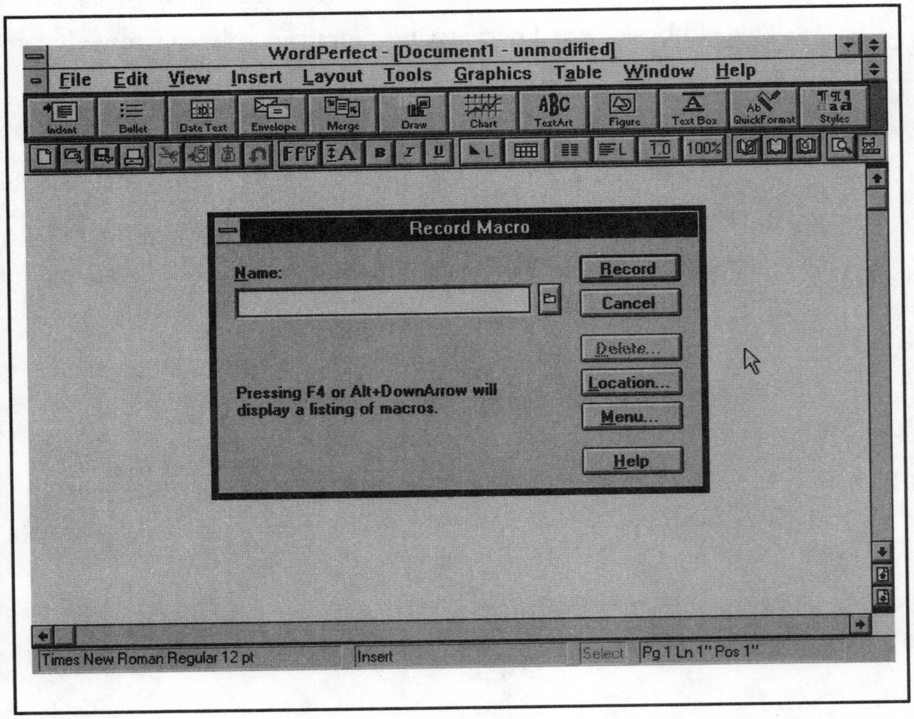

2 Type the macro name, then press Enter (or click on Record).

3 Type your keystrokes or select menu and dialog box options. Note that while recording a macro, you cannot use the mouse to select text or move the insertion point.

4 Select Tools ➤ Macro ➤ Record.

To play a macro:

1 Select Tools ➤ Macro ➤ Play (Alt+f10)

2 Enter the name of the macro and then select Play; or click on the folder icon or press F4 to see a list of macros, then double-click on the macro you want to play.

tip

Macro locations

If you are using a custom template, your macros will be stored with the template itself. Otherwise, macros are stored in the WPWIN60\MACROS directory.

tip

To convert a WordPerfect 5.1 macro

Select Tools ➤ Macro ➤ Play, pull down the Location button, and select File On Disk. Type the path and name of the macro, then select Play. A dialog box will appear reporting that the macro must be converted to 6.0 format. Select Save As, enter a new path and macro name for the converted macro, then click on OK.

CUSTOMIZING THE POWER BAR

The Power Bar offers a quick and convenient way to execute the most popular WordPerfect commands, but its display might not be exactly right for you. If so, you can customize the Power Bar by adding or removing buttons, changing their order, and by changing the bar's position on the screen. You can also change the fonts and font sizes that will be listed when you select the Font Face and Font Size buttons.

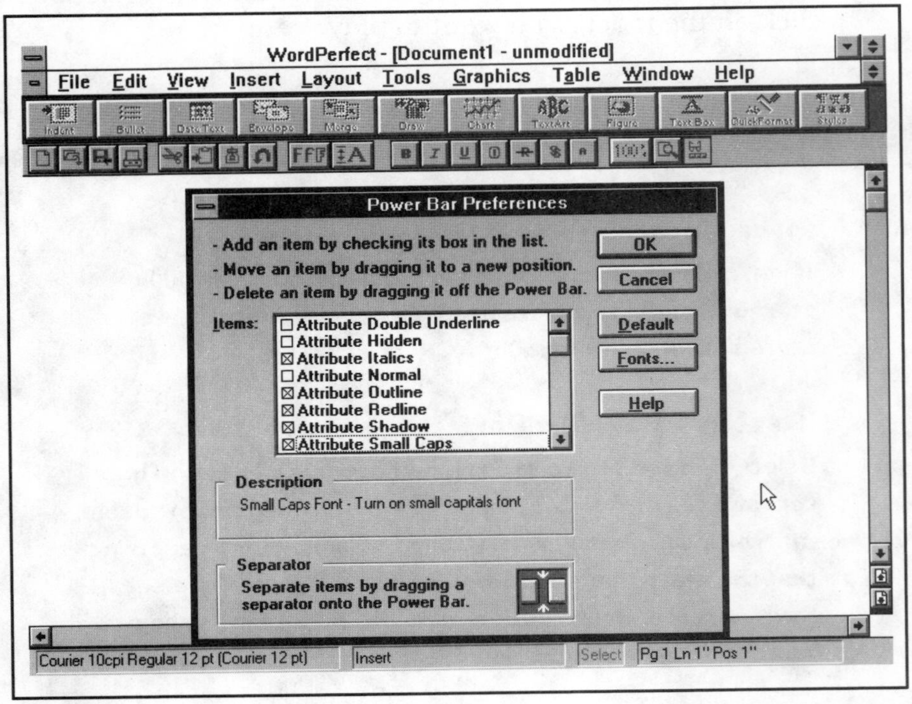

Power Bar Preferences dialog box with customized power bar in the background

To customize the Power Bar:

1 Select File ➤ Preferences ➤ Power Bar.

2 To add a button, scroll the list to see the function you want to perform, then click in the check box.

3 To delete a button, drag it down off of the Power Bar.

4 To change the position of a button, drag it to a new location.

5 Select Fonts to see a dialog box where you choose the fonts and font sizes that will be listed when you pull down the Font Face and Font Size buttons.

6 Click on OK.

tip

Customizing Button Bars

Select File ➤ Preferences ➤ Button Bar. From the dialog box, click on Options to change the size and position of the bar and to change the appearance of the button faces. To add features to the Button Bar, click on Edit to display the Button Bar Editor.

tip

Adding macro buttons

If you have a macro that you play often, add it as a button on the Button Bar. In the Button Bar Editor, click on Play a Macro. Click on Add Macro, then type the name of the macro, or press F4 then double-click on the macro you want to add as a button. Choose Select to add the macro to the Button Bar and to return to the Button Bar Editor.

CORRECTING SPELLING ERRORS

To many users, the spelling checker is the most important tool WordPerfect provides. Typographical and spelling errors can occur no matter how careful you are.

To check a document for spelling:

1 Position the insertion point in the text you want to spell check. If you do not want to check the entire document, place the insertion point on the word or page you want to check. To check a block of text, select the text first.

Speller dialog box

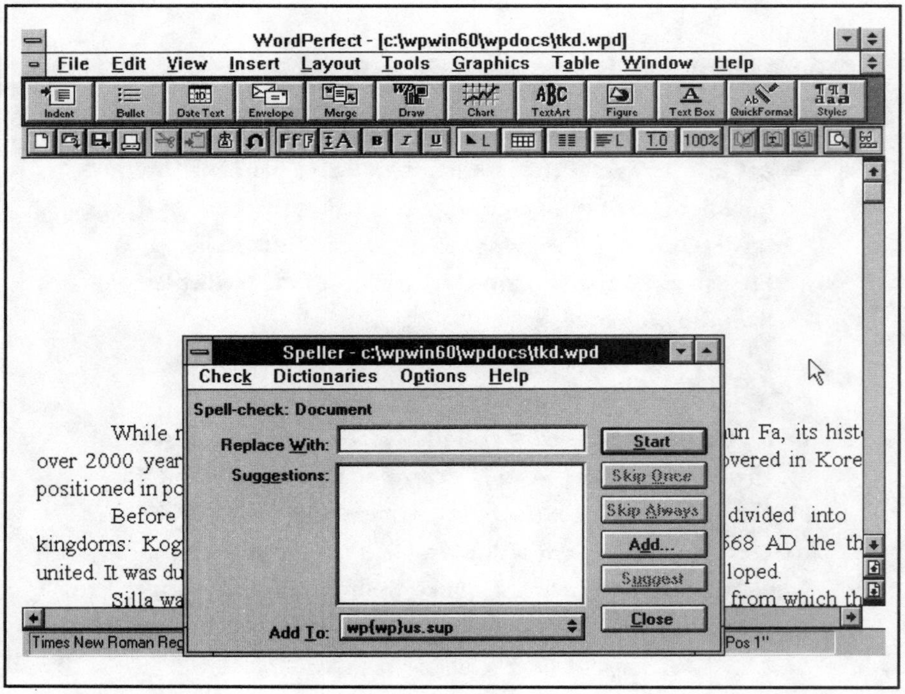

2 Select Tools ➤ Speller ➤ Start. WordPerfect finds the first possible error and displays a list of alternative spellings, as shown in the figure.

3 Double-click on the correctly spelled word in the list (scroll the list if necessary) to replace the misspelled word, or select Skip Always to accept the word as it is spelled for the remainder of the session.

Extra! Extra!

tip **Other spelling options**

To edit the word manually, type the correct spelling in the Replace With text box, then press Enter or click on Replace. The Speller dialog box has several options in addition to Replace and Skip Always. Select Skip Once to leave the word as it is one time. If the correctly spelled word is not in the list, type an alternate spelling in the Replace With text box, then click on Suggest to have WordPerfect look up additional words.

tip **How much do you want to check?**

To check the entire document, the insertion point can be anywhere in the document. If you selected a block of text first, only that block will be checked. To check just a word, page, paragraph, or section from the location of the insertion point, pull down the Check menu in the Speller dialog box, then select the amount of text you want to check.

IMPROVING YOUR VOCABULARY

Sometimes the hardest part of writing is selecting just the right word. You know what you want to say but you're not sure of the best word. Other times, you find yourself repeating a word frequently in a paragraph and you'd like to find another way to say the same thing without sounding repetitious. Try the WordPerfect thesaurus.

To find a synonym:

1. Place the insertion point anywhere in the word you want to replace with a synonym.

Thesaurus dialog box

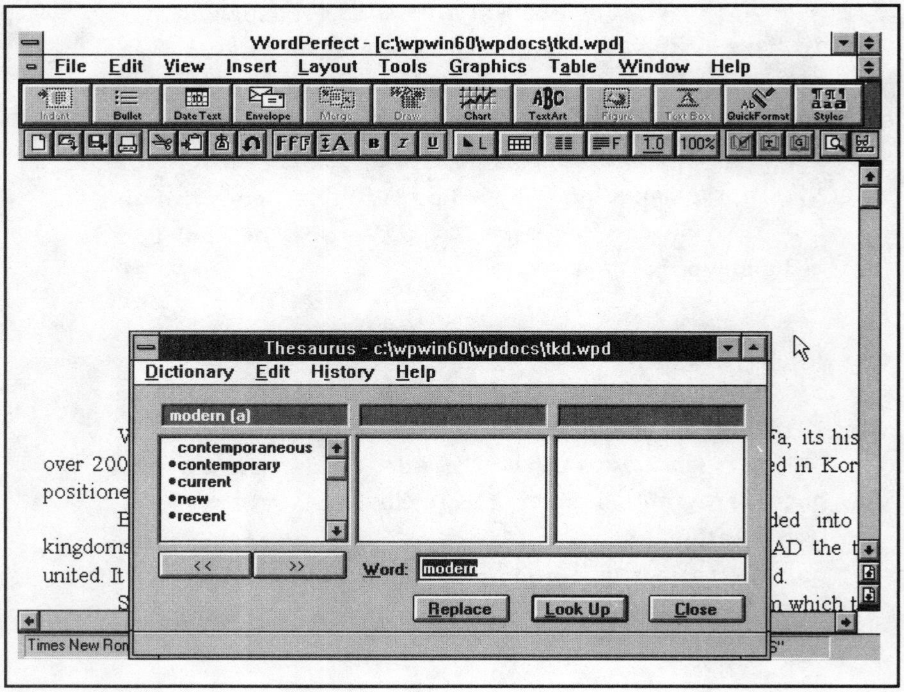

2 Select Tools ➤ Thesaurus to display the Thesaurus dialog box. Several synonyms for the word may be listed, as shown in the figure.

3 Scroll the list box to highlight the desired word.

4 Select Replace.

tip

More words

Some words in the list box had bullets (large dots) next to them to indicate that the Thesaurus contains additional synonyms for that word. If none of the words in the list are quite right, search for the proper word by double-clicking on a bulleted word, or selecting it and clicking on Lookup.

tip

Word Not Found

If WordPerfect cannot find a synonym for your word, the message Word Not Found will appear. To return to the document, select Close.

arning!

Beware the parts of speech

Depending on the word you are looking up, the thesaurus may list both nouns and verbs, or adjectives. Make sure you replace the word with one of the correct type. Also, select a word that has the same connotation, and avoid using words simply because of their size or novelty. Substituting a simple *I love you, please marry me* with *I philos you, please espouse me*, may not make the impression you want.

IMPROVING YOUR GRAMMAR

WordPerfect's speller cannot determine if you used the wrong word when it is correctly spelled. For instance, it won't report that you used *too* instead of *to* or *two,* or used *effect* when you should have used *affect*. Fortunately, WordPerfect includes Grammatik, a powerful program that checks your grammar as well as spelling and punctuation.

To check your grammar:

1. Type or open the document you want checked.
2. Select Tools ➤ Grammatik ➤ Start.

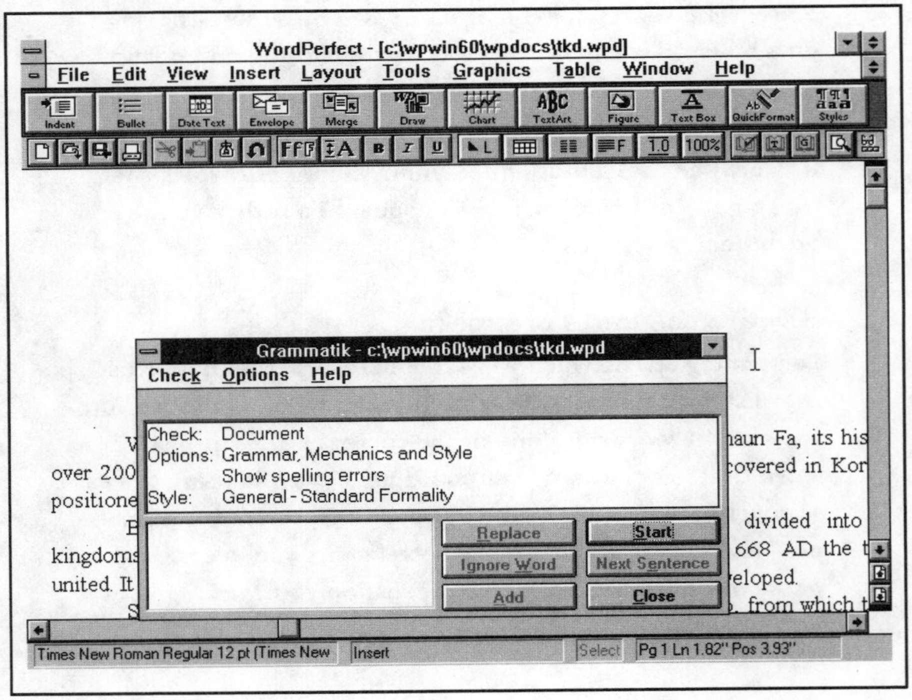

The Grammatik dialog box

3 Grammatik finds the first possible error and displays a description of the problem and, in some cases, a suggested correction.

4 Select Replace to replace the text with Grammatik's suggested phrase, or select Ignore Phrase to move on to the next problem.

5 After the last detected error, a dialog box appears asking if you want to close Grammatik—select Yes.

tip

How much do you want to check?

To check the entire document, the insertion point can be anywhere in the document. To check just a sentence, paragraph, or from the location of the insertion point, pull down the Check menu, then select the amount of text you want to check.

tip

Document statistics

To check the writing level of the document, select Options ➤ Statistics, then click on Start. A dialog box will appear listing the number of words, syllables, paragraphs, sentences, long sentences, and short sentences in the document. It also lists the average sentences per paragraph, words per sentence, and syllables per word, as well as an overall readability level.

It's So Easy

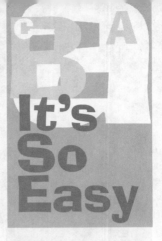

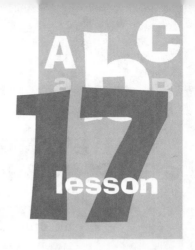

lesson 17

Desktop Publishing with Graphics

As you become familiar with WordPerfect's graphics commands, you'll see that you can create some rather sophisticated documents. Not only can you produce some very dramatic effects, but you can have some fun doing it.

There's really much more to graphics than can be covered in a book of this length, but this lesson will show you the basics you'll need to use graphic images in your documents.

RETRIEVING A GRAPHICS IMAGE

The first step in using a graphic image is to retrieve it into your document. You must know the name of the graphic file, including its file extension, and the drive and directory in which the file is located.

To retrieve a graphic image:

1. Select Graphics ➤ Figure to display the Insert Image dialog box.

Graphics image retrieved into document

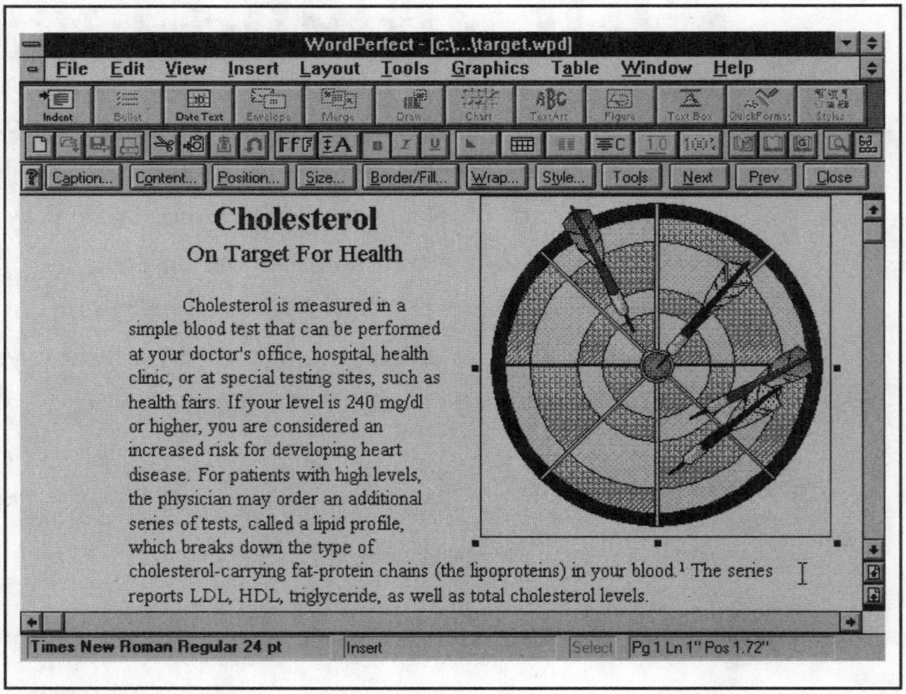

WordPerfect - [c:\...\target.wpd]
File Edit View Insert Layout Tools Graphics Table Window Help
Indent Bullet Date Text Envelope Merge Draw Chart TextArt Figure Text Box QuickFormat Styles
Caption... Content... Position... Size... Border/Fill... Wrap... Style... Tools Next Prev Close
Cholesterol
On Target For Health
Cholesterol is measured in a simple blood test that can be performed at your doctor's office, hospital, health clinic, or at special testing sites, such as health fairs. If your level is 240 mg/dl or higher, you are considered an increased risk for developing heart disease. For patients with high levels, the physician may order an additional series of tests, called a lipid profile, which breaks down the type of cholesterol-carrying fat-protein chains (the lipoproteins) in your blood.1 The series reports LDL, HDL, triglyceride, as well as total cholesterol levels.
Times New Roman Regular 24 pt
Insert
Select
Pg 1 Ln 1" Pos 1.72"

2 Double-click on the name of the image you want to insert, or type the name of the image file and click on OK. The image appears in a box on the right of the document, and a Graphics Feature Bar appears under the Power Bar, as in the figure. The small boxes around the image are called handles, and they indicate that the graphic is selected.

3 Click outside of the graphics box to deselect the graphic.

oops!

This File Does Not Exist!

If you see this message, make sure you are typing the correct name and extension of the file. WordPerfect expects graphics files to be in the WPWIN60\GRAPHICS directory and with the WPG extension. If your image is in another directory, use the Directories, Drives, and List Files of Type boxes to display the file name, or type the complete path of the file in the Filename text box.

tip

Printing graphics

In the Print dialog box, pull down the Print Quality list under Document Settings. Select High, Medium, or Draft. High results in the best quality but slowest printing. Use Draft for quick draft copies. If you do not have a color printer, screen colors will print in shades of gray.

CHANGING THE SIZE AND POSITION OF GRAPHICS

You change the size, shape, and position of a graphics box just as you do for graphic horizontal and vertical lines. With a mouse it's easy.

To change the size and position of graphics:

1 Click on the graphics box to surround it in a selection box with eight handles.

2 To move the image, point inside the selection box and drag the mouse.

Graphic in several sizes

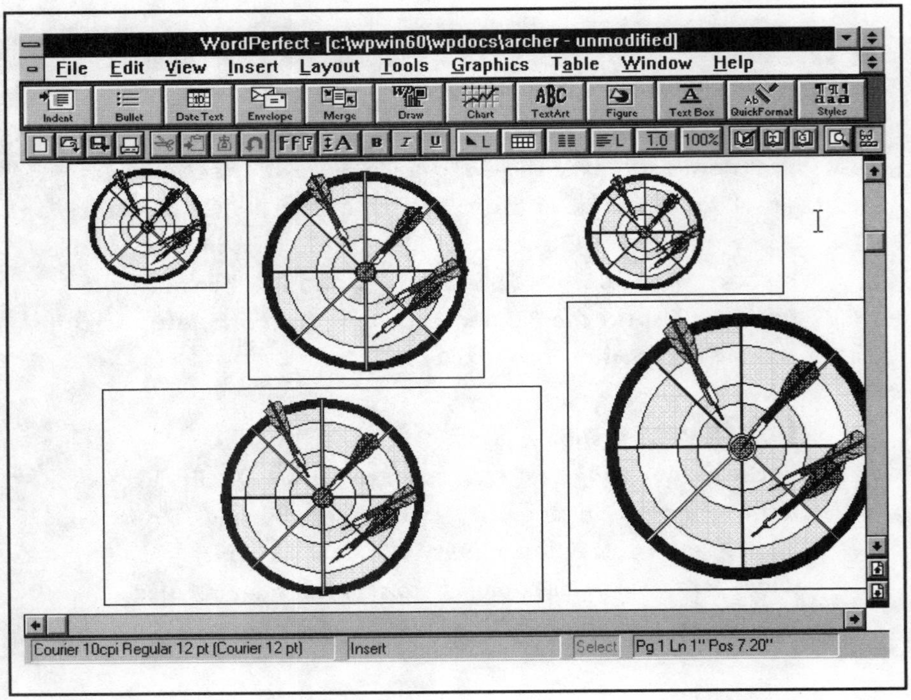

3 To change the size of the box, drag one of the handles.

tip ▶ **Graphics boxes and images**

Think of a graphic as having two separate parts—the image (drawing or picture) and the graphics box that surrounds the image. When you change the size of a graphics box, WordPerfect maintains the proper width-to-height ratio of the image within it, preventing you from distorting the image. If you triple the width of the box without changing the height, for example, the height of the graphic within the box will not change.

tip ▶ **To delete a graphics box**

Select the graphic, then press Del.

tip ▶ **Beyond the screen**

To change the size and position of the image while viewing the overall page design, click on the Page Full Zoom button.

oops! ▶ **I started WordPerfect Draw!**

If WordPerfect Draw starts when you click to select a graphic box, Windows has interpreted the click as a double-click. Select File ➤ Exit and Return ➤ No to return to your document. WordPerfect Draw is discussed later in this lesson.

EDITING A GRAPHICS BOX

If you don't care for the plain-vanilla square graphics box, you can customize its appearance. You can change the lines that surround the box, make round rather than square corners, and even have text follow the image's contour.

To edit a graphics box:

1 Select the graphic you want to customize.

2 Click on the button in the Graphics Feature Bar that refers to the attribute you want to customize. The categories are caption, content, position, size, border/fill, wrap, and style.

Wrap Text dialog box with edited box in the background

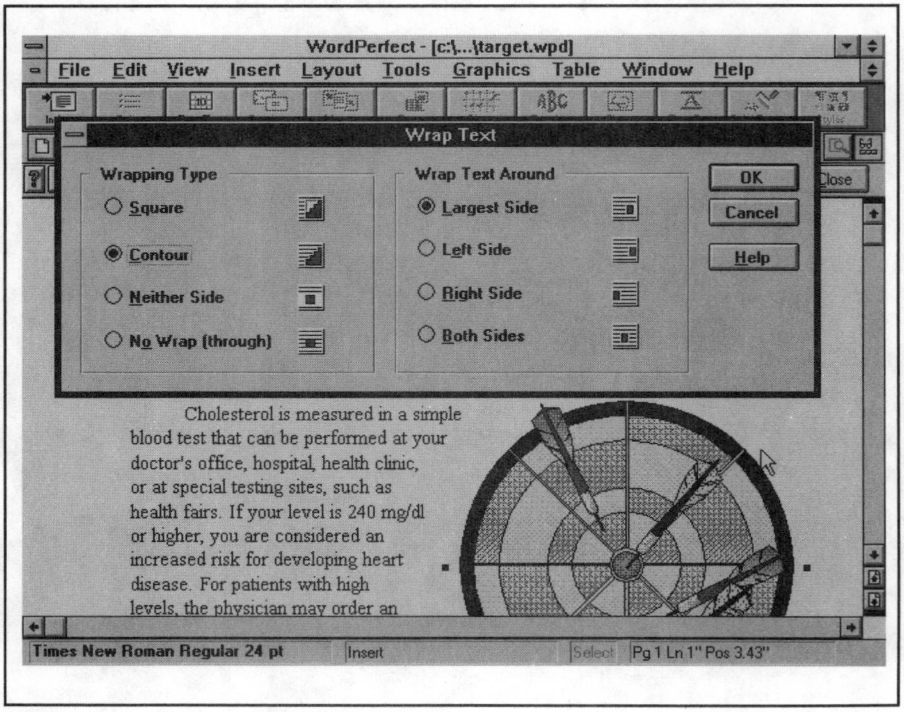

3 Complete the dialog box that appears, then click on OK to see the effects of your choices on the graphic.

If the Feature Bar is not displayed, point to the graphic and click the right mouse button to display the same options in a Quick menu. Select the category from the Quick menu, or select Feature Bar to display the Feature Bar.

tip

Graphic editing options

Here are a few ways to edit your graphics box:

***Changing box lines*: Select Border/Fill from the quick menu or Feature Bar. Choose a line option from the Border Style list; a fill pattern from the Fill Style list. Select Customize Style to customize the corners and lines, or create a shadow box.**

***Positioning the image in the box*: By default, the image is centered within the graphics box. To change its position, select Content from the Quick menu or Feature Bar to display the Box Content dialog box.**

EDITING GRAPHICS IMAGES

In addition to editing the graphics box that surrounds the image, you can change the image itself. Editing the graphic changes only how it appears in your document—it does not affect the actual graphics file itself.

To edit the image:

1 Select Tools from the Feature Bar, or Image Tools from the Quick menu. The graphics Toolbar will appear, as shown in the figure.

2 Use the tools to change the appearance, size, and position of the image within the box.

Graphics Toolbar with edited image

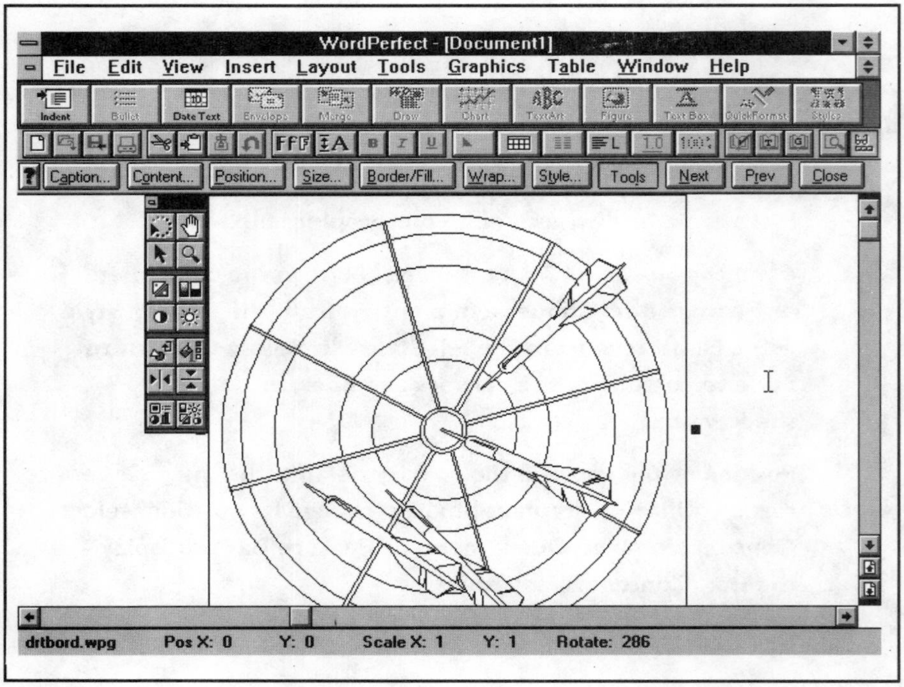

new feature

New feature

The graphics Toolbar is new to version 6.0.

tip

Editing images

A thorough discussion of the image editing capabilities could fill an entire lesson. Here are the functions of the Toolbar buttons (from left to right, starting in the top row) to get you started:

***Rotate*: Rotates the graphic within the box.**
***Move*: Moves the graphic within the box.**
***Mouse*: Moves the box within the document.**
***Scale*: Changes the size of the image.**
***Complementary Colors*: Changes to a complementary color scheme.**
***Black and White*: Displays the image in black and white.**
***Contrast*: Determines the contrast between colors and shades.**
***Brightness*: Sets the overall brightness of the image.**
***Reset*: Returns the graphic to its original settings.**
***Image Fill*: Selects filled or outline images.**
***Mirror Vertically*: Flips the image from left to right.**
***Mirror Horizontally*: Flips the image from top to bottom.**
***Edit Image*: Displays the WordPerfect Draw application.**
Image Settings: Displays a dialog box for making multiple changes.

ROTATING TEXT IN BOXES

A graphics text box contains text instead of a graphic image. It is, however, still a graphics box because you can change the box's size and position using the mouse—something you cannot do to a paragraph with borders. But more importantly, you can rotate the text in the box 90, 180, or 270 degrees.

To create a rotated text box:

1 Select Graphics ➤ Text. A text box appears on the screen along with the Graphics Feature Bar.

2 Select Content to display the Box Content dialog box.

Document showing rotated text in customized and overlapped boxes

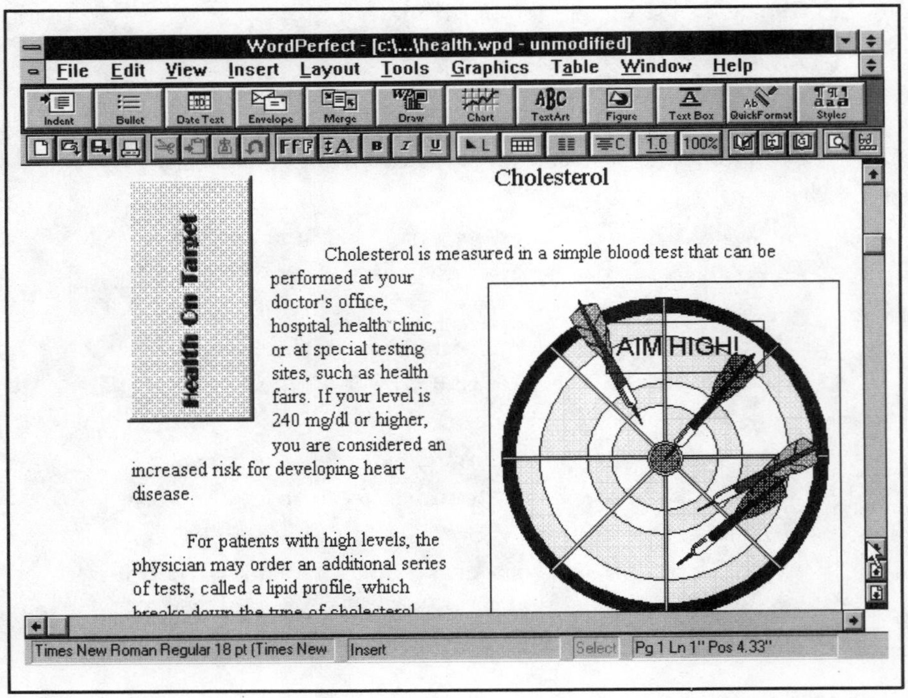
WordPerfect - [c:\...\health.wpd - unmodified]
File Edit View Insert Layout Tools Graphics Table Window Help
Indent Bullet Date Text Envelope Merge Draw Chart TextArt Figure Text Box QuickFormat Styles
Cholesterol
Health On Target
Cholesterol is measured in a simple blood test that can be performed at your doctor's office, hospital, health clinic, or at special testing sites, such as health fairs. If your level is 240 mg/dl or higher, you are considered an increased risk for developing heart disease.
For patients with high levels, the physician may order an additional series of tests, called a lipid profile, which
AIM HIGH!
Times New Roman Regular 18 pt (Times New
Insert
Select
Pg 1 Ln 1" Pos 4.33"

3 Select 90, 180, or 270 degrees, then select OK. The text box editor appears where you enter and format the text of the box.

4 Type and format the text you want in the box, then click on Close.

5 Use the mouse, Feature Bar, or Quick menu options to customize the box.

If you do not want to rotate text, select Graphics ➤ Text, then simply type the text in the box.

tip ▶ **Reducing box size**

The default box size may be much larger than the text within it. Drag the handles to reduce the box size, or use the Size dialog box.

tip ▶ **Printer compatibility**

Some printers may not be able to print rotated graphics in all fonts. Experiment to see what your printer's capabilities are.

tip ▶ **Combining text and graphics**

By selecting No Wrap (through) for figure and text boxes, you can overlap graphics boxes to create some dramatic visual effects.

CREATING CUSTOM DRAWINGS

WordPerfect Draw is a powerful application for creating artwork and for customizing WPG and other graphics files. To use the application to its fullest requires some knowledge of computer graphics and a degree of creativity. Here's how to create a drawing:

1 Select Graphics ➤ Draw. To edit an image already in a graphics box, double-click on the figure. The Draw screen will appear and you can then create your own image or edit an existing graphic.

Customized WPG file in Draw

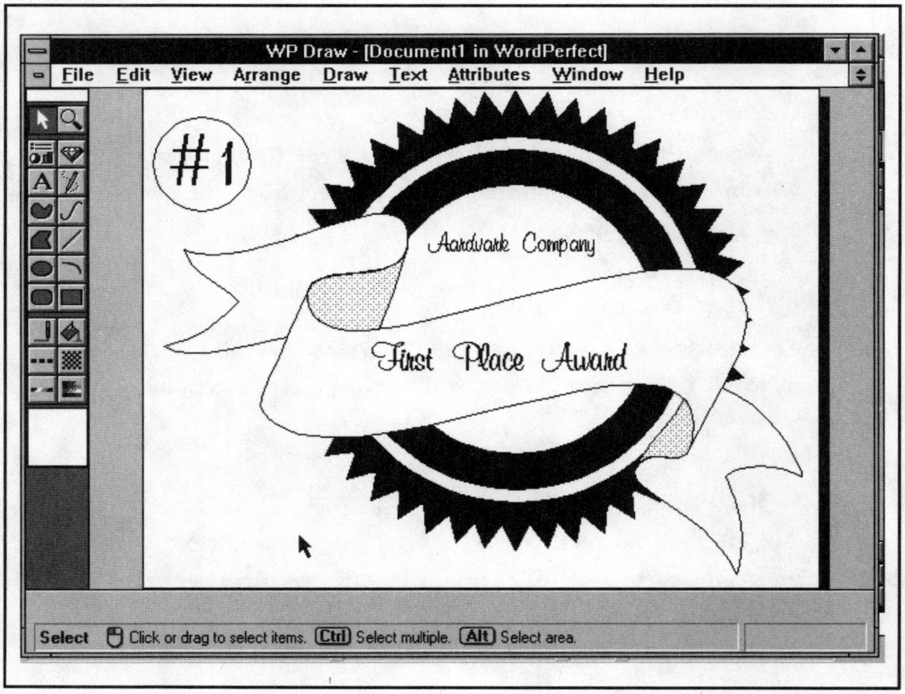

2 Use the mouse, tools in the Toolbar, or the menu options, to customize the image.

3 Select File ➤ Update to insert the image into WordPerfect and remain in Draw, or select File ➤ Close and Return, or File ➤ Exit and Return, to insert the drawing and return to WordPerfect.

new feature

New feature

WordPerfect Draw is new to version 6.0.

tip

Using WordPerfect Draw

You can use the Toolbar or menu options to create and customize graphics. Here are the functions of the tools in the Toolbar, from left to right starting in the top row.

Select area	Zoom area
Create chart	Insert image
Enter text	Draw freehand
Draw closed curve	Draw curve
Draw polygon	Draw line
Draw ellipse	Draw arc
Draw rounded rectangle	Draw rectangle
Outline/no outline	Fill/no fill
Line type	Fill type pattern
Line color	Fill color

CREATING CHARTS AND GRAPHS

WordPerfect Chart creates bar, line, pie, and other types of charts and inserts them into your document.

1. Select Graphics ➤ Chart. The chart editor will appear with a default sample chart and data, as shown in the figure.
2. Select File ➤ Clear to clear the sample.
3. Click in the spreadsheet grid and enter your data.

WordPerfect Chart with sample data and graph

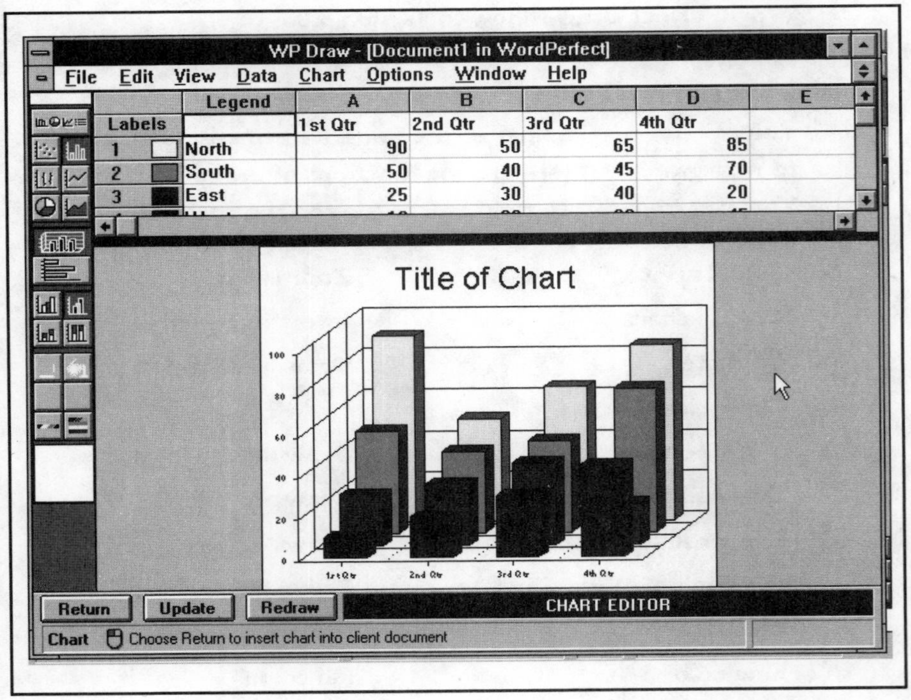

4 Select a chart type in the Toolbar.

5 Click on Redraw to display the chart.

6 Click on Update to copy the chart to your WordPerfect document and remain in Chart, or click on Return to copy the chart and return to WordPerfect.

WordPerfect inserts the chart into the document in a box without border lines.

tip ▶ Instant charts

To chart data you've already typed in a table, select the rows and columns you want to chart, then select Graphics ➤ Chart.

tip ▶ Customizing the chart

Select Options from the Menu Bar to enter a title, create a legend or labels, change the perspective of three-dimensional charts, and set the attributes of a series, axis, or grid.

CREATING SPECIAL TEXT EFFECTS

TextArt is a new WordPerfect feature that lets you create slanted, curved, filled, and rotated text. Use it to create headlines, watermarks, eye-catching graphics, even text for round buttons.

To create a special text effect:

1 Select Graphics ➤ TextArt. The figure shows the TextArt window with customized text.

2 Select a font and style to be used for the characters. You can choose any TrueType font. The styles include regular, bold, italic, and bold italic.

3 In the Enter Text box, type the text you want to use for the special effect. You can enter up to 58 characters, divided into as many as three lines.

4 Select the desired effect from the group of buttons next to the sample window.

5 Select File ➤ Exit & Return to WordPerfect, then select Yes, to insert the text art into the document.

WordPerfect inserts the text art into the document in a box without border lines. Use the mouse, Graphics Feature Bar, or Quick menu, to customize the box. To edit the chart itself, double-click on the chart to display the TextArt window. Change the text or the design, then exit and return to WordPerfect.

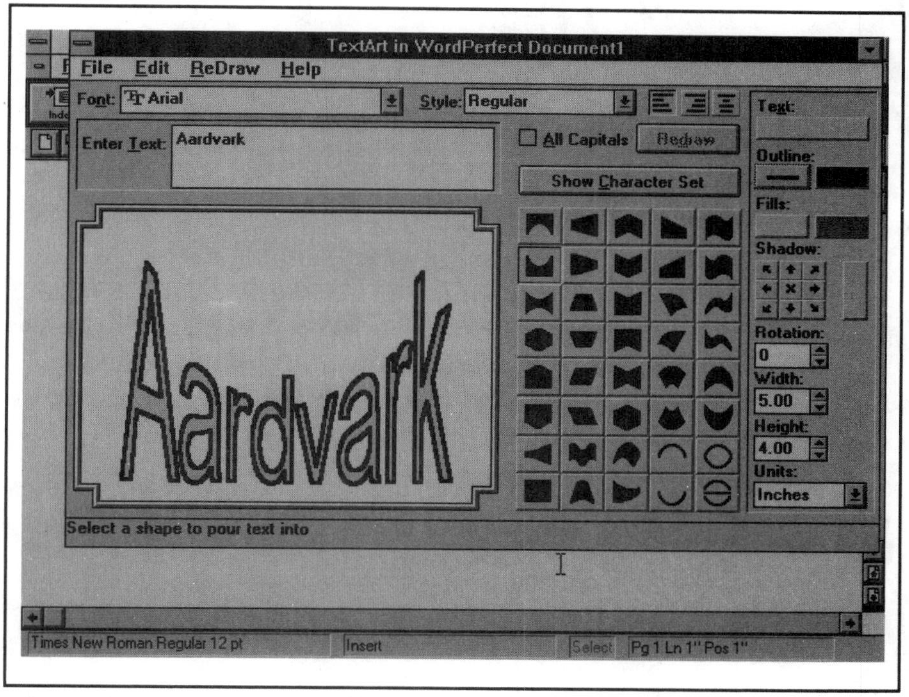

Special text effects showing outlined characters

button bar

Quick art

Click on the TextArt button to create a special effect.

tip

TextArt options

The options in the TextArt window allow you to further customize the special text effect.

tip

Printing samples

In the TextArt window, select File ➤ Print to print a sample of the text.

Let's Do It!

PART FOUR ▶ **Exercises**

Even the most powerful features of WordPerfect are easy to use. It just takes a few clicks of the mouse to add lines, borders, and graphics to your document. You can also speed up your work by recording macros that perform functions that you use often. And don't forget to spell check your document and improve it using the thesaurus and Grammatik.

Once you feel comfortable with these special WordPerfect features, you'll be able to create a wider variety of documents, and you'll work more efficiently and comfortably.

Creating Tables

When you want to make a point with numbers, place them in a table. A table makes direct impact by letting the numbers stand out. A table draws the eye, getting immediate attention and placing the reader's focus just where you want it.

Let's create a small table now.

1. Select Table ➤ Create.
2. Type **3**, then press Tab.
3. Type **4**, then press Enter or click on OK.
4. Press → to move to cell B1.

▶▶▶▶▶▶▶

5 Type **1993**.

6 Press → to move to cell C1.

7 Type **1994**.

8 Move to cell A2 and type **Income**.

9 Press → and type **64500**.

10 Press → and type **75600**.

11 Move to cell A3 and type **Expenses**.

12 Press → and type **14250**.

13 Press → and type **13780**.

14 Move to cell A3, and type Profit. (We'll add the profit amounts later.)

15 Select File ➤ Save.

16 Type **Profit**, then select OK.

17 Select File ➤ Close.

Using Formulas to Create a Spreadsheet

When we created the table named Profit, we didn't manually calculate and insert the net profit amounts. That's because we can have WordPerfect do this for us automatically by using formulas. Add the formulas now, and format the calculated cells.

1 Open the document named Profit.

2 Place the insertion point in cell B4 (the one below the cell containing 14250).

3 Select Table and confirm that a check mark appears next to the Cell Formula Entry option. If there is no check mark, click on that option.

4 Type **B2-B3**, then press → to select sell C4. The amount, 50250, is calculated and displayed in the cell. (If the number is not calculated, select Table ➤ Calculate, click on Calculate Table in the Automatic Calculation Mode section, then click on OK.)

5 In cell C4, type **C2-C3**.

6 Select Table ➤ Calculate ➤ Calc Table to calculate the figure before you move the insertion point to another cell.

If you change any of the income or expense amounts, select Table ➤ Calculate ➤ Calc Table again to recalculate the formulas.

Formatting Tables

Now, let's center the labels in the first row, format the numbers to appear like dollar amounts, and add a gray pattern to highlight the calculated cells.

1 Drag the mouse across cells B1 and C1 to select both cells.

2 Select Table ➤ Format. Because cells are selected, the Format dialog box appears with cell format options.

3 Pull down the Justification list and select Center.

▶▶▶▶▶▶▶

4 Select OK.

5 Drag the mouse to select cells B2 to C4.

6 Select Table ➤ Number Type.

7 Choose Currency, then click on OK. The numbers now appear with dollar signs, commas as a thousands separator, and two decimal places.

8 Click outside of the table to deselect the cells, then drag to select cells B4 and C4.

9 Select Table ➤ Lines/Fill.

10 Pull down the Fill Style list and choose 20%.

11 Select OK.

12 Click outside of the table to deselect the cells, then select File ➤ Save.

13 Select File ➤ Print ➤ Print. Check your work against Figure 4.1.

14 Select File ➤ Close.

Working with Columns

Let's see how easy it is to create newsletters.

1 Open one of your documents—you can use TKD.DOC if you saved it after the Part 3 Let's Do It exercise.

2 Place the insertion point in front of the first paragraph.

Figure 4.1:
Formatted table

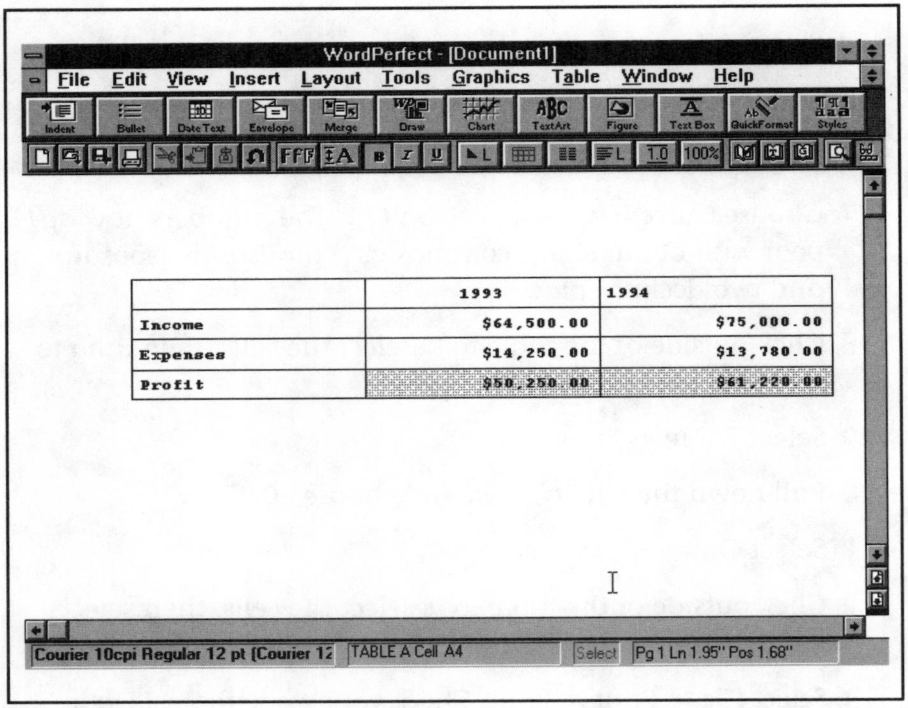

3 Pull down the column button in the power Bar and select 3 Columns. (As an alternative, select Layout ➤ Columns ➤ Define, type **3**, then click on OK.) The text automatically adjusts to the default 1.83-inch column width.

4 Click on the Page Zoom Full button. Figure 4.2 shows how the TKD document will look with some additional text in three columns.

▶▶▶▶▶▶▶

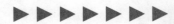

5 Click on the button again to return to the previous magnification and mode.

6 Select File ➤ Close ➤ No.

7 Select File ➤ Exit if you are not ready to continue.

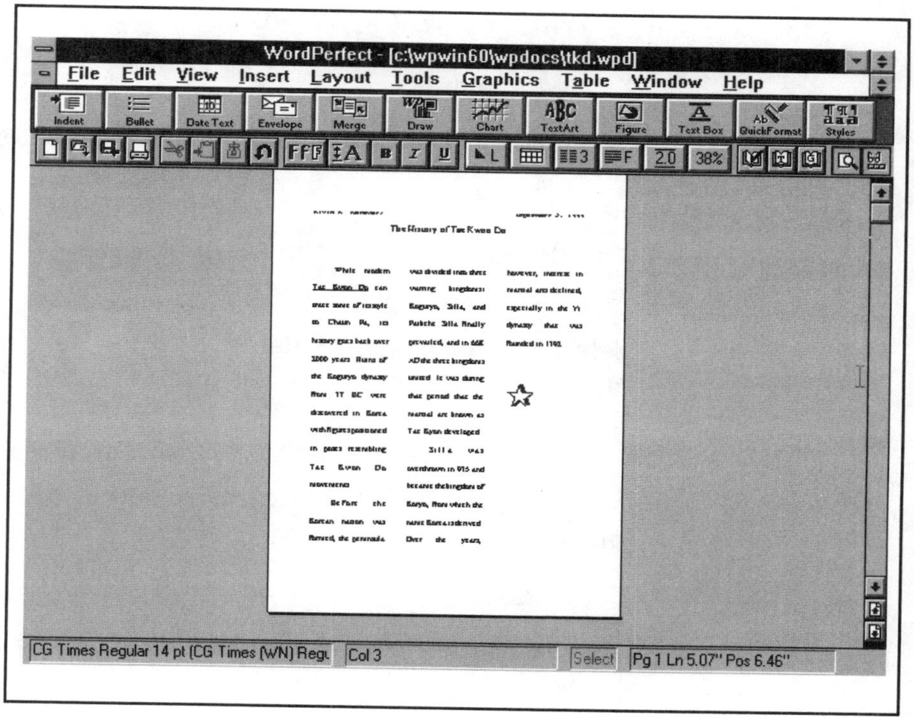

Figure 4.2: The finished three-column newsletter

Adding Lines and Boxes

Graphic lines and borders add visual interest to your work. In this exercise, we'll get some practice with graphics by creating a letterhead template complete with a horizontal line and a shaded page border. Because the letterhead will be stored as a template, you can open it when you want to write a letter without worrying about how you save it.

1. Start WordPerfect.
2. Select File ➤ Template ➤ Options ➤ Create Template.
3. Type **Lhead**, then click on OK.
4. Pull down the font button in the Power Bar and select a scalable font, such as TrueType.
5. Select Layout ➤ Font ➤ Relative Size ➤ Very Large, then click on OK.
6. Type your name.
7. Select Layout ➤ Font ➤ Relative Size ➤ Normal, then click on OK.
8. Press Enter.
9. Select Graphics ➤ Horizontal Line to insert the default horizontal line.
10. Press Enter.

▶▶▶▶▶▶▶

11 Select Layout ➤ Line ➤ Flush Right (or press Alt+F7) for right flush alignment, type your address and telephone number, then press Enter.

Now let's add a custom border around the page.

12 Select Layout ➤ Page ➤ Border/Fill.

13 Pull down the Border Style list and select Shadow.

14 Pull down the Fill Style list and select 10%.

15 Click on OK to return to the template.

16 Click on the Page Zoom Full button to see the entire page.

17 Click on the button again to return to the previous magnification and view.

18 Select File ➤ Save. Check your work against Figure 4.3.

19 Select File ➤ Print ➤ Print.

20 Click on Exit Template.

21 Select File ➤ Exit if you're not ready to go on.

When you want to type a letter, select File ➤ Template, then double-click on LHEAD in the template list.

Figure 4.3: Template for letterhead

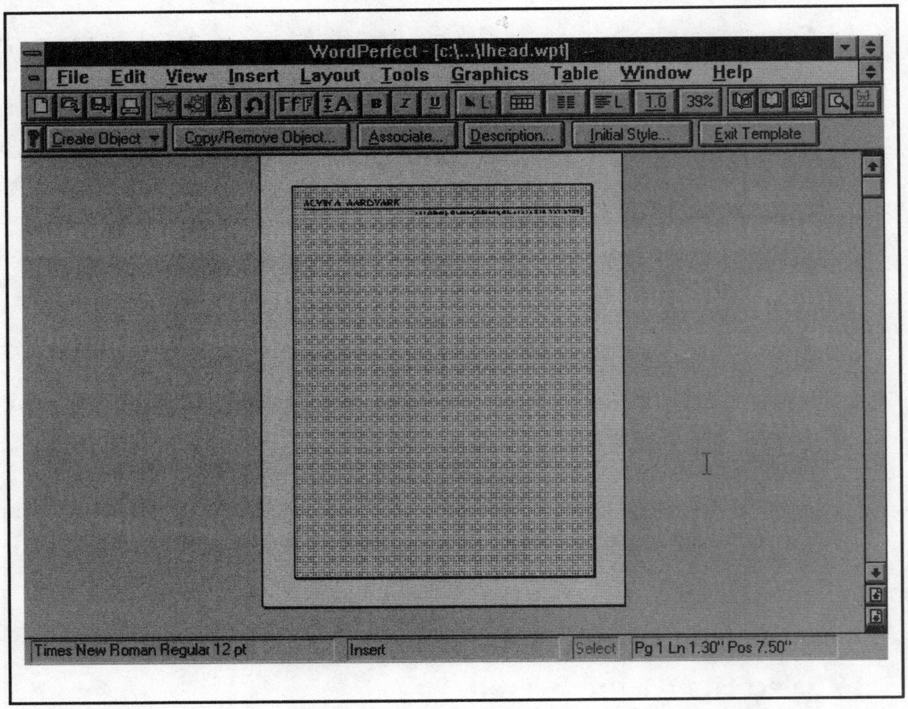

Creating Form Documents

WordPerfect's merge commands make it as easy to write thousands of letters as it is to create just one. But don't think form letters are only for mass mailings. Use them even if you send just one or two form-type letters per week, such as employment applications or requests for information.

In this exercise we'll create a form letter and envelopes.

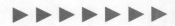

Constructing the Data File

The first step is to create a data file containing the variable information you want inserted into the letters. Just follow these steps.

1 Select Tools ➤ Merge.

2 Choose Place Records in a Table, then click on Data.

Now enter the field names.

3 Type **Name**, then press Enter.

4 Type **Address**, then press Enter.

5 Type **City**, then press Enter.

6 Type **State**, then press Enter.

7 Type **Zip**, then press Enter.

8 Select OK to display the Quick Data Entry dialog box.

Next, enter the information for each copy of the form document.

9 Type **Watson, Inc.**, then press Enter.

10 Type **246 Walnut St.**, then press Enter.

11 Type **Philadelphia,** then press Enter.

12 Type **PA**, then press Enter.

13 Type **19101**, then press Enter.

WordPerfect saves the record, clears the text boxes, and places the insertion point in the first field box for the next record.

14 Type **Mellow Marshmallow, Inc.**, then press Enter.

15 Type **92 Park Ave.**, then press Enter.

16 Type **New York**, then press Enter.

17 Type **NY**, then press Enter.

18 Type **12002**.

19 Select Close.

20 Select Yes to save the table, type **MAILLIST.DAT**, then select OK. The table will appears on screen, as in Figure 4.4.

21 Select File ➤ Close.

22 Select File ➤ Exit if you're not ready to go on.

Writing the Form Letter

The second big step is to write the form letter itself, inserting merge codes where you want variable information from the data file to be inserted.

1 Select Tools ➤ Merge ➤ Form.

2 Type **MAILLIST.DAT**, then select OK.

3 Select Layout ➤ Justification ➤ Center.

4 Type your name and address, then press Enter twice.

▶▶▶▶▶▶▶

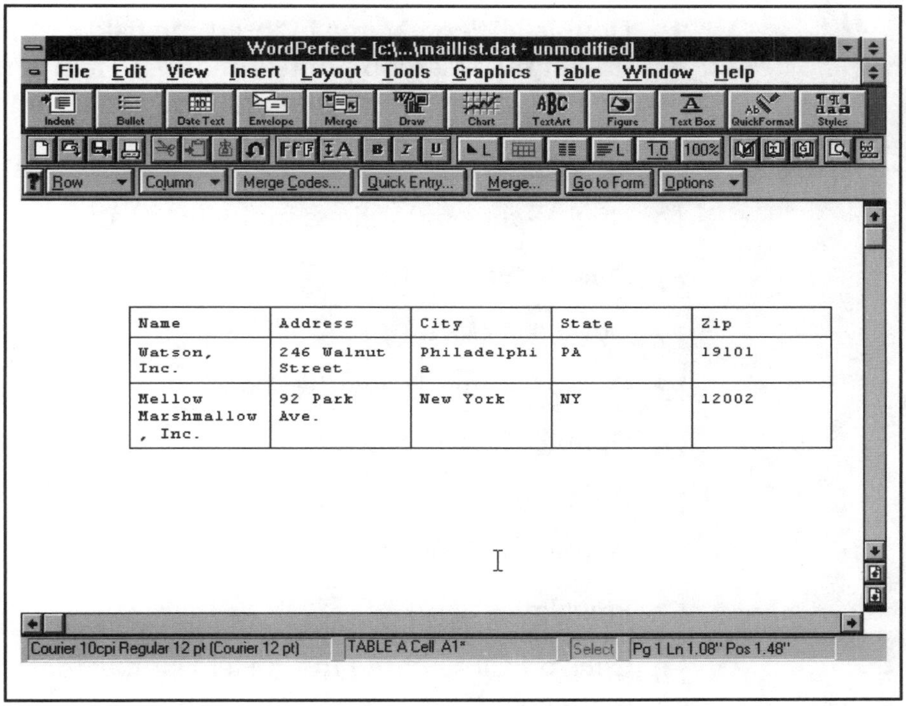

Figure 4.4: Completed data file table

5 Select Insert ➤ Date ➤ Date Code, then press Enter twice.

6 Select Layout ➤ Justification ➤ Left.

Now add the codes to print the address in the merged letters.

7 Click on Insert Field in the Feature Bar to display a list of fields.

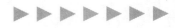

8 Double-click on Name to insert the field's code at the position of the insertion point. The Insert Field Name or Number dialog box will remain on the screen.

9 Press Enter.

10 Double-click on Address in the field list.

11 Press Enter.

12 Double-click on City.

13 Press , (comma) then the spacebar.

14 Double-click on State.

15 Press the spacebar twice.

16 Double-click on Zip.

17 Press Enter twice.

18 Click on Close in the Insert Field Name or Number dialog box.

Next, complete the letter.

19 Type a short letter:

Dear Sirs:

I represent a group of investors in your company. Please send me a copy of your latest annual report.

Sincerely,

▶▶▶▶▶▶▶

20 Press Enter five times.

21 Type your name. The form letter should now look like Figure 4.5.

22 Select File ➤ Save.

23 Type **Request**, then select OK.

24 Select File ➤ Close.

25 Select File ➤ Exit if you're not ready to go on.

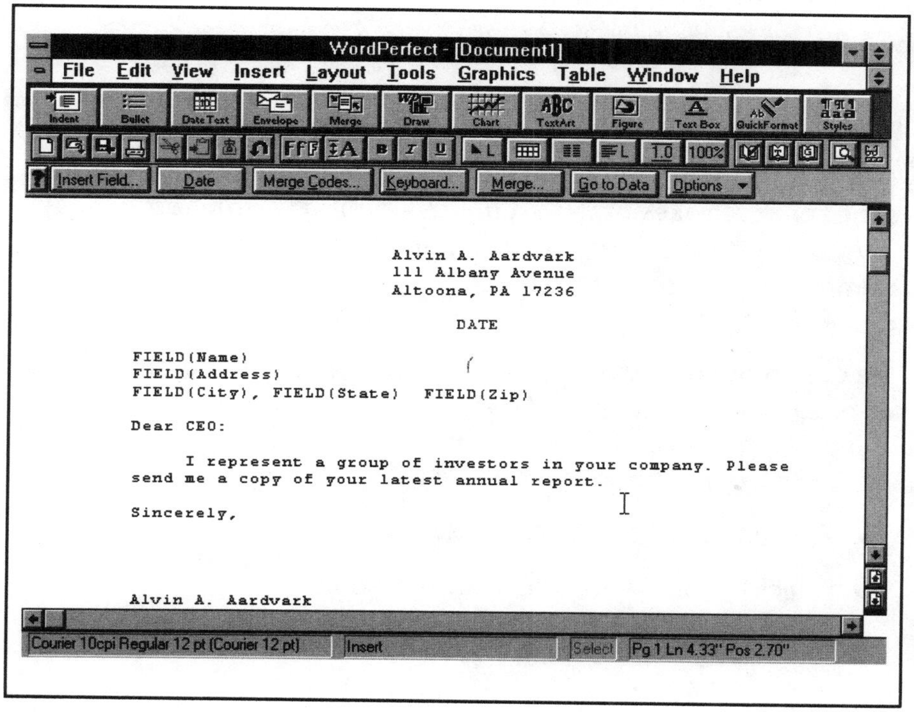

Figure 4.5: Completed form letter

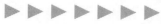

Merging Form Letters

To generate the form letters, just tell WordPerfect the name of the form file.

1. Select Tools ➤ Merge ➤ Merge to display the Perform Merge dialog box.
2. Type **Request** then press Enter. Because the form document is associated with a data file, WordPerfect will locate the data, merge the documents, and then display the letters on the screen.
3. Select File ➤ Close ➤ No.
4. Select File ➤ Exit.

Macros

If you do much typing, you'll find yourself repeating the same series of keystrokes time and again—typing your letterhead, applying a certain format, adding page numbers or graphics elements. You can save time by creating macros to automate these chores.

Let's create and use two macros, starting with one macro that inserts your letterhead and date.

1. Select Tools ➤ Macro ➤ Record.
2. Type **LHEAD**, then click on Record.
3. Select Layout ➤ Justification ➤ Center.
4. Type your name and address, then press Enter.

►►►►►►►

5 Select Insert ➤ Date ➤ Date Code, then press Enter.

6 Select Layout ➤ Justification ➤ Left.

7 Press Enter twice.

8 Select Tools ➤ Macro ➤ Record to save the macro.

Next, create a macro that performs a common editing task—swapping the position of two paragraphs.

9 Type **This is paragraph one**, and press Enter.

10 Type **This is paragraph two**, and press Enter.

11 Place the insertion point anywhere in the second paragraph.

12 Select Tools ➤ Macro ➤ Record, type **Swap**, and click on Record.

13 Select Edit ➤ Select ➤ Paragraph.

14 Select Edit ➤ Cut (or press Ctrl+X) to delete the paragraph and place it into the Clipboard.

15 Press Ctrl+↑ then Home to move the insertion point to the beginning of the first paragraph. (Pressing Home insures that this macro will work with an indented paragraph.)

16 Select Edit ➤ Paste (or press Ctrl+V) to insert the deleted paragraph.

17 Select Tools ➤ Macro ➤ Record to save the macro.

18 Select File ➤ Close ➤ No.

Using Macros

Now let's see how easy it is to use a macro.

1. Select Tools ➤ Macro ➤ Play.
2. Type **LEAD**, or press F4, then double click on the macro file lhead.wcm.
3. Select Play.

Your address appears on the screen just as you typed it. Now we'll try using the Swap macro.

4. Type **I want this to be the second paragraph**, and press Enter.
5. Type **I want this to be the first paragraph**, and press Enter.
6. Place the insertion point in the second paragraph.
7. Select Tools ➤ Macro ➤ Play.
8. Type **swap**, or press F4 then double click on the macro file swap.wcm.
9. Select Play.

The Swap macro is recalled from the disk and run, switching the two paragraphs.

10. Select File ➤ Close ➤ No to clear the document window.

▶▶▶▶▶▶▶

Writing Tools

Even if you rarely use most features of WordPerfect, you'll find the speller and thesaurus to be invaluable. In fact, many writers believe these the most useful tools that WordPerfect provides.

Speller

Get into the habit of spell-checking every document before your print it. It doesn't take very long and it can save you quite a few headaches.

Let's practice using the speller now. We'll type a short document—riddled with errors—and let WordPerfect help correct it.

1 Type the following paragraphs exactly as they appear. Be sure to type in any spelling and typographical errors.

> **Nellie Watson, former burlesq leading lady and wife of show operator and star Sliding Billy WAtson, was shot and killed at at the Three Hundred Club on April 7, 1926.**
>
> **Mrs. Watson, who retirred from burlesque in 1918, appeared with her husband in Girls from Happyland between 1910 and 1911.**

2 Select Tools ➤ Speller ➤ Start.

WordPerfect finds the first possible error and displays the dialog box shown in Figure 4.6. In this case, the name Nellie is not in WordPerfect's dictionary. The word will become highlighted in the text and suggested spellings will appear in the Suggestions list box.

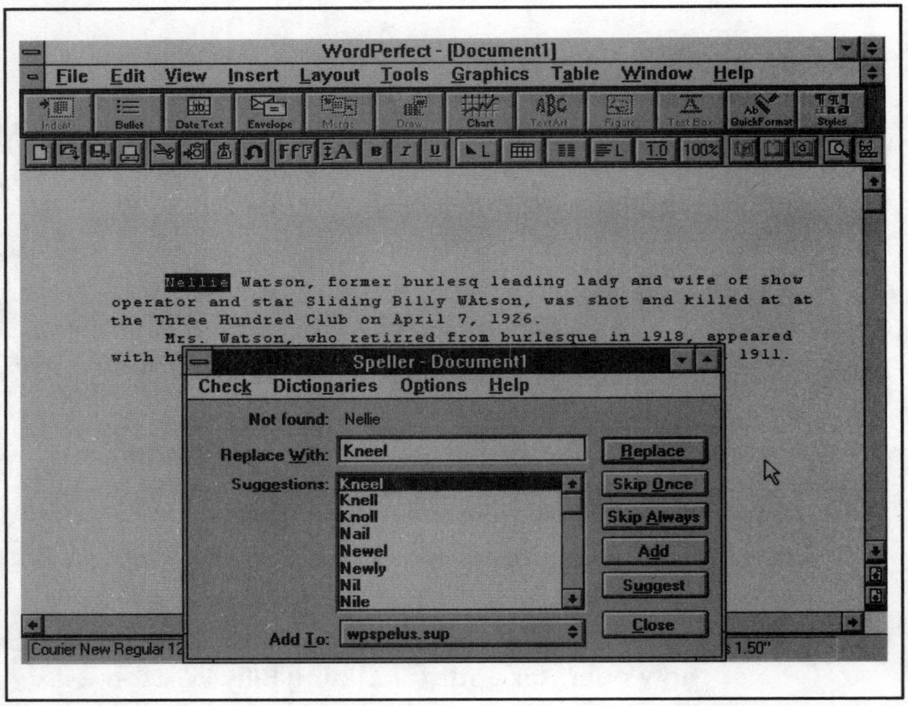

Figure 4.6: Spelling dialog box

The misspelled word will appear at the Not Found prompt in the dialog box. If the highlighted word is hidden by the dialog box, and you want to see the word in its context, drag the box out of the way.

4 Since the word is spelled correctly, select Skip Always.

5 WordPerfect continues checking the document until it finds the next unknown word, *burlesq*. The correct spelling of the word is shown highlighted in the list box. Double-click on the word burlesque in the list box, or select Replace.

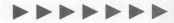

6 The next error located is the capitalization in *WAtson*. WordPerfect suggests replacing the word with Watson. Select Replace.

7 WordPerfect now detects the repetition of the word at. Select Replace to delete one of the words. The next word found is *retirred.*

8 Double-click on the word retired in the list box, or select Replace.

Finally, WordPerfect stops at the word *Happyland*. WordPerfect cannot find any alternative spellings for this word. Let's add the word to the dictionary so it will no longer be reported as a possible error. If you add the word to the *document dictionary* (the default setting), the word will only be associated with this document. Let's change to the supplemental dictionary so the word will not be reported if it is found in any document.

9 Pull down the Add To list and select wpspelus.sup.

10 Select Add.

11 A box appears with the message **Spell Check Completed** indicating that the entire document has been checked. Click on Yes.

Thesaurus

Use the thesaurus when you can't think of the correct word, or when you find yourself using the same word over and over again. But make your selections wisely—don't choose words just because they are long or unusual.

Let's look for a synonym for the word former in the document you used for the spelling check.

1 Place the insertion point anywhere in the word *former*. If you do not still have the document on the screen, just type the word **former**.

2 Select Tools ➤ Thesaurus to display the Thesaurus dialog box.

Several synonyms for the word *former* are shown in the list box on the left. WordPerfect will use the other, now empty, list boxes when necessary.

3 Scroll down the list box. At the bottom, you'll see two antonyms for *former—future and modern.*

4 Scroll back up to highlight the word past, then select Replace. The word past replaces former in the document.

5 Select File ➤ Close ➤ No to clear the screen without saving.

6 Select File ➤ Exit if you're not ready to go on.

Working with Graphics

A well-chosen graphic image can transform the look of your document. But as with lines and borders, don't overdo it with graphics. Avoid graphics that have no relation to the text or that will distract from your words rather than support then.

For practice, let's add a graphic image to a document. We'll use HOTROD.WPG, a graphics file supplied with WordPerfect in the WPWIN60\GRAPHICS directory. We'll display the ruler to help in positioning the graphic.

▶▶▶▶▶▶▶

1 Select View ➤ Ruler Bar

2 Type the following:

Watson Automotive has announced the release of its first convertible model, the Laser Z486. With 250 horsepower and fuel injection, the Laser Z486 is one of the fastest stock cars on the market. The basic model features dual air-bags, anti-lock breaks, and four-speaker stereo with CD player.

The basic model is priced at only $22,512, suggested dealer price. A special anniversary model is also available with custom interior and exterior trim, for a suggested dealer price of $26,246.

3 Select File ➤ Save, type **CARS**, then click on OK.

4 Press Ctrl+Home to move the insertion point to the start of the document.

5 Select Graphics ➤ Figure.

6 Double-click on HOTROD.WPG, or select it then click on OK. The graphic appears selected in a box on the right of the screen, and the graphics Feature Bar appears below the Power Bar, as in Figure 4.7.

Now, let's customize the image by creating a shadow box and rotating the image using the graphics Toolbar.

7 Drag the box down, so it is below the second line in the sentence.

Figure 4.7: Picture inserted into a document

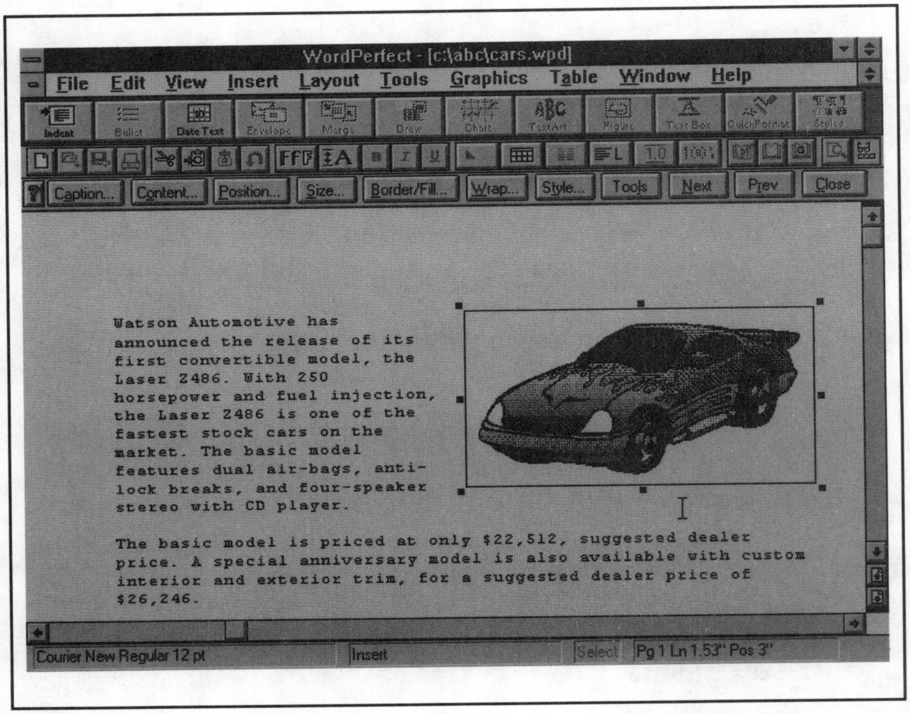
WordPerfect - [c:\abc\cars.wpd]
File Edit View Insert Layout Tools Graphics Table Window Help
Indent Bullet Date Text Envelope Merge Draw Chart TextArt Figure Text Box QuickFormat Styles
Caption... Content... Position... Size... Border/Fill... Wrap... Style... Tools Next Prev Close
Watson Automotive has announced the release of its first convertible model, the Laser 2486. With 250 horsepower and fuel injection, the Laser 2486 is one of the fastest stock cars on the market. The basic model features dual air-bags, anti-lock breaks, and four-speaker stereo with CD player.
The basic model is priced at only $22,512, suggested dealer price. A special anniversary model is also available with custom interior and exterior trim, for a suggested dealer price of $26,246.
Courier New Regular 12 pt
Insert
Select
Pg 1 Ln 1.53" Pos 3"

8 Drag the box to the left, so the right edge of the box is at the 6 ½-inch position.

9 Click on the Border/Fill button in the Feature Bar.

10 Click on the Customize Style button.

11 Pull down the Type options (in the Drop Shadow section).

12 Select the fourth drop shadow style, with the shadow on the lower-right corner.

13 Select OK twice.

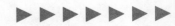

14 Click on the Tools button in the Feature Bar.

15 Click on the Rotate tool (on the left of the first row). Small markers appear in the corners of the graphics box.

16 Point to the marker in the top right corner, then drag it slightly down to rotate the image.

17 Click on the document to unselect the graphics box and remove the Toolbar from display. Check your document against Figure 4.8.

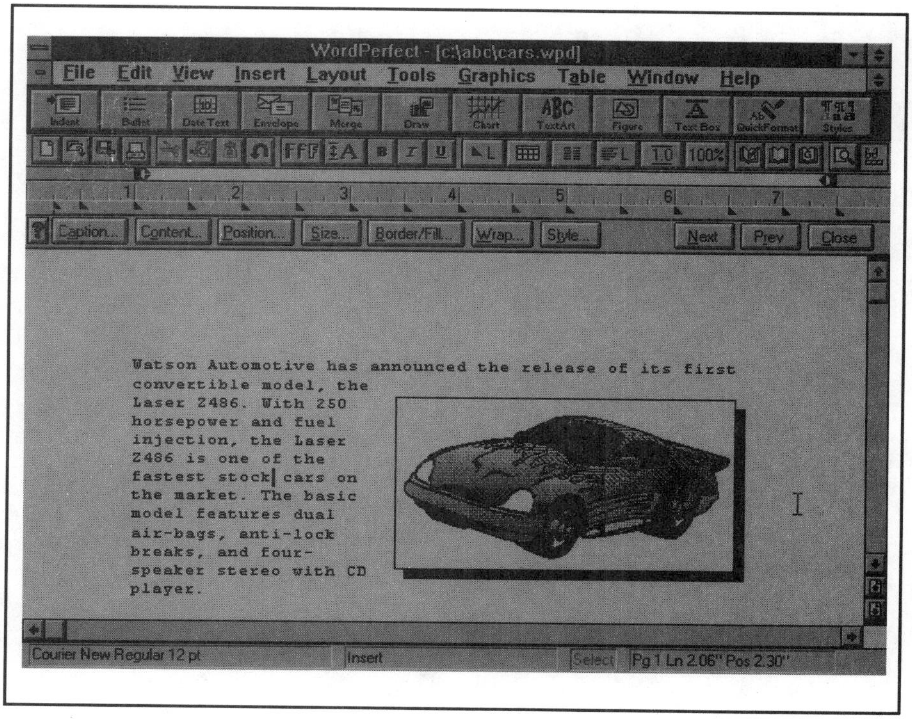

Figure 4.8: Customized picture and graphics box

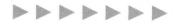

18 Click in the graphics box to select it.

19 Click on the Border/Fill button in the Feature Bar to display the Border/Fill dialog box. Now let's remove the border lines and see how the graphic appears with text following its contour.

20 Pull down the Border Style list and select None.

21 Select OK.

22 Click on the Wrap button in the Feature Bar.

23 Choose Contour, then click on OK.

WordPerfect adjusts the text to follow the shape of the graphic. Check your work against Figure 4.9.

24 Select File ➤ Save.

25 Select File ➤ Print ➤ Print.

26 Select File ➤ Exit.

▶▶▶▶▶▶▶

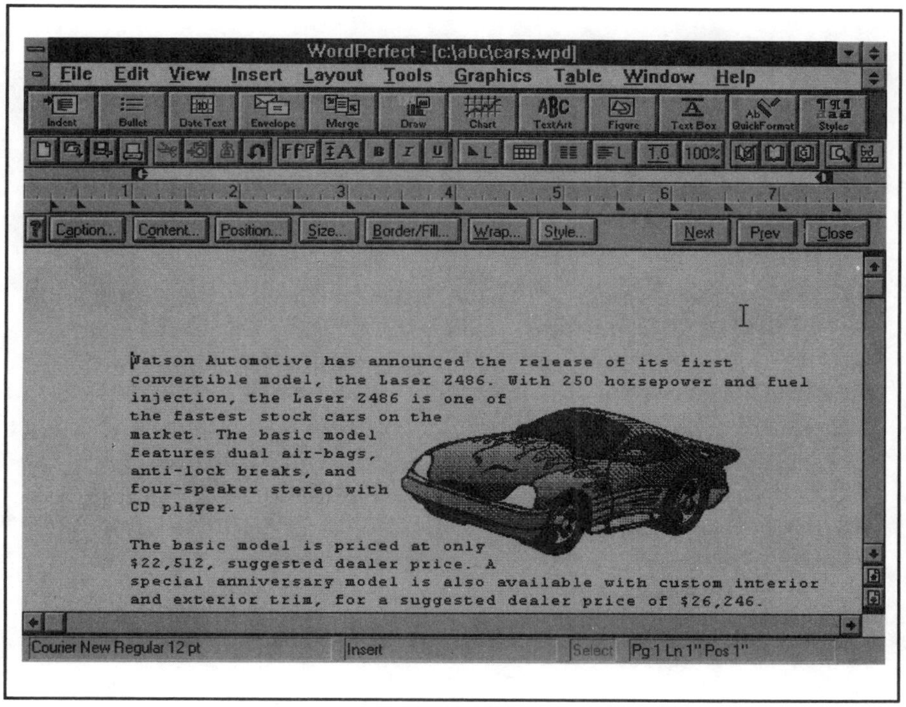
WordPerfect - [c:\abc\cars.wpd]
File Edit View Insert Layout Tools Graphics Table Window Help
Indent Bullet Date Text Envelope Merge Draw Chart TextArt Figure Text Box QuickFormat Styles
Caption... Content... Position... Size... Border/Fill... Wrap... Style... Next Prev Close
Watson Automotive has announced the release of its first convertible model, the Laser Z486. With 250 horsepower and fuel injection, the Laser Z486 is one of the fastest stock cars on the market. The basic model features dual air-bags, anti-lock breaks, and four-speaker stereo with CD player.
The basic model is priced at only $22,512, suggested dealer price. A special anniversary model is also available with custom interior and exterior trim, for a suggested dealer price of $26,246.
Courier New Regular 12 pt
Insert
Select
Pg 1 Ln 1" Pos 1"

Figure 4.9: Text wrapped to the picture contour

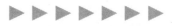

index

Boldfaced page numbers indicate the principal discussions of topics.
Italic page numbers indicate illustrations.

C

▶▶▶▶▶▶▶

D

▶▶▶▶▶▶

H

I

S

T

U

V

W

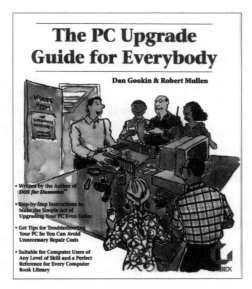

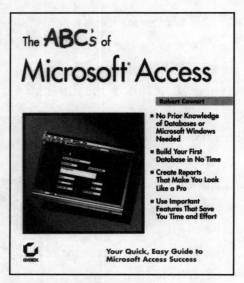

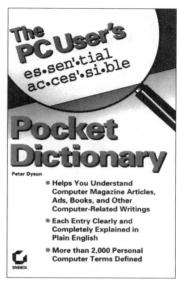

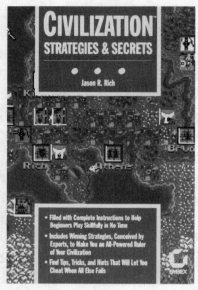

Which of the following best describes your job title?

____ Administrative/Secretarial ____ President/CEO

____ Director ____ Manager/Supervisor

____ Engineer/Technician ____ Other ____________________
(please specify)

Comments on the weaknesses/strengths of this book: ____________________

____

____

____

____

Name ____________________

Street ____________________

City/State/Zip ____________________

Phone ____________________

PLEASE FOLD, SEAL, AND MAIL TO SYBEX

SYBEX, INC.

Department M
2021 CHALLENGER DR.
ALAMEDA, CALIFORNIA USA
94501

SYBEX

SEAL

Function	CUA Key Sequence	Menu Selection
Print	F5	File ➤ Print
Print Current Document	Ctrl+P	
Replace	Ctrl+F2	Edit ➤ Replace
Reveal Codes	Alt+F3	View ➤ Reveal Codes
Ruler	Alt+Shift+F3	View ➤ Ruler Bar
Save As	F3	File ➤ Save As
Save File	Shift+F3 and Ctrl+S	File ➤ Save
Select Mode	F8	
Show Symbols	Ctrl+Shift+F3	View ➤ Show ¶
Sort	Alt+F9	Tools ➤ Sort
Speller	Ctrl+F1	Tools ➤ Speller
Table Sum	Ctrl+=	Table ➤ Sum
Table Format	Ctrl+F12	Table ➤ Format
Table Number Type	Alt+F12	Table ➤ Number Type
Table Lines/Fill	Shift+F12	Table ➤ Lines/Fill
Table Data Fill	Ctrl+Shift+F12	Table ➤ Data Fill
Table Create	F12	Table ➤ Create
Thesaurus	Alt+F1	Tools ➤ Thesaurus
Undelete	Ctrl+Shift+Z	Edit ➤ Undelete
Undo	Ctrl+Z	Edit ➤ Undo